Tenants' Right of First Refusal

Tenants' Right of First Refusal

Anthony Radevsky LLB
Barrister

Wayne Clark LLB, BCL (Oxon)
Barrister

Butterworths
London, Edinburgh and Dublin
2001

United Kingdom	Butterworths, a Division of Reed Elsevier (UK) Ltd, Halsbury House, 35 Chancery Lane, LONDON WC2A 1EL and 4 Hill Street, EDINBURGH EH2 3JZ
Australia	Butterworths, a Division of Reed International Books Australia Pty Ltd, CHATSWOOD, New South Wales
Canada	Butterworths Canada Ltd, MARKHAM, Ontario
Hong Kong	Butterworths Hong Kong, a division of Reed Elsevier (Greater China) Ltd, HONG KONG
India	Butterworths India, NEW DELHI
Ireland	Butterworth (Ireland) Ltd, DUBLIN
Malaysia	Malayan Law Journal Sdn Bhd, KUALA LUMPUR
New Zealand	Butterworths of New Zealand Ltd, WELLINGTON
Singapore	Butterworths Asia, SINGAPORE
South Africa	Butterworths Publishers (Pty) Ltd, DURBAN
USA	Lexis Law Publishing, CHARLOTTESVILLE, Virginia

A CIP Catalogue record for this book is available from the British Library.

ISBN 0 406 91104 5

ISBN 0-406-91104-5

9 780406 911049

Printed and bound in Great Britain by Antony Rowe Ltd, Chippenham, Wilts

Preface

In the 14 years since the Landlord and Tenant Act 1987 was passed, we have frequently had to consider the complexities of Part I, which gives residential tenants the right of first refusal when their landlord wants to dispose of his interest. For some years we have thought that a detailed work devoted to these provisions would be of real assistance to property practitioners. We hope that this book will go some way to providing the answers to the many questions which arise under the Act.

We would like to thank Jason Hunter and his colleagues at Russell-Cooke for sending us problems found in practice, which we have tried, but probably failed, to answer. We also wish to thank our colleagues in Chambers including, in particular, Barry Denyer-Green.

The law is stated as at 10 April 2001.

Anthony Radevsky
Wayne Clark

Falcon Chambers

Contents

CHAPTER 3
Relevant disposal 15

CHAPTER 4
The offer notice 39

CHAPTER 8
Subsequent purchasers 87

CHAPTER 9
Termination of rights against purchaser or subsequent purchaser 95

CHAPTER 10
Miscellaneous 103

CHAPTER 11
Prospective purchasers: section 18 115

Appendix I 119

Table of statutes

References in this table are to paragraph numbers.

Table of statutory instruments

References in this table are to paragraph numbers.

Table of cases

Y

CHAPTER 1

Introduction

1.01 The Landlord and Tenant Act 1987 ('LTA 1987') was enacted following the Report of the Committee of Inquiry on the Management of Privately Owned Blocks of Flats (October 1985) chaired by Edward Nugee QC. That Report had considered the strong support in the evidence it had gathered for a general right to collective enfranchisement[1], but had concluded that giving tenants a right of first refusal when the reversion was disposed of by their landlord would suffice[2], given that they also proposed a right to have a manager appointed in the event of serious default by the landlord. The Report did not append a draft Bill, but a suggested procedure was outlined in the body of the Report[3]. A right to collective enfranchisement would have to wait for six more years[4].

1 The Report of the Committee of Inquiry on the Management of Privately Owned Blocks of Flats (October 1985), para 7.9.13.
2 The Committee were not convinced that management by lease-holders would solve all the problems which had been identified.
3 The Report of the Committee of Inquiry on the Management of Privately Owned Blocks of Flats (October 1985), para 7.9.16.
4 See the Leasehold Reform, Housing and Urban Development Act 1993.

1.02 The LTA 1987 was rushed through Parliament before the 1987 general election by a government keen to be seen to be tackling the well-publicised problems of lessees in large mansion blocks, many in key constituencies in Central London. It was not unusual for freeholds to change hands on more than one occasion without the knowledge of the tenants from one off-shore company to another. In the hurry, many of the provisions in the LTA 1987 were not properly thought through, and there was a view at the time that, once on the statute book, it would be possible to amend the legislation before bringing it into force. As it happened, it came into force unamended and was roundly (and justifiably) criticised by the courts, probably to a greater extent than any other piece of legislation. In *Denetower Ltd v Toop*[1] Sir Nicolas Browne-Wilkinson V-C referred[2] to the difficulty 'in construing such an ill-drafted, complicated and confused Act as this'. In *Belvedere Court Management Ltd v Frogmore Developments Ltd*[3] Sir Thomas Bingham MR (referring to *Denetower*) said[4]: 'The argument in this case has given new force to this understated criticism'. He continued:

> '... one could wish that the Act provided as many answers as it raised problems. I can readily appreciate the complexity of the task which confronted the draftsman in seeking to give legislative effect to this ambitious scheme. But the history of these proceedings is a dismal commentary on a measure intended to help tenants of mansion blocks, many of them of limited means. As it is, the legal profession would appear to be the main beneficiaries of this obscure statute.'

In *Kay Green v Twinsectra Ltd* Staughton LJ said[5]:

> 'This is the most remarkable case of statutory interpretation that I have ever seen. It is as plain as can be what the purpose of Part I of the Landlord and Tenant Act 1987 was – to enable tenants of flats to buy their landlord's interest in the building if the landlord proposed to sell it to someone else, and to buy it from the purchaser if the landlord had actually done so. But nowhere does the statute say expressly that the tenants shall have that right against the new landlord. If that omission is fatal, Part I of the Act is not worth the paper which it is written on.'

1 [1991] 1 WLR 945.
2 [1991] 1 WLR 945 at 952G.
3 [1997] QB 858.
4 [1997] 1 QB 858 at 881D.
5 [1996] 1 WLR 1587, 1603B.

1.03 It was, perhaps, not appreciated by the original draftsman just how significant were the changes being made to the law by the LTA 1987. Hitherto, tenants of flats had no right to acquire their landlord's interest. Their only statutory rights concerned service charges, and those had been introduced as recently as 1972[1]. The main difficulties with the right of first refusal, including those identified by the Court of Appeal, were a lack of comprehensive definitions[2], inadequate detail[3], the existence of loopholes which could easily be exploited by determined landlords[4], and no criminal or civil sanction against a defaulting landlord.

1 By s 90 of the Housing Finance Act 1972. Those provisions are now contained in the Landlord and Tenant Act 1985, itself amended by the LTA 1987.
2 Eg of 'building': see *Denetower Ltd v Toop* [1991] 1 WLR 945.
3 Eg concerning sales by auction, or the entry into conditional contracts to sell the reversion.
4 Such as the sale of the landlord's interest to a newly formed associated company, as to which see para **3.52** ff.

1.04 It was not until 1996 that substantial amendments were made to the LTA 1987[1]. This involved the wholesale replacement of most of Part I. Although many problems of interpretation still remain, some of the more serious defects have been tackled successfully. In particular, the introduction of criminal penalties[2] seems to have been an effective deterrent, with no reports of prosecutions to date.

1 By the Housing Act 1996.
2 See para **10.09** ff.

1.05 In November 1998, the government issued a consultation paper on leasehold reform[1]. The only proposals concerning Part I of the LTA 1987 were to widen its scope to include houses within the right of first refusal, and to extend the six-month time limit for prosecutions for flouting tenants' rights. The Analysis of Responses to the Consultation Paper[2] indicated that three-quarters of the respondents favoured extending the right to leaseholders of houses[3]. However, the Lord Chancellor's Draft Bill and Consultation Paper on Commonhold and Leasehold Reform[4] omitted all reference to including houses within Part I; the problem which has been identified is that many house reversions are sold in large lots and it is not clear how best to deal with them. The Commonhold and Leasehold Reform Bill introduced into the House of Lords on 20 December 2000 contained no proposals to reform Part I. However, in a proposed amendment made at the committee stage in the House of Lords, Baroness Hanham has sought to include an individual house in the definition of premises to which the LTA 1987 applies. However, on 22 March 2001 she withdrew the amendment when the government would not support it in the present Bill. There has been no further mention of the proposed extension to the prosecution time limit.

1 Residential Leasehold Reform in England and Wales – A Consultation Paper, Department of the Environment, Transport and the Regions.
2 Published in December 1999.
3 Analysis of Responses to the Consultation Paper, para 53.
4 Presented to Parliament in August 2000.

1.06 It seems possible that the proposals in the Commonhold and Leasehold Reform Bill to give long lessees a right to manage their building without showing fault on the part of the landlord, together with an extension of the right to collective enfranchisement, will be seen as the grant of sufficient tenants' rights for the immediate future; if so, we can expect the present provisions in Part I of the LTA 1987 to remain as they are.

1.07 No modern legal textbook would be complete without mentioning the Human Rights Act 1998 which, in October 2000, incorporated the European Convention on Human Rights into our domestic law. However, we consider that no arguable infringement of a landlord's human rights arises as a result of Part I of the LTA 1987. It does not deprive the landlord of his property, it merely requires him, if he chooses to sell, to sell to his tenants rather than a third party. It should be noted, in addition, that the European Court of Human Rights has held that the Leasehold Reform Act 1967 (which gives long lessees of houses the more radical right to buy the freehold for less than market value) does not contravene the landlord's human rights[1].

1 *James v United Kingdom* (1986) 8 EHRR 123.

CHAPTER 2

Premises, landlords and qualifying tenants

2.01 Part I of the LTA 1987 grants to certain tenants of certain premises a statutory right of first refusal. It does so in a negative way, by prohibiting the landlord from making a relevant disposal[1] without first serving a notice[2] and ensuring that the disposal is made in accordance with the statutory requirements[3]. The relevant disposal must be one 'affecting any premises to which at the time of the disposal this Part applies'.

1 See Chapter 3.
2 Under s 5 of the LTA 1987, as to which see Chapter 4.
3 LTA 1987, s 1(1). The statutory requirements are those contained in ss 6–10.

Premises

2.02 Subject to two important exceptions, Part I of the LTA 1987 applies to premises if three conditions are satisfied[1]. The premises must (i) consist of the whole or part of a building; (ii) contain two or more flats held by qualifying tenants; and (iii) the number of flats held by qualifying tenants must exceed 50% of the total number of flats contained in the premises.

1 LTA 1987, s 1(2).

'The whole or part of a building'

2.03 The LTA 1987 does not define 'building'. The word 'covers an immense range of all sorts of structures' and, as a matter of law, 'to give a defined or precise meaning to the word "building" is an impossibility'[1]. In one LTA 1987 case[2] it was said that one should apply the ordinary meaning of the word as being 'an inclosure of brick or stone covered in by a roof'[3]. The building must, of course, contain at least two flats. It is considered that the lack of a definition will not usually cause a problem; the Act was intended to apply particularly to mansion blocks of residential flats, and will plainly do so. Difficult questions might arise, however, if one is seeking to define the extent of the building for the purposes of the Act, where one is not dealing with a single, detached block. The following situations need to be considered:

(a) A terrace of buildings divided into flats

Consider a row of terraced buildings, each divided vertically from each other, and each divided into two flats. They may have been constructed as terraced houses, and later converted into flats, or originally built as flats. It is considered that each vertical building is a separate building for the purposes of the LTA 1987, even though it is attached to its neighbour[4]. It should be noted that if more than one building is being disposed of by the landlord, each building must be dealt with separately[5]. However, if flats within the terrace straddle more than one building, then the building will comprise the smallest property that can be divided vertically from its neighbours[6]. In effect, the test for a building should be the same as that expressly set out in s 3(2) of the Leasehold Reform, Housing and Urban Development Act 1993, namely can the building in question be divided vertically and independently developed?

(b) A building sharing a common wall with another building

A similar question arises in the case of a building containing flats which is attached to another building (perhaps commercial), by reason of sharing an outside wall, but which has no other connection with it. Applying the test in (a) above, it is only the building containing flats which will be considered. Accordingly, the landlord will not be able to rely on the mixed use exception[7] in such a case.

(c) An estate comprising a number of residential blocks

The LTA 1987 does not make express provision for the common situation of a residential estate comprising a number of blocks of flats being disposed of together. It is clear that even though it will often be convenient to deal with the estate as a whole, each building must be dealt with separately[8]. The fact that the tenants in each block have rights over the common roads, gardens and grounds of the estate creates problems which are simply not addressed in the Act[9]. A building includes appurtenances to that building, which (depending on the particular property in question) may comprise gardens, roadways and paths[10].

(d) Houses

In one case[11] it was held that premises containing seven flats and three terraced houses comprised one building which could be the subject of a purchase notice under the (old) s 12.

1 *Bardrick v Haycock* (1976) 31 P & CR 420, per Scarman LJ at 424.
2 *Saga Properties Ltd v Palmeira Square Nos 2–6 Ltd* [1995] 1 EGLR 199 LT.
3 [1995] 1 EGLR 199 LT, per Judge Marder QC at 209M.
4 See *Saga Properties Ltd v Palmeira Square Nos 2–6 Ltd* [1995] EGLR 199 LT.
5 LTA 1987, s 5(3), and see para **4.02**.

6 As in *Saga Properties Ltd v Palmeira Square Nos 2–6 Ltd* [1995] 1 EGLR 199 LT.
7 See para **2.06**.
8 LTA 1987, s 5(3); and see para **4.02**.
9 See eg *Denetower Ltd v Toop* [1991] 1 WLR 945, CA; *Twinsectra Ltd v Jones* [1998] 2 EGLR 129 LT.
10 *Denetower v Toop* [1991] 1 WLR 945, CA.
11 *Kay Green v Twinsectra Ltd* [1996] 1 WLR 1587, CA.

Flats in building

2.04 The premises must contain two or more flats held by qualifying tenants[1] for the LTA 1987 to apply. This must be the case as at the date of the disposal[2]. The status of the premises may change from time to time – flats may be vacated or filled. A statutory tenant under the Rent Act 1977 (who is a qualifying tenant) may leave and be replaced by an assured tenant (who is not). The number of flats held by qualifying tenants must *exceed* 50% of the total number of flats in the premises. Accordingly, if a building contains only two flats, both must be occupied by qualifying tenants for the LTA 1987 to apply.

1 For qualifying tenants, see para **2.13**.
2 See the LTA 1987, s 1(1).

'Flat'

2.05 The word 'flat' is defined[1] as a separate set of premises[2], whether or not on the same floor, which:

(a) forms part of the building;
(b) is divided horizontally from some other part of that building; and
(c) is constructed or adapted for use for the purposes of a dwelling.

'Dwelling' means a building or part of a building occupied or intended to be occupied as a separate dwelling, together with any yard, garden, outhouses and appurtenances belonging to it or usually enjoyed with it[3].

The words 'whether or not on the same floor' make it clear that maisonettes are included[4]. The word 'separate' suggests both 'physically separate' or 'set apart' and 'single' or 'regarded as a unit'; subject to questions of fact and degree it may be possible for the rooms forming part of a flat not to be contiguous[5].

It is considered that where there is a tenancy of, say, a single room, with the tenant sharing essential living accommodation such as a kitchen[6] with other tenants in the building, the demised premises are not a separate dwelling and, accordingly, not a flat. The tenant of such accommodation might, nevertheless, be deemed to have a protected tenancy, by virtue of s 22 of the Rent Act 1977. However, the LTA 1987 contains no equivalent provision to s 22.

1 In the LTA 1987, s 60(1).
2 See *Cadogan v McGirk* [1996] 4 All ER 643, CA for a useful discussion of this expression in a case under the Leasehold Reform, Housing and Urban Development Act 1993.
3 LTA 1987, s 60(1).

4 *Cadogan v McGirk* [1996] 4 All ER 643, per Millet LJ at 649. That case concerned the same words in the definition of 'flat' in s 101(1) of the Leasehold Reform, Housing and Urban Development Act 1993.
5 *Cadogan v McGirk* [1996] 4 All ER 643.
6 See eg *Neale v Del Soto* [1945] KB 144.

Exceptions

(a) Mixed use buildings

2.06 The right of first refusal does not apply to premises which would otherwise fall within the definition if two conditions apply. The first condition is that a part or parts of the premises is or are occupied (or intended to be occupied) otherwise than for residential purposes[1]. The second condition is that the internal floor area of the part(s) taken together exceeds 50%[2] of the internal floor area of the premises taken as a whole[3]. The internal floor area of any common parts is disregarded[4]. In passing, it should be noted that a disposal of a purely non-residential part of a mixed use building will not be caught by the LTA 1987[5]. Accordingly, a landlord is free to grant a lease of shop premises alone on the ground floor of premises where the upper floors comprise residential flats.

There is no limitation as to whose intention to occupy is to be considered, nor how long any future intention must be. An empty part of the building will be treated as non-residential if there is an intention to occupy it for non-residential purposes at any time in the future. If part of the building is occupied residentially, but there is an intention to change the nature of occupation to non-residential in the future, it would appear that that part must be classified as non-residential.

1 LTA 1987, s 1(3)(a).
2 LTA 1987, s 1(5) gives the Secretary of State power to change the percentage; there is no sign of an order being made.
3 LTA 1987, s 1(3)(b).
4 LTA 1987, s 1(3). 'Common parts', in relation to any building or part of a building, includes the structure and exterior of that building or part and any common facilities within it: LTA 1987, s 60(1). In *Woodfall on Landlord and Tenant*, vol 4, para 28.008, n 13, it is pointed out that common facilities outside the building (eg car parks, gardens or grounds, swimming pools, tennis courts) appear not to be common parts, unless they can be said to be part of the exterior of the building, which seems unlikely. The relevance of that comment is puzzling; the definition only takes into account internal floor areas.
5 See para **3.05** dealing with what is a relevant disposal.

'Residential purposes'

2.07 It is considered that the fact that a flat is used for residential purposes does not preclude it from being used for business purposes as well. For instance, a doctor might reside in a flat but use part of it as a consulting room for seeing patients[1]. It is thought that the consulting room would not be excluded from consideration as residential accommodation, but rather that the flat as a whole would be measured as residential. A difficult question could arise if part of a building was used by a tenant for the business of providing residential accommodation, eg a student hostel, where the students were licensees. The students would not be qualifying tenants. On one view, the hostel is being used for residential purposes, namely as a residence for the occupying students. On the other hand, it is being occupied by the tenant for business purposes.

1 *Cheryl Investments Ltd v Saldanha* [1978] 1 WLR 1329.

(b) Excluded landlords

2.08 Part I of the LTA 1987 does not apply at a time when the interest of the landlord in the premises is held by an exempt landlord or a resident landlord[1]. The use of the expression 'at a time' makes it clear that applicability of the Act to the premises may change from time to time if the identity of the landlord changes.

1 LTA 1987, s 1(4).

Exempt landlord

2.09 There is a long list of public authority bodies which are exempt landlords[1]. They are:

(a) a district, county, county borough or London borough council; the Common Council of the City of London, the Council of the Isles of Scilly, a police authority[2], the Service Authority for the National Criminal Intelligence Service, the Service Authority for the National Crime Squad, or a joint authority established by Part IV of the Local Government Act 1985;

(b) the Commission for the New Towns or a development corporation established by an order made (or having effect as if made) under the New Towns Act 1981;

(c) an urban development corporation[3];

(d) a housing action trust[4];

(e) the Development Board for Rural Wales;

(f) the Broads Authority;

(g) the Housing Corporation;

(h) Housing for Wales;

(i) a housing trust[5] which is a charity;

(j) a registered social landlord[6], or a fully mutual housing association[7] which is not a registered social landlord;

(k) an authority established under s 10 of the Local Government Act 1985[8].

1 They are set out in s 58(1) of the LTA 1987.
2 Established under s 3 of the Police Act 1996.
3 Within the meaning of Pt XVI of the Local Government, Planning and Land Act 1980.

4 Established under Pt III of the Housing Act 1988.
5 As defined in s 6 of the Housing Act 1996.
6 By s 58(1A) of the LTA 1987, this has the same meaning as in the Housing Associations Act 1985, as to which see s 1(1), (2).
7 By s 58(1A) of the LTA 1987, this has the same meaning as in the Housing Act 1985, as to which see s 5(4), (5).
8 Joint arrangements for waste disposal functions.

Resident landlord

2.10 The landlord of any premises consisting of the whole or part of a building is a resident landlord of the premises at any time if three conditions are fulfilled[1]. First, the premises must not be, or must not form part of, a purpose-built block of flats. 'Purpose-built block of flats' means a building which is contained as constructed, and contains two or more flats[2]. It will, therefore, include a house converted into flats[3].

Secondly, at the time in question the landlord must be occupying a flat contained in the premises as his only or principal residence. There being no difference between 'main' and 'principal' nor between 'residence' and 'home', this test is the same as that under a number of housing statutes, namely the Leasehold Reform Act 1967[4], the Housing Act 1985[5], the Housing Act 1988[6] and the Leasehold Reform, Housing and Urban Development Act 1993[7]. Which of two or more residences is a person's principal residence is a question to be considered objectively. All residences, wherever in the world situated, must be taken into account. It is often difficult to decide between, say, a town house where someone works during the week and a country house which is occupied at weekends. The question is one of fact and degree which has to be looked at in a commonsense way, and there may be many circumstances to be considered[8].

A company cannot be a resident landlord even if it lets a director occupy a flat within the building as his only or principal residence.

The third condition is that the landlord has so occupied a flat throughout a period of not less than 12 months ending with the time in question, eg the date of the disposal. Accordingly, a landlord who moves into premises must wait for at least 12 months before he is entitled to dispose of them without giving the tenants the right of first refusal.

1 LTA 1987, s 58(2).
2 LTA 1987, s 58(3).
3 *Barnes v Gorsuch* (1981) 43 P & CR 294, CA, a decision on similar wording in the Rent Act 1977. O'Connor LJ, at 297, referred to the possibility that, in certain circumstances, an old building which had been completely gutted and rebuilt inside might well be a new and different building.
4 Leasehold Reform Act 1967, s 1(2).
5 Housing Act 1985, s 81.
6 Housing Act 1988, s1(1)(b) and Sch 1, para 10(1)(b).
7 Leasehold Reform, Housing and Urban Development Act 1993, ss 6(2), 10(1)(b), 39(2A), (2B).
8 See eg *Byrne v Rowbotham* (1969) 210 Estates Gazette 823, CA; *Frost v Feltham* [1981] 1 WLR 452. For a detailed discussion of the cases under the similarly worded Leasehold Reform Act 1967, see *Hague on Leasehold Enfranchisement* (3rd edn), paras 4.03, 4.07.

Landlords

2.11 Subject to two cases[1], the landlord, for the purposes of Part I of the LTA 1987, in relation to premises consisting of the whole or part of a building, is the immediate landlord of the qualifying tenants of the flats contained in those premises[2]. Where any of the qualifying tenants are statutory tenants[3], the person who, apart from the statutory tenants, would be entitled to possession of the flat is the landlord[4].

Accordingly if, in a block of flats, there is a freeholder, an intermediate lessee, and then underleases of the individual flats, the intermediate lessee is normally the landlord for the purposes of the LTA 1987. Accordingly, a disposal of the intermediate lease will attract the right of first refusal, but not a disposal of the freehold. In one case[5], there were two long leases superior to that of the qualifying tenants, one of 99 years and the other of 1992 years. They were both sold to a purchaser in breach of the LTA 1987, s 5, but there was a declaration that the two leases did not merge. The tenants argued that they were entitled to acquire both leases under ss 12 and 16 because the purchaser was 'the landlord' and it was immaterial, once it was identified, that it owned two interests in the premises. The Court of Appeal held, however, that it was only the interest held as immediate landlord, ie the 99 years' lease, that could be acquired by the tenants. It is considered that the same principle would probably apply to an offer notice under the LTA 1987, s 5, ie a landlord holding two unmerged interests would only have to offer the right of first refusal in respect of the lease immediately superior to the interests of the qualifying tenants.

1 Dealt with at para **2.12**.
2 LTA 1987, s 2(1)(a).
3 Within the meaning of the Rent Act 1977. A statutory tenancy is within the meaning of the word 'tenancy' (LTA 1987, s 60(1)) even though it is not a tenancy as such but merely a statutory right to occupy.
4 LTA 1987, s 2(1)(b).
5 *Belvedere Court Management Ltd v Frogmore Developments Ltd* [1997] QB 858.

Exceptions

2.12 First, if the intermediate landlord has a tenancy for a term of less than seven years, or for a longer term but with an option for the superior landlord to terminate it within the first seven years, the superior landlord is also regarded as the landlord for the purposes of the LTA 1987[1]. This provision may be illustrated by an example. Assume four interestes in reversion to that of the tenant, namely the owner of the freehold, an intermediate lease ('lease A') of five years, an intermediate lease ('lease B') of three years and an intermediate lease ('lease C') of one year. All such persons are 'landlord' for the purposes of the LTA 1987. Thus a relevant disposal by any of them would be a relevant disposal by 'the landlord'[2]. If lease B were, instead of a lease of three years, a lease of 15 years, a disposal of lease A or of the freehold would not be a disposal by 'the landlord'. A disposal of lease B or C in these circumstances would be a disposal by 'the landlord'. This would be unlikely to occur in practice. The second exception is where a disposal is made by a mortgagee of the landlord's estate or interest in exercise of the mortgagee's power of sale or leasing (whether or not made in the landlord's name). In such a case, the mortgagee is regarded as the landlord for the purposes of Part I[3].

1 LTA 1987, s 2(2). If the superior landlord is himself a tenant under such a short tenancy, his landlord is also a landlord under the LTA 1987.
2 For the purposes of s 4 of the LTA 1987. This is not to say that the occupying tenants would necessarily be the qualifying tenants having regard to the provisions of the LTA 1987, s 3(4). See para **2.15**.
3 LTA 1987, s 4(1A).

Qualifying tenants

2.13 The basic rule is that a person is a qualifying tenant for the purposes of Part I of the LTA 1987 if he is the tenant of a flat under a tenancy[1]. 'Tenancy' includes a sub-tenancy[2] and an agreement for a tenancy or sub-tenancy[3]. It is clear from this that there must be a tenancy, and not a licence. However, unlike, for example, rights under Part I of the Leasehold Reform, Housing and Urban Development Act 1993, a qualifying tenant need not have a long lease. A short fixed term or a periodic tenancy, or even a tenancy at will, is sufficient. Moreover, a statutory tenant under the Rent Act 1977 is specifically included[4]. It is considered that if there are joint tenants, all together are to be regarded as the qualifying tenant, although the LTA 1987 does not contain a specific reference to joint tenants. Accordingly, any notices served on or by joint tenants must name them all to be valid[5].

There are a number of types of tenancy which are excluded from the definition:

(a) a protected shorthold tenancy as defined in s 52 of the Housing Act 1980. There are not many of these remaining, and no new protected shorthold tenancies can be created (since the Housing Act 1988 came into force);
(b) a tenancy to which Part II of the Landlord and Tenant Act 1954 applies. Accordingly, if the business use of a flat is sufficient to bring it within the 1954 Act[6], the tenant will not be a qualifying tenant;
(c) a tenancy terminable on the cessation of the tenant's employment. This will exclude a resident caretaker whose accommodation is provided as part of his job;
(d) an assured tenancy or assured agricultural occupancy within the meaning of Part I of the Housing Act 1988. This, of course, includes assured shorthold tenancies which are a species of assured tenancy. There is therefore a marked contrast between a regulated tenant under the Rent Act 1977, who is a qualifying tenant, and an assured tenant, who is not. The exemption was presumably introduced to increase the incentive for landlords to grant assured tenancies, which was the main purpose of the Housing Act 1988. One consequence is that if a statutory tenant dies and a member of his family succeeds to an assured tenancy (under the Rent Act 1977, Sch 1, Part 1) the

flat will automatically cease to have a qualifying tenant. If, however, a tenancy is granted so that the Housing Act 1988 does not apply, eg to a company[7] or at a rent of more than £25,000 per annum[8], the tenant will be a qualifying tenant for the purposes of Part I of the LTA 1987.

1 LTA 1987, s 3(1). There is no requirement that a qualifying tenant should occupy his flat.
2 As to which, see para **2.15**.
3 LTA 1987, s 59(1).
4 LTA 1987, s 60(1).
5 See eg in different statutory contexts *T M Fairclough & Sons Ltd v Berliner* [1931] 1 Ch 60; *Jacobs v Chaudhuri* [1968] 2 QB 470; *Featherstone v Staples* [1986] 1 WLR 861.
6 See para **2.07**.
7 By the Housing Act 1988, s 1(1) an assured tenancy must be to an individual occupying the dwelling-house as his only or principal home.
8 Housing Act 1988, Sch 1, para 2. If the rent under an assured tenancy is increased to more than £25,000 under ss 13 and 14 of the Housing Act 1988, it will cease to be assured: *R v London Rent Assessment Panel, ex p Cadogan Estates Ltd* [1998] QB 398.

Multiple tenancies

2.14 If a person is the tenant[1] of at least three flats in the same building (or part), then he is not the qualifying tenant of any of the flats[2]. If the tenant of a flat or flats is a body corporate, then this exclusion applies if the tenancy of the other flat or flats is held by an associated company[3].

1 Other than under one of the four types of tenancy referred to in para **2.13**.
2 LTA 1987, s 3(2).
3 LTA 1987, s 3(3). 'Associated company' is defined as another body corporate which is (within the meaning of s 736 of the Companies Act 1985) that body's holding company, a subsidiary of that body or another subsidiary of that body's holding company: LTA 1987, s 20(1).

Sub-tenant

2.15 A tenant whose landlord is a qualifying tenant of the flat is not to be regarded as being a qualifying tenant of that flat[1]. The purpose of this provision is to ensure that there can only be one qualifying tenant of a flat at any one time.

Examples

A has a 99-year lease of a flat. He grants a four-year sublease to B. The qualifying tenant is A. A then acquires the leases of three other flats in the same building. Since he cannot be a qualifying tenant of any of the flats, B becomes the qualifying tenant of the flat, unless his tenancy is an assured tenancy (in which case there will be no qualifying tenant for that flat).

1 LTA 1987, s 3(4).

Requisite majority

2.16 The acceptance of an offer contained in a s 5 notice and subsequent steps in the process require the participation of 'the requisite majority of qualifying tenants of the constituent flats'. That expression is defined[1] as qualifying tenants of constituent flats with more than 50% of the available votes.

1 By the LTA 1987, s 18A(1).

2.17 The total number of available votes is determined depending on which procedure is being considered[1]. Where a s 5 offer notice has been served, the total number is equal to the total number of constituent flats let to qualifying tenants on the date when the period specified in that notice as the period for accepting the offer expires[2]. There could, in theory, be a different number of such flats from that which existed on the date the s 5 notice was served. Where no s 5 notice has been served, and a notice is served under s 11A of the LTA 1987, the total number is equal to the total number of constituent flats let to qualifying tenants on the date of service of the s 11A notice[3]. Where no s 5 or s 11A notice has been served, and a notice under the LTA 1987, ss 12A, 12B or 12C is served, the total number is equal to the total number of constituent flats let to qualifying tenants on the date of service of such notice[4]. Each flat let on the date in question has only one available vote, and that is attributed to the qualifying tenant to whom it is let[5]. It is specifically provided that the persons constituting the requisite majority may be different for different purposes[6]. It should also be noted that the LTA 1987 applies to a tenant's successor in title[7]. Accordingly, if the requisite majority accept an offer contained in a s 5 notice and appoint a nominee to act on the purchase, and then one of the tenants assigns his lease, the tenants can continue with the purchase, with the assignee taking over as qualifying tenant of the flat which has been assigned. On the other hand, if the original group of tenants only have a bare majority, and the assignee does not wish to proceed, the claim will have to be withdrawn[8].

1 LTA 1987, s 18A(2).
2 LTA 1987, s 18A(2)(a).
3 LTA 1987, s 18A(2)(b). See para **6.01** ff for the procedure of serving a s 11A notice.
4 LTA 1987, s 18A(2)(c). See para **7.01** ff for the procedure for serving a s 12A, s 12B or s 12C notice.
5 LTA 1987, s 18A(3).
6 LTA 1987, s 18A(4).
7 LTA 1987, s 20(3).
8 By virtue of the LTA 1987, s 14(2); see para **9.06**.

CHAPTER 3

Relevant disposal

Relevant disposal

3.01 The LTA 1987 applies only where there has been a 'relevant disposal' affecting any premises to which Part I of the LTA 1987 applies. It is provided[1] that references to a relevant disposal affecting any premises to which Part I applies are:

> '... references to the disposal by the landlord of any estate or interest (whether legal or equitable) in any such premises, including the disposal of any such estate or interest in any common parts of any such premises.'

1 LTA 1987, s 4(1).

'Disposal'

3.02 'Disposal' is defined as meaning a disposal whether by the creation or the transfer of an estate or interest, and:

(a) includes the surrender of a tenancy and the grant of an option or right of pre-emption[1]; but

(b) excludes a disposal under the terms of a will or under the law relating to intestacy[2].

The most obvious disposal is that of the freehold estate. However, the grant of an overriding lease would equally be a relevant disposal[3].

A disposal[4] of a registered estate, for the purposes of Part I of the LTA 1987, takes place on the execution (in unconditional form, not in escrow) of the transfer, just as a disposal of an unregistered estate takes place on the execution of the conveyance[5]. The date of registration is, in practice, the date of the application to register[6]. In some cases that application may not be processed, and therefore the registration may not be confirmed for some considerable time. Accordingly, it has been said that it would be quixotic to take the date of registration as the date of the disposal[7].

1 As to the surrender of a tenancy, the grant of an option or a right of pre-emption see paras **3.48, 3.43** and **3.44**.
2 LTA 1987, s 4(3)(a) and (b).
3 *Belvedere Court Management Ltd v Frogmore Developments Ltd* [1997] QB 858, CA.
4 Being a disposal other than by entry into a contract.
5 *Michaels v Harley House (Marylebone) Ltd* [1997] 3 All ER 446, [1997] 1 WLR 967, per Lloyd J. This part of the decision was not subject to the appeal.
6 Land Registration Rules 1925, SI 1925/1093, rr 83, 85.
7 Lloyd J, in *Michaels v Harley House (Marylebone) Ltd* [1997] 3 All ER 446, [1997] 1 WLR 967 was of this view as he considered that it would make, for example, the exception in the LTA 1987, s 4(2)(f) very difficult to apply since the land would change from being functional land of the transferor charity to that of the transferee charity on completion and not on registration.

3.03 Prior to the amendments brought about by the Housing Act 1996[1], the provisions of Part I of the LTA 1987 did not apply to the entry into a contract to create or transfer an estate or interest in land. It had been held, for the purposes of the Act as originally enacted[2], that an exchange of contracts was not a relevant disposal. The right of first refusal now applies to a contract to create or transfer an estate or interest in land as it applies in relation to a disposal which consists of the creation or transfer of such an interest or estate[3].

1 Housing Act 1996, s 89.
2 *Mainwaring v Henry Smith's Charity Trustees* [1998] QB 1, CA.
3 LTA 1987, s 4A discussed in para **3.56** ff.

'Estate or interest'

3.04 The LTA 1987 applies to any disposal of any 'estate or interest' in the qualifying premises. The only estates in land which are capable of subsisting or of being conveyed or created at law are (a) an estate in fee simple absolute in possession, and (b) a term of years absolute[1]. The only interests in or over land which are capable of subsisting or being conveyed or created at law are:

(a) an easement, right or privilege in or over land for an interest equivalent to an estate in fee simple absolute in possession or a term of years absolute;
(b) a rentcharge in possession issuing out of or charged on land being either perpetual or for a term of years absolute;
(c) a charge by way of legal mortgage[2];
(d) any other similar charge on land which is not created by an instrument;
(e) rights of entry exercisable over or in respect of a legal term of years absolute, or annexed, for any purpose, to a legal rent charge.

All other estates, interests and charges in or over land take effect as equitable interests[3].

1 Law of Property Act 1925, s 1(1)(a), (b).
2 Law of Property Act 1925, s 1(2) includes two forms of charge which are capable of subsisting or of being conveyed or created at law, namely a 'charge by way of legal mortgage' or 'any other

similar charge on land which is not created by an instrument': Law of Property Act 1925, s 1(2)(c) and (d) respectively. Although s 4(1) of the LTA 1987 refers only to 'estate or interest' and does not specifically include charge, it is clear that the grant of a mortgage is a relevant disposal. Not only is this not an excluded disposal under s 4(2) of the LTA 1987, but the grant of a mortgage is clearly the grant of either a legal estate (if the mortgage takes effect by way of a sub-demise) or the grant of a legal interest in land.

3 Law of Property Act 1925, s 1(3).

3.05 The estate or interest which may be the subject matter of the disposal may be legal or equitable. Thus the creation of a trust of the landlord's estate or interest confers upon the beneficiaries only an equitable interest but would, nonetheless, be a relevant disposal. Similarly, where the interest of the landlord consists of an agreement for a lease which takes effect in equity as an equitable lease[1], the disposal of such a lease would constitute a relevant disposal. However, the LTA 1987 appears unconcerned with a disposal where the subject matter of the disposal consists only of a beneficial interest in the premises to which the Act applies, eg where the freehold is held on trust for a nominee, the disposal by the beneficiary of his entire beneficial interest will not be caught, for such a disposal, albeit a disposal of an equitable interest in land, is not a disposal 'by the landlord'.

1 *Walsh v Lonsdale* (1882) 21 Ch D 9, CA.

'Any'

3.06 It is to be noted that the disposal is of 'any' estate or interest, whether legal or equitable, in the qualifying premises. It is considered that the disposal need not be of an estate or interest in the entirety of the qualifying premises. This can best be illustrated by an example. L is the freehold owner of a four-storey building, with each storey containing two self-contained flats held by qualifying tenants. Disposal of the freehold interest of one floor, ie the disposal of the reversionary interest in respect of two of the flats held by qualifying tenants, would nevertheless be a relevant disposal, for it is a disposal 'affecting ... premises to which this Part applies'. The building does contain two or more flats held by qualifying tenants, for it contains eight flats held by qualifying tenants. To construe the requirement of the disposal of the estate or interest to relate to the entirety of the qualifying premises would enable the landlord to avoid the LTA 1987 with ease. Two provisions of the LTA 1987 support this view. First, the provisions of the Act relating to relevant disposals 'in any common parts of any such premises'[1] make it clear that in considering whether a disposal is a relevant disposal one asks whether the disposal affects qualifying premises as opposed to asking whether that part of the qualifying premises affected by the disposal itself constitutes qualifying premises. Secondly, the exclusion of a disposal which consists of a grant of any tenancy of a single flat[2] equally suggests that, but for the exclusion, a disposal of part of the qualifying premises would be a relevant disposal. However, it is considered that the grant of a lease of only a shop below residential premises would not amount to a relevant disposal, provided the demise did not include common parts used by residential tenants. Indeed, although the contrary has been suggested[3], the grant of such leases has continued without difficulty. It was plainly not the intention of Parliament to include such transactions. Of course, the disposal of the whole building would be caught (subject to the 50% rule, discussed in para **2.06**).

1 LTA 1987, s 4(1).
2 LTA 1987, s 4(1)(a). See para **3.11** ff.
3 See the article by R Budge entitled 'Unwitting Criminals' (Estates Gazette 9707, p 141).

Common parts

3.07 A disposal of any legal or equitable estate or interest in any common parts of qualifying premises is equally a relevant disposal[1]. 'Common parts' are defined 'in relation to any building or part of a building' as including 'the structure and exterior of that building or part and any common facilities within it'[2]. Thus the grant of the freehold or a lease of part of the qualifying premises, eg its roof or outside walls, would be a relevant disposal. It is unclear whether a disposal of an estate or interest in communal gardens would be a qualifying disposal. The definition of 'common parts' refers to matters which are 'within' the building. However, the definition is not exhaustive[3].

1 LTA 1987, s 4(1).
2 LTA 1987, s 60(1).
3 LTA 1987, s 60(1).

3.08 The express reference to a relevant disposal (including the disposal of an estate or interest), whether legal or equitable, in the common parts causes a problem with, but does not prevent, one of the methods of seeking to avoid the consequences of the LTA 1987. As will be seen, the grant of a tenancy under which the demised premises consist of a single flat (whether with or without any appurtenant premises) is not a relevant disposal[1]. It was, prior to the amendments brought about by the Housing Act 1996[2], and remains, common for landlords to seek to avoid the LTA 1987 by granting individual tenancies of flats within the block. Provided such tenancies are tenancies for terms of not less than seven years, the landlord is then able to dispose of the freehold of the flats, for, in relation to the flats, the landlord is not a qualifying landlord[3]. However, this scheme fails to deal with the 'common parts' of the qualifying premises. Any disposition of the freehold interest of the common parts would be caught[4].

1 LTA 1987, s 4(1)(a). See also para **3.11** ff.
2 Which criminalise the failure to comply with the provisions of the LTA 1987 in relation to any relevant disposal. See para **10.09**.
3 Having regard to the provisions of the LTA 1987, s 2(2)(a). See para **2.12**.
4 The problem with common parts is not a particularly difficult hurdle to overcome in an attempt to avoid the provisions of the LTA 1987. A lease of the common parts could be granted, say, in excess of seven years. This would, of course, have to be offered to the qualifying tenants. It may or may not be accepted by the qualifying tenants. Assuming it is, the landlord, nevertheless, disposes of his freehold interest in the entirety immediately after the grant of the leases, including

the lease of the common parts (even if this has been taken up by the qualifying tenants). Upon the expiry of the seven-year lease of the common parts, the qualifying tenants' interest therein disappears and the new reversioner steps in free of the qualifying tenants' previous leasehold interest therein. The problem, if any, is simply a practical one, namely that the new reversioner must accept that his freehold may be subject to a seven-year lease of the common parts. The idea behind the scheme is that in light of the limited extent and short term nature of the interest offered to the qualifying tenants, the qualifying tenants will be unlikely to accept the offer.

Disposal by mortgagee

3.09 Where an estate or interest of the landlord has been mortgaged, the reference to a disposal of an estate or interest by the landlord includes a reference to its disposal by the mortgagee in exercise of a power of sale or leasing, whether or not the disposal is made in the name of the landlord[1]. The grant of a mortgage, where it is for the purposes of security for a loan[2], is not a relevant disposal. The grant of a mortgage may possibly be utilised as a means of avoiding the provisions of the LTA 1987[3].

1 LTA 1987, s 4(1A). In relation to such a proposed disposal by the mortgagee, any reference in the provisions of Part I of the LTA 1987 to 'the landlord' is to be construed as a reference to the mortgagee: LTA 1987, s 4(1A).
2 LTA 1987, s 4(2)(aa); see para **3.19**.
3 As to which see further para **3.20**.

Excluded disposals

3.10 There are numerous disposals which do not initiate the right of first refusal as they are excluded from being relevant disposals.

Grant of tenancy of flat

3.11 The grant of any tenancy under which the demised premises consists of a single flat (whether with or without any appurtenant premises) is not a relevant disposal[1].

1 LTA 1987, s 4(1)(a).

3.12 'Any tenancy' of a single flat is exempt. No conditions are imposed as to the terms upon which the tenancy is to be granted, eg as to the rent or its duration. Thus it matters not whether the lease is 99 years or the grant of a periodic tenancy.

3.13 'Flat' is defined as meaning a 'separate set of premises, whether or not on the same floor, which (a) forms part of a building, and (b) is divided horizontally from some other part of that building, and (c) is constructed or adapted for use for the purposes of a dwelling'[1].

1 LTA 1987, s 60(1). As to this definition, see para **2.05**.

3.14 The tenancy of the single flat may be with or without 'any appurtenant premises'[1]. It is provided[2] that in relation to a flat 'appurtenant premises' means any yard, garden, outhouse or appurtenance (not being a common part of the building containing the flat) which belongs to, or is usually enjoyed with, the flat.

1 LTA 1987, s 4(1).
2 LTA 1987, s 4(4).

3.15 A similar provision is to be found in the Leasehold Reform Act 1967[1]. In the context of that Act, which applies only to houses, the tenant is entitled to require a conveyance not only of the house but of the 'house and premises', and the reference to 'premises' is to be taken as referring to any 'garage, outhouse, garden, yard and appurtenances which at the relevant time were let to [the tenant] with the house and are occupied with and used for the purposes of the house or any part of it by him or by another occupant'[2]. It has been held for the purposes of the Leasehold Reform Act 1967 that 'appurtenances' extended to land within the curtilage of the house[3]. It has been said that 'for one corporeal hereditament to fall within the curtilage of another, the former must be so intimately associated with the latter as to lead to the conclusion that the former in truth forms part and parcel of the latter'[4]. That decision was distinguished in a case involving a claim to a new lease of a flat under the Leasehold Reform, Housing and Urban Development Act 1993[5]. A storeroom on the sixth floor of a building was held to be an appurtenance of a flat on the second floor, each being demised by a lease granted for the same term. In the context of the LTA 1987 an obvious appurtenance to a flat would be, for instance, a garage[6].

1 Leasehold Reform Act 1967, s 2(3).
2 Leasehold Reform Act 1967, s 2(3).
3 *Methuen-Campbell v Walters* [1979] QB 525.
4 *Methuen-Campbell v Walters* [1979] QB 525, per Buckley LJ at 544.
5 *Cadogan v McGirk* [1996] 4 All ER 643.
6 Unless let under a separate lease, in which case it would not be an 'appurtenance': *Denetower Ltd v Toop* [1991] 1 WLR 945.

3.16 If the tenancy is of a *single* flat but includes non-appurtenant premises, then it is considered that the disposal is a relevant disposal. The grant of a tenancy of *more* than one flat is not within the terms of the exclusion. What of the grant of a single tenancy consisting of business premises on the ground floor with residential accommodation above? Assume a building with four shops on the ground floor and eight flats above on first and second floors[1], with each shop having two flats above. The building thus consists of two or more flats and, assuming that the other conditions for the application of the LTA 1987 are satisfied[2], the grant of a single tenancy of the shop premises and of the two flats above would appear to be caught[3].

1 It is also to be assumed that the provisions of s 1(3) of the LTA 1987 are not satisfied so that the Act applies to the whole of the building.
2 LTA 1987, s 1(2).
3 As to whether the grant of a tenancy of just the shop could be a relevant disposal, see para **3.06**.

Interest of beneficiary in settled land

3.17 A disposal of any interest of a beneficiary in settled land within the meaning of the Settled Land Act 1925 is not a relevant disposal[1]. Under the terms of the Settled Land Act 1925 the beneficiary in whom the estate is vested for life (the tenant for life) holds the legal estate on trust for himself and those who succeed thereafter upon his death[2]. As the legal estate is vested in the tenant for life, the tenant for life may transfer the legal estate during the course of his life. The tenant for life has a statutory power to transfer the legal estate[3]. It is considered that the reference to 'the interest of a beneficiary in settled land' is referring to the tenant for life's estate for life in equity and not the ownership of the legal estate of which he is trustee. The tenant for life's interest is a conditional one[4], such that his interest determines before his death, the tenant for life must convey the legal estate to the new owner[5]. The provisions of the LTA 1987 appear to make no distinction between voluntary disposals by the tenant for life and disposals by him required by the provisions of the Settled Land Act[6].

1 LTA 1987, s 4(2)(a)(i). It should noted that, subject to minor exception, it has not been possible to create new settlements under the Settled Land Act 1925 after 1996: the Trusts of Land and Appointment of Trustees Act 1996, s 2. Any new settlements are governed by the 1996 Act. The exceptions are set out in s 2(2) of the 1996 Act and are not material for present purposes.
2 Settled Land Act 1925, ss 16(1). The tenant for life is constituted the 'estate owner'; see s 117(1)(xi) as to the meaning of 'estate owner'.
3 Settled Land Act 1925, s 38(i). The power is left untouched by the Trustee Act 2000.
4 Ie determinable upon an event, eg where land is settled upon A for life or until he shall reach 30 years of age, remainder to B for life and remainder to C in fee simple. Upon reaching 30, A must convey to B by a vesting deed.
5 Settled Land Act 1925, s 7(4).
6 However, it is considered that the transfer by the tenant for life of the legal estate to the new tenant for life is exempt under the LTA 1987, s 4(2)(g), as the tenant for life is a trustee of the legal estate: Settled Land Act 1925, s 16(1).

A disposal of an incorporeal hereditament

3.18 The disposal of any incorporeal hereditament is not a relevant disposal[1]. Thus the grant to a third party of a right to use, in common with the tenants of a block of flats, the communal gardens[2] is not a relevant disposal. One can imagine cases where the landlord would wish to grant rights of way, eg over estate roads, where the estate consists or more than one building. The grant of various rights over the road is not, therefore, hampered by having to comply with the provisions of the LTA 1987.

1 LTA 1987, s 4(2)(a)(iii).
2 Provided of course that this is permitted by the terms of the tenants' leases. It may be, in any event, that the grant of rights over communal gardens or estate roads is not a relevant disposal as such premises do not constitute 'a building', nor do they fall within the definition of 'common parts'; see paras **2.03** and **3.07**.

A disposal by way of security for a loan

3.19 A disposal by way of security for a loan is not a relevant disposal[1]. It is clear that the grant of a mortgage over the landlord's interest in respect of qualifying premises would not constitute a relevant disposal, provided it is a disposal by way of security for a loan. There is, however, no requirement that the security and the loan be simultaneous transactions. There is no reason why, therefore, the provision of further security for a loan already made should not qualify as an exempt disposal. Nor, it should be noted, is there any requirement that the loan be a loan to the landlord. One can well imagine security being provided, for instance, in the context of group companies by one member of the group for a loan made by the mortgagee. No conditions are laid down as to the minimum or maximum duration of the period of the loan.

1 LTA 1987, s 4(2)(aa).

3.20 This category of exclusion would appear to be one capable of, albeit limited, exploitation. L could grant a mortgage to the prospective purchaser, P, for a loan which reflects the market value of the rents receivable from occupational tenants within the property. For X number of years, the mortgage agreement provides that the loan is repayable by the mortgagee, P, recouping the money from the occupational tenants. P can enter into possession immediately, since a legal mortgage gives the mortgagee a legal estate in possession[1]. The mortgagee can take possession of the mortgaged property even if there is no default[2]. In the case of a block of flats the mortgagee cannot, of course, take physical possession. He may, however, take possession constructively by directing the tenants to pay their rents to him instead of to the mortgagor[3]. A mortgagee in possession is entitled to sue the tenants on their covenants[4].

1 This is subject to any agreement to the contrary in the mortgage deed.
2 *Four-Maids Limited v Dudley Marshall (Properties) Ltd* [1957] Ch 317.
3 *Horlock v Smith* (1842) 6 Jur 478.
4 Landlord and Tenant (Covenants) Act 1995, s 15 in respect of a new lease governed by that Act, ie one granted after 1 January 1996. A disposal by the mortgagee in exercise of a power of sale or leasing is not an exempt disposal: LTA 1987, s 4(1A); see para **3.09**.

A disposal to a trustee in bankruptcy or to the liquidator of a company

3.21 Neither a disposal to a trustee in bankruptcy or to a liquidator of a company is a relevant disposal[1]. Oddly, the LTA 1987 does not state expressly that the trustee or the liquidator should be the trustee or liquidator of the landlord, although this was presumably the intention.

1 LTA 1987, s 4(2)(b).

Disposal to a trustee in bankruptcy

3.22 Upon the bankruptcy of the landlord, the landlord's estate or interest will vest in the trustee in bankruptcy once appointed[1]. Any disposition by the bankrupt after the presentation of the petition for bankruptcy and prior to the vesting in the trustee, without the leave of the court, is void[2]. Property held by the bankrupt on trust for others is excluded from the transfer to the trustee[3]. This includes property in which the bankrupt is beneficially entitled[4]. This exclusion of property which would otherwise vest in the trustee will accordingly cover the case of a person who constitutes one of two or more joint landlords of the reversion[5]. A disposal *by* the trustee in bankruptcy is not an exempt disposal.

1 Insolvency Act 1996, s 306.
2 Insolvency Act 1996, s 284(3).
3 Insolvency Act 1996, s 283(3).
4 *Re a Solicitor (1951 M 234)* [1952] Ch 328.
5 Law of Property Act 1925, ss 34, 36 as amended by the Trusts of Land and Appointment of Trustees Act 1996.

Disposal to a liquidator of a company

3.23 On the making of a winding-up order the property of a company does not vest in the liquidator. The liquidator may, however, apply to the court for an order vesting property of the company in the liquidator[1]. A disposal *by* the liquidator will not be an exempt disposal.

1 Insolvency Act 1996, s 145(1).

Disposals made in connection with matrimonial proceedings

3.24 Several disposals are excluded from being relevant disposals where they are made in connection with matrimonial proceedings. One can see the sense behind these exclusionary provisions. It is unlikely that frequent resort will have to be made to these provisions in practice and are likely to be confined to fairly small property holdings. It is not a relevant disposal if a disposal is made in pursuance of an order made under:

(1) the Matrimonial Causes Act 1973, ss 238 or 24 (property adjustment orders in connection with matrimonial proceedings);
(2) the Matrimonial Causes Act 1973, s 24A (orders for the sale of property in connection with matrimonial proceedings) where the order includes provision

requiring the property concerned to be offered for sale to a person or class of persons specified in the order;

(3) the Inheritance (Provision for Family and Dependants) Act 1975, s 2 (orders as to financial provision to be made from estate);

(4) the Matrimonial and Family Proceedings Act 1984, s 17(1) (property adjustment after overseas divorce, etc);

(5) the Matrimonial and Family Proceedings Act 1984, s 17(2) (orders for the sale of property after overseas divorce, etc) where the order includes provision requiring the property concerned to be offered for sale to a person or class of persons specified in the order; or

(6) the Children Act 1989, Sch 1, para 1 (orders for financial relief against parents)[1].

1 LTA 1987, s 4(2)(c)(i)–(vi) inclusive.

Compulsory purchase

3.25 A disposal in pursuance of a compulsory purchase order or in pursuance of an agreement entered into in circumstances where, but for the agreement, such an order would have been made or (as the case may be) carried into effect[1].

1 LTA 1987, s 4(2)(d).

3.26 The latter part of this exclusion is intended to deal with the situation of an agreement entered into with the acquiring authority either to pre-empt an order which would be made or, where an order has been made, to pre-empt it being carried into effect.

Collective enfranchisement

3.27 A disposal of any freehold or leasehold interest in pursuance of Ch 1 of Part I of the Leasehold Reform, Housing and Urban Development Act 1993 is not a relevant disposal[1]. Chapter 1 of Part I of the 1993 Act deals with collective enfranchisement in the case of tenants' flats. Thus where the tenants of a block of flats have gone through the various procedural requirements of the 1993 Act a disposal pursuant to the 1993 Act is not caught by the provisions of the LTA 1987. In order to implement the collective enfranchisement provisions, notice has to be served by not less than two-thirds of the qualifying tenants of the flats contained in the relevant premises as at the date when the notice is given[2]. In addition, not less than one-half of the qualifying tenants by whom the notice is given must satisfy a residence condition[3]. In the context of the LTA 1987, any acceptance of an offer notice need be made only by 51% of the qualifying tenants[4].

Thus under the Leasehold Reform, Housing and Urban Development Act 1993 there is a greater proportion of involvement of the qualifying tenants than there is in the case of acceptance under the LTA 1987. However, it should be remembered that, unlike the LTA 1987, the 1993 Act gives rights only to long lessees. The landlord is not prevented from selling his interest after an initial notice under s 13 of the 1993 Act has been served; however, he must in those circumstances serve an offer notice on the tenants under the LTA 1987.

1 LTA 1987, s 4(2)(da).
2 Leasehold Reform, Housing and Urban Development Act 1993, s 13(2).
3 Leasehold Reform, Housing and Urban Development Act 1993, s 13(2A). The recently introduced Commonhold and Leasehold Reform Bill proposes to abolish the residence requirement and reduce the required number to 50%.
4 LTA 1987, ss 6(3), 18A.

Gifts

3.28 A disposal by way of gift to a member of the landlord's family or to a charity is not a relevant disposal[1].

1 LTA 1987, s 4(2)(e).

Disposal by way of gift to members of landlord's family

3.29 This category of exclusion is limited to disposals by way of gift to members of the landlord's family. A person is a member of another's family for the purposes of this category of exclusion if:

(a) that person is the spouse of that other person, or the two of them live together as husband and wife[1], or
(b) that person is that other person's parent, grandparent, child, grandchild, brother, sister, uncle, aunt, nephew or niece[2].

For the purposes of category (b):

(a) a relationship by marriage shall be treated as a relationship by blood;
(b) a relationship of the half-blood shall be treated as a relationship of the whole blood;
(c) the stepchild of a person shall be treated as his child; and
(d) an illegitimate child shall be treated as the legitimate child of his mother and reputed father[3].

1 The requirement that the two live together as 'husband and wife' excludes couples of the same sex: *Fitzpatrick v Sterling Housing Association Ltd* [2001] AC 27, HL dealing with similar wording in para 2(2) of Sch 1 to the Rent Act 1977.

2 LTA 1987, s 4(5).
3 LTA 1987, s 4(6).

3.30 'Gift' is not defined. It would include a disposal in consideration of 'love and affection'.

Gifts to charity

3.31 'Charity' means a charity within the meaning of the Charities Act 1993[1].

1 LTA 1987, s 60(1).

Disposals by charities

3.32 A disposal by one charity to another of an estate or interest in land which, prior to the disposal, is functional land of the first-mentioned charity and which is intended to be functional land of the other charity once the disposal is made is not a relevant disposal[1]. 'Functional land' in relation to a charity means land occupied by the charity, or by trustees for it, and wholly or mainly used for charitable purposes[2], and 'charitable purposes' means charitable purposes whether of that charity or of that charity and other charities[3].

1 LTA 1987, s 4(2)(f).
2 LTA 1987, s 60(1).
3 LTA 1987, s 60(1).

Appointment or discharge of trustee

3.33 A disposal consisting of the transfer of an estate or interest held on trust for any person where the disposal is made in connection with the appointment of a new trustee or in connection with the discharge of any trustee is not a relevant disposal[1].

1 LTA 1987, s 4(2)(g). For a possible avoidance scheme, see para **10.05**.

3.34 No more than four trustees of settled land or land held on a trust of land can be appointed, whether the title is unregistered or registered[1]. Where more than four persons are named as trustees, the first four named who are able and willing to act become trustees to the exclusion of the others[2]. The limitation on the number of trustees does not apply to land held on trust for charitable, ecclesiastical or public purposes, where there is no limit to the number of trustees[3]. There is no minimum number of trustees even in respect of land[4].

1 Trustee Act 1925, s 34(2) (as amended by the Trusts of Land and Appointment of Trustees Act 1996, s 25(1), Sch 3, para 3); Land Registration Act 1925, s 95 (as amended by the Trusts of Land and Appointment of Trustees Act 1996, s 25(1), Sch 3, para 5).

2 Trustee Act 1925, s 34(2) (as amended by the Trusts of Land and Appointment of Trustees Act 1996, s 25(1), Sch 3, para 3).
3 Trustee Act 1925, s 34(3).
4 However, where land is settled or held on a trust of land a sole trustee cannot give a valid receipt for capital money, notwithstanding any contra-provision, unless that trustee is a trust corporation: Settled Land Act 1925, s 94(1); Law of Property Act 1925, s 27(2) (as amended).

3.35 Trustees of settled land have no property vested in them[1]. In such cases no question of vesting of property arises upon the appointment, retirement, removal or death of such a trustee.

1 Megarry and Wade, *The Law of Real Property* (6th edn), para 8.108. The legal estate is vested in the tenant for life: see para **3.17**.

3.36 Where new trustees of a trust of land are appointed, the trust property will need to be vested in the new trustees jointly with any continuing trustees. Where the appointment is made by deed, a declaration therein by the appointer that the property shall vest in the trustees ('a vesting declaration') is sufficient to vest the property in the new and continuing trustees[1]. This is not the case, however, in relation to land held under a lease with a provision against assigning or disposing of the land without consent, unless the requisite consent has been obtained or the vesting declaration would not be a breach of covenant or give rise to a forfeiture[2]. In this case the trust property would need to be transferred other than by a vesting declaration and be transferred in the normal way. Where the land is registered land, the new trustee must be registered as a proprietor of the land. This is done either by executing a transfer in the usual form in favour of all the new trustees or by submitting a deed of appointment to the registrar, which appointment is deemed to be a conveyance of the land[3] and which the registrar will give effect to by making a proper entry on the register[4].

1 Trustee Act 1925, s 40(1)(a).
2 Trustee Act 1925, s 40(4)(b).
3 Trustee Act 1925, s 40(5).
4 Land Registration Act 1925, s 47(1).

3.37 Where a trustee retires or is discharged from the trust without any new trustee being appointed, the land can be divested from the former trustee and vested solely in the continuing trustee by means of a vesting declaration[1]. The same exception as in the appointment of new trustees applies[2] where the land is held under a lease.

1 Trustee Act 1925, s 40(2)(a). The deed must be executed by the retiring/removed trustee, the continuing trustees and any person with power to appoint new trustees.
2 See para **3.33**.

3.38 Upon the death of one trustee the estate or interest vested in him passes to the surviving trustee by the doctrine of survivorship[1].

1 This arises where two or more persons are made joint tenants or joint owners of the trust property. On the death of one joint tenant the remaining or sole remaining joint tenant holds the land by the right of survivorship (jus accrescendi). Trustees are always made joint tenants because of the convenience of trust property passing automatically by the right of survivorship to the other trustees when one trustee dies. For a full discussion of the nature of a joint tenancy see Megarry and Wade, *The Law of Real Property* (6th edn), para 9.002.

Inter-family transfers

3.39 A disposal is not a relevant disposal where it consists of a transfer by two or more persons who are members of the same family either:

(a) to fewer of their number, or

(b) to a different combination of members of the family (but one that includes at least one of the transferors)[1].

1 LTA 1987, s 4(2)(h).

3.40 The question of who is a member of another's family is considered in para **3.29**.

Disposal pursuant to contractually binding obligations

3.41 The entry into a contract for the disposal of the landlord's interest in respect of qualifying premises is a relevant disposal[1]. A disposal *in pursuance* of a contract, option or right of pre-emption binding on the landlord is not, subject to an exception, a relevant disposal[2].

1 See para **3.57**.
2 LTA 1987, s 4(2)(a)(i).

Contract

3.42 If there is a pre-existing contractual obligation, that is to say one which affected the premises prior to their becoming premises to which the LTA 1987 applies, then, upon the premises subsequently becoming premises to which the Act applies, any transfer of the landlord's interest will be immune from the provisions relating to the right of first refusal. A common example of where this category of exclusion is advantageous arises in connection with residential developments where it is proposed to transfer the freehold interest to a management company or to grant to the management company a long leasehold interest, with the management company eventually being owned by the tenants as shareholders. In this form of development the management company is usually retained by the developer/owner until the sale of all the flats within the development and it is then transferred to the tenants. Upon the incorporation of the management company and prior to the commencement of the sale of the flats, it is advantageous for the developer/owner to enter into a contractual obligation with the management company to transfer to the management company the landlord's interest or to grant to the management company of the head lease upon the completion of the development (as defined by the terms of the relevant contract between the developer/owner and the management company). If no provision for this is made then upon the completion of the development, a transfer of the freehold interest or a long intermediate leasehold to the management company would be a relevant disposal and, therefore, the provisions of the LTA 1987 would need to be complied with, albeit the disposal is effectively to the tenants themselves.

Option

3.43 The *grant* of an option *is* a relevant disposal. The grant of an option is the grant of an equitable interest in land[1]. The qualifying tenants of qualifying premises will, therefore, have their opportunity of acquiring the interest the subject matter of the option upon its grant not upon a disposal pursuant to the exercise of an option once granted[2]. There is no definition of 'option'. It is considered that it would include a put option[3] as well as the more usual call option.

1 *London and South Western Rly Co v Gomm* (1882) 20 Ch D 562.
2 As to disposals pursuant to an option, see **3.45**.
3 That is one where the landlord has the option of calling upon a party to purchase his interest, usually within a specified time and for a calculable consideration.

Pre-emption

3.44 A right of pre-emption is one whereby the owner of the land has agreed not to dispose of it without first giving the grantee the opportunity of acquiring it. Although there is no obligation upon the grantor to sell the property, if he should do so he is required first to offer it to the grantee who is then free to accept or reject it. The *grant* of a right of pre-emption does not create an equitable interest in land until the terms upon which the right of pre-emption become exercisable have arisen, ie from the time that the owner decides to dispose of the property within the terms of the pre-emption granted[1]. Thus ordinarily the grant of a right of pre-emption would not be a relevant disposal for it is not the disposal of 'any estate or interest (whether legal or equitable)' in respect of premises to which Part I of the LTA 1987 applies. However, 'disposal' is expressly defined so as to include the grant of a right of pre-emption[2].

1 *Pritchard v Briggs* [1980] Ch 338, CA.
2 LTA 1987, s 4(3)(a).

The exception: disposal pursuant to option or pre-emption

3.45 A disposal *in pursuance* of an option or right of pre-emption is *not* a relevant disposal[1]. However, the disposal pursuant to the option or right of pre-emption can qualify as a relevant disposal if it is made soon after the creation of the option or right pursuant to which the disposal is being made. If the disposal in pursuance of the option or right or pre-emption is made before the expiry of the period for notification to the requisite majority of qualifying tenants of the constituent flats of the *grant*[2] of the option or right of pre-emption, then the disposal qualifies as a relevant disposal. Moreover, if the disposal pursuant to the option or right of pre-emption is made before the expiry of the relevant period[3], the provisions of the LTA 1987, ss 11–17 have effect as if the later disposal and not the original disposal (ie the grant) were the relevant disposal[4].

1 LTA 1987, s 4(2).
2 Which itself will have given rise to a relevant disposal: see para **3.43**.
3 As to which see para **3.46**.
4 LTA 1987, s 8D(1)(b).

3.46 The period prior to which a disposal *in pursuance* of an option or right of pre-emption is caught by the provisions of Part I of the LTA 1987 is a period of four months beginning with the date by which:

(a) notices under s 3A of the Landlord and Tenant Act 1985[1] relating to the original disposal[2]; or

(b) where that section does not apply, documents of any other description:
   (i) indicating that the original disposal has taken place, and
   (ii) alerting the tenants to the existence of their rights under Part I of the LTA 1987 and the time within which any such rights must be exercised,

have been served on the requisite majority of qualifying tenants of the constituent flats[3].

Thus the minimum period between grant and disposal pursuant to the grant is four months beginning with one of the above dates. The disposal is exempt if it takes place outside the four-month period.

1 It is difficult to see how this section has any relevance in the context of an original disposal which is the grant of an option or a right of pre-emption. A notice under the Landlord and Tenant Act 1985, s 3A is to be served only if the 'new landlord' is required to serve a notice under s 3 of the 1985 Act. Section 3 of the 1985 Act applies only where there has been an assignment of the landlord's interest under the tenancy. The grant of an option or right of pre-emption in respect of the landlord's reversionary estate is not, however, an assignment of the landlord's interest. As to ss 3 and 3A, see paras **6.05–6.08**.
2 An 'original disposal' is one which has been made without complying with the notice requirements of the Act: LTA 1987, s 11(1).
3 LTA 1987, s 8D.

3.47 By way of summary:

(a) a disposal consisting of the grant of an option or right of pre-emption ('the original grant') is a relevant disposal[1];

(b) a disposal pursuant to the original grant is ordinarily an exempt disposal[2];

(c) a disposal pursuant to the original grant is not exempt if made before the expiry of the relevant four-month period. Where the disposal is not exempt, the disposal pursuant to the original grant, and not the original grant, is to be treated as the relevant disposal for the purposes of the exercise of the tenants' rights. It is considered that if the grant was preceded by service of an appropriate offer notice, the disposal pursuant to the original grant will ordinarily be exempt[3].

1 LTA 1987, s 4(1).

2 LTA 1987, s 8D.

3 It has been suggested that s 8D of the LTA 1987 can apply, albeit the landlord has served a s 5C notice prior to the grant of the option. If the landlord has complied with his statutory duty and given the tenants the chance to acquire the interest granted by serving an appropriate s 5C notice, it would seem odd that the qualifying tenants may have a further right (by virture of s 8D treating the *exercise* of the grant as the relevant disposal) to acquire the subject matter of the grant upon its exercise. If, for instance, the landlord, during the two-month period for acceptance of the offer, *grants* the option or right of pre-emption in breach of the provisions of the LTA 1987, s 6, the relevant disposal is still the grant; s 8D has no application. The qualifying tenants have their rights to acquire the option or pre-emption so granted pursuant to s 12B of the LTA 1987. If the landlord has served a s 5C notice, the landlord has to give a minimum of two months for acceptance and a further minimum period of two months for nomination of the nominated person: LTA 1987, s 5C(4), (5). If the qualifying tenants do not accept the offer within the two-month period for acceptance, the landlord may effect the disposal, ie grant the option or right of pre-emption. However, the landlord cannot effect the disposal (the grant) before the expiry of the period expiring with the time for nomination (ie four months), notwithstanding that acceptance has not been given in the two-month period: LTA 1987, s 7(1); see para **5.06**. It is difficult, therefore, to see how, if the landlord complies with those time limits, the option, when exercised, will be exercised within the period specified by sub-s (2) of s 8D, for the landlord is not required to serve any notices upon making the disposal in circumstances where the tenants have declined the offer and the landlord has waited for the protected period to expire. An 'original disposal' is one which does not comply with the Act: LTA 1987, s 11(1). The premise of s 8D is that the original disposal was not in accordance with the Act. The exercise of the grant after a prior s 5C notice should be exempt. It would seem therefore that s 8D will apply after service of a s 5C notice only where the landlord does not wait for the tenants to decide whether or not to accept the offer and grants the option *and effects a disposal pursuant to it* contrary to s 6.

Surrender of tenancy

3.48 Ordinarily a surrender of a tenancy other than in pursuance of a covenant, condition or agreement, is a relevant disposal[1]. A disposal consisting of the surrender of a tenancy in pursuance of any covenant, condition or agreement contained in it is not a relevant disposal[2]. Thus if L, the freehold owner, wishes to take a surrender of the intermediate lessees' long leasehold interest so as to acquire the immediate reversion to the qualifying tenants of flats within the building, any variation of the intermediate lease to provide for its surrender in the future or for its immediate surrender will, in the absence of any covenant, condition or agreement contained within the tenancy agreement, be a relevant disposal. What if the parties avoid entering into an agreement of surrender of the tenancy but make provision for its termination by service of a break notice either by L or the intermediate lessee subject to payment of the appropriate 'purchase' price? The break clause does not reduce the original term. A break notice is a unilateral act of one of the parties, whereas surrender is bilateral. A break notice exercisable by the intermediate lessee does not give rise to the grant of any equitable interest in favour of the landlord or of the intermediate lessee. 'Disposal' is expressly defined to include 'the grant of an option'[3]. In context it would appear that the draftsman of the statutory wording was considering that the option referred to was that of the acquisition of an interest in land, ie principally the grant of an option to acquire the reversion. It is considered that the grant of a break-clause is not a relevant disposal, albeit the tenants may desire to acquire the grant of the 'option' to determine in order to frustrate the landlord's scheme.

1 LTA 1987, s 4(3).
2 LTA 1987, s 4(2)(j).
3 LTA 1987, s 4(3)(a).

3.49 There is no definition of 'surrender of a tenancy'. It would presumably include both an express surrender and surrender by operation of law. Surrender by operation of law will arise by the grant by the landlord of a valid new lease to the tenant, where the new lease is to commence during the currency of the existing lease[1]. However, a variation of the terms of an existing lease will not necessarily give rise to a surrender. It is only if the variation cannot be effected without the grant of a new lease that it would take effect as a surrender and re-grant. It has been held that a variation of the term or an expansion of the premises demised will take effect as a surrender and re-grant[2]. A variation in the terms of the lease (eg as to user or alienation) or in the rent is unlikely to give rise to a surrender and re-grant[3].

1 *Lyon v Reed* (1844) 13 M & W; *Jenkin R Lewis v Kerman* [1971] Ch 477. The landlord has no power to make such a grant unless the old lease has been surrendered.
2 *Friends' Provident Life Office v British Railways Board* [1996] 1 All ER 336.
3 *Friends' Provident Life Office v British Railways Board* [1996] 1 All ER 336.

3.50 The LTA 1987 talks of 'a surrender of *a tenancy*'. If there is a surrender of part only of the premises demised by the relevant tenancy can this be described as a surrender of a tenancy[1]? One can imagine, for instance, a situation where the intermediate lessee surrenders all of the premises demised by the relevant tenancy save, for example, one vacant flat within the block, and then grants a tenancy only of that flat back to the landlord so the landlord effectively acquires entire control over the block[2].

1 It would not appear that it gives right to a re-grant in relation to the remainder: *Holme v Brunskill* (1878) 3 QBD 495, CA.
2 It will undoubtedly be argued that the arrangement was a 'sham' and that effectively there was a surrender of the entirety back to the landlord. However, one must keep in mind the words of Sir Thomas Bingham MR in *Belvedere Court Management Ltd v Frogmore Developments Ltd* [1997] QB 858, CA where he said that: 'I am not for my part satisfied that in the field of real property the

principles in *W T Ramsay Ltd v IRC* [1982] AC 300 and *Furniss v Dawson* [1984] AC 474 entitle the courts simply to ignore or override apparently effective transactions which on their face confer an interest in land on the transferee. Many transactions between group companies may be artificial. That does not entitle the court in ordinary circumstances to treat such transactions as null'.

3.51 The surrender of the tenancy must, of course, be by the 'landlord'[1]. It may be possible to bring about the desired surrender by seeking first to grant to the superior landlord a lease of the reversion[2], say, for a term of seven years plus one day, followed by a surrender of the landlord's lease to the superior landlord. If the requisite majority of qualifying tenants of constituent flats wish to take this lease up they will do so, but in the knowledge that at the expiration of the term that is the end of their interest in the building. But taking the seven-year lease will not prevent the landlord surrendering. The surrender of the landlord's tenancy may be effected for the disposal by way of the surrender is not then a disposal by the 'landlord'[3].

1 As to the meaning of landlord, see para **2.11**.
2 So that the superior landlord will become tenant of the landlord and immediate reversioner of the qualifying tenants.
3 See also the discussion of a similar scheme to avoid the LTA 1987 in para **3.08**.

A disposal to the Crown

3.52 A disposal to the Crown is not a relevant disposal[1]. Although the expression 'Crown interest' is not used in the LTA 1987, s 4(2)(k), which expression is defined in s 56 of the LTA 1987, it is considered that the Crown will be given the same meaning. Accordingly, there is no relevant disposal where there is a disposal to the Crown Estate, the Duchy of Lancaster or Cornwall, or to a government department.

1 LTA 1987, s 4(2)(k).

Disposals to associated companies

3.53 A disposal is not a relevant disposal if it is one by a body corporate to a company which has been an associated company of that body for at least two years[1]. This category of exclusion was inserted by the Housing Act 1996[2]. Prior to this amendment a disposal to an associated company was not a relevant disposal. Thus a common avoidance route was for the landlord to transfer its interest to an associated company and then sell the shares of the associated company. Since there was no transfer of the freehold, Part I of the LTA 1987 did not apply. Parliament has not sought to remove this avoidance route but has made it more difficult to undertake by reason of the requirement that the association of the companies should have existed for a period of at least two years.

1 LTA 1987, s 4(2)(l).
2 Housing Act 1996, s 90.

3.54 An 'associated company' means another body corporate which is (within the meaning of s 736 of the Companies Act 1985) that body's holding company, a subsidiary of that body or another subsidiary of that body's holding company[1]. A company is a 'subsidiary' of another company, its 'holding company', if that other company (a) holds a majority of the voting rights in it; (b) is a member of it and has the right to appoint or remove a majority of its board of directors; or (c) is a member of it and controls alone, pursuant to an agreement with other shareholders or members, a majority of the voting rights in it, or if it is a subsidiary of a company which is itself a subsidiary of that other company[2].

1 LTA 1987, s 20(1).
2 Companies Act 1985, s 736(1).

3.55 The rights held by a company in a fiduciary capacity are to be treated as not held by it[1]. The issue of when voting rights of shares are held in a fiduciary capacity has recently been considered[2]. A registered shareholder who is absolute beneficial owner can vote as he pleases, subject only to imprecise constraints imposed by company law[3]. A registered shareholder who is a nominee must vote in accordance with the directions of the absolute beneficial owner to whom his voting rights are attributed. A registered shareholder who is vendor under an uncompleted contract is in an intermediate position. He is a fiduciary but not a nominee, and his voting rights are for the purposes of the LTA 1987, s 736 in abeyance[4].

3.56 The arrangement to avoid the LTA 1987 by effecting a transfer of the land to an associated company commonly involves three elements: (i) the creation of the associated company; (ii) the transfer of the land to the associated company; and (iii) the transfer of the shares in the associated company to the purchaser. It is essential where the land has not previously been transferred to the associated company that the transfer of the shares in the subsidiary to the purchaser occurs before the transfer of the land. Thus where the landlord entered into an agreement with the purchaser to (i) transfer to the purchaser the shares in the subsidiary, and (ii) transfer the land to the subsidiary on the basis that the transfer of the land was conditional on the purchase of the shares, it was held that (i) the transfer of the land was not on a proper analysis conditional, and (ii) at the time of the transfer of the land the landlord held its shares in the company as a fiduciary for the purchaser and therefore the transfer was not to an associated company[5].

1 Companies Act 1985, s 736A(5).
2 *Michaels v Harley House (Marylebone) Ltd* [2000] Ch 104, CA.
3 *Smith v Croft (No 2)* [1988] Ch 114, 186.
4 *Michaels v Harley House (Marylebone) Ltd* [2000] Ch 104, CA.
5 *Michaels v Harley House (Marylebone) Ltd* [2000] Ch 104, CA.

Application of provisions of the LTA 1987 to contracts

3.57 The provisions of Part I of the LTA 1987 apply to a contract to create or transfer an interest in land, whether conditional or unconditional and whether or not enforceable by specific performance[1]. The Act also applies to an assignment of rights under such a contract[2] as well as contracts to make such an assignment of such rights[3]. All relevant expressions in the LTA 1987 are to be construed accordingly[4]. Thus:

(a) references to a disposal of any description shall be construed as references to a contract to make such a disposal[5];

(b) references to making a disposal of any description shall be construed as references to entering into a contract to make such a disposal[6];

(c) references to the transferee under the disposal shall be construed as references to the other party to the contract and include a reference to any party to whom an estate or interest is to be granted or transferred in pursuance of the contract[7];

(d) references to a disposal of any description shall be construed as references to an assignment of rights under a contract to make such a disposal[8];

(e) references to making a disposal of any description shall be construed as references to making an assignment of rights under a contract to make such a disposal[9];

(f) references to the landlord shall be construed as references to the assignor[10]; and

(g) references to the transferee under the disposal shall be construed as references to the assignee of such rights[11].

1 LTA 1987, s 4A(1).
2 LTA 1987, s 4A(2).
3 LTA 1987, s 4A(3).
4 LTA 1987, s 4A(1), (2).
5 LTA 1987, s 4A(1)(a).
6 LTA 1987, s 4A(1)(b).
7 LTA 1987, s 4A(1)(c).
8 LTA 1987, s 4A(1)(a).
9 LTA 1987, s 4A(1)(b).
10 LTA 1987, s 4A(1)(c).
11 LTA 1987, s 4A(1)(d).

3.58 Under the unamended provisions of the LTA 1987[1] a conditional contract to dispose of the landlord's interest in respect of premises to which the Act applied, which contract was conditional upon the approval by the Leasehold Valuation Tribunal ('LVT') of an estate management scheme pursuant to s 70(1) of Part 1, Ch IV of the Leasehold Reform, Housing and Urban Development Act 1993, was held not to be a relevant disposal[2]. The effect of the amendments is that such a contract would now be a relevant disposal.

1 See now the LTA 1987, s 4A which was inserted by the Housing Act 1996, s 90.
2 *Mainwaring v Henry Smith's Charity Trustees* [1998] QB 1, CA.

3.59 If the landlord proposes to make a relevant disposal affecting premises to which Part I of the LTA 1987 applies, he is required to serve a notice (an 'offer notice') on the qualifying tenants of the flats contained in the premises ('the constituent flats')[1]. It has been held that a landlord 'proposes' to make a relevant disposal albeit he may not have formed a fixed and settled intention to do it[2]. The expression 'proposes' describes a state of mind somewhere between mere consideration of a possible course of action at one extreme and a fixed and irrevocable determination to pursue that course of action at the other[3]. It has been held, prior to the application of the right of first refusal to contracts to create an estate or interest in land, that a landlord proposes to make a relevant disposal by contractually binding himself to sell, albeit the contract is conditional and is one in respect of which specific performance could not be granted[4]. Now that the right of first refusal applies to the entry into a contract to create an estate or interest in land it would seem that, logically, the time at which the landlord can be said to 'propose' within s 5 of the LTA 1987 to make a relevant disposal is, therefore, going to be earlier than the date of actual entry into the contract. The entry into the contract is the latest date by which the landlord 'proposes' to make the relevant disposal. Arguably negotiations which have been concluded but which remain 'subject to contract' will be sufficient to establish that the landlord 'proposes' to make the relevant disposal. Applying the well known dictum of Asquith LJ[5], it has been said that a 'proposal' means a project which has moved out of the 'zone of contemplation ... into the valley of decision'[6]. There is undoubtedly room for argument that albeit the contract has yet to be concluded, nevertheless the landlord has moved out of the zone of contemplation and into the valley of decision.

1 LTA 1987, s 5(1).
2 *Magdalen and Lasher Charity, Hastings (Trustees) v Shelower* (1968) 19 P & CR 389, per Lord Denning MR at 392; approved in *Mainwaring v Henry Smith's Charity Trustees* [1998] QB 1, CA.
3 *Mainwaring v Henry Smith's Charity Trustees* [1998] QB 1, CA.
4 *Mainwaring v Henry Smith's Charity Trustees* [1998] QB 1, CA.
5 Made in the context of the provisions of s 18(1) of the Landlord and Tenant Act 1927 (an intention to undertake structural works so as to render repairs valueless) made in *Cunliffe v Goodman* [1950] 2 KB 237 at 254.
6 *Mainwaring v Henry Smith's Charity Trustees* [1998]QB 1, CA, per Sir Thomas Bingham MR.

3.60 Now that the right of first refusal applies to contracts for the grant of an estate or interest in land as well as contracts for the assignment of the benefit of such a contract, the criminalisation[1] of a failure to comply with the requirements of Part I of the LTA 1987 must be paramount in the mind of advisers of landlords who seek advice as to their legal obligations in relation to the service of offer notices[2].

1 See para **10.09**.
2 LTA 1987, s 10A, inserted by the Housing Act 1996, s 91. A landlord commits an offence if, without reasonable excuse, he makes a relevant disposal affecting premises to which Pt I of the LTA 1987 applied without having first complied with the requirements of s 5 as regards service of notices on the qualifying tenants of flats contained in the qualifying premises: LTA 1987, s 10A(1)(a). See further paras **10.08–10.11**.

3.61 If a landlord has effected a relevant disposal by entry into a contract and the tenants do not (upon the landlord having complied with the provisions of serving the relevant offer notice) acquire the interests so disposed of, the subsequent disposal pursuant to the contract so granted will *not* be a relevant disposal[1]. The wording of this category of exclusion was, prior to the substitution of a new provision by the Housing Act 1996, confined to a contractual obligation binding on the landlord which was created before the commencement of the LTA 1987, ie the contractual obligation was entered into before the commencement of the Act. In light of the extension of the rights of first refusal to entry into contracts generally, it was necessary to make provision to exempt disposals pursuant to the contract entered into where the entry into the contract constitutes the relevant disposal. As has been said it would be absurd if, in a transaction involving the entry into a contract prior to conveyance, there were two relevant disposals, one on the exchange of contracts and another on completion[2]. It is obvious that provision had to be made to avoid this absurdity and thus once the transaction has been entered into and the relevant disposal is the exchange of contracts, the disposal pursuant to the contract so entered into is excluded from being a relevant disposal[3].

1 LTA 1987, s 4(2)(i). The terms of s 4(2)(i) were substituted by the Housing Act 1996, s 89(2).
2 *Mainwaring v Henry Smith's Charity Trustees* [1998] QB 1, per Sir Thomas Bingham MR.
3 Compare the provisions relating to the grant of options and rights of pre-emption and disposals pursuant to the original grant: see para **3.42** ff.

CHAPTER 4

The offer notice

4.01 The landlord gives effect to the tenant's right of first refusal by serving a notice under s 5 of the LTA 1987, called an 'offer notice'[1]. An offer notice must be served 'where' the landlord proposes[2] to make a relevant disposal affecting premises to which the Act applies. The use of the word 'where' as the opening word of s 5(1) has been described as 'somewhat odd' for a draftsman to use[3]. An expression such as 'as soon as', 'once', 'when' or 'if' might have been clearer; however, since the notice must be served a sufficient time before the proposed disposal to allow the tenants to respond, the natural meaning of the provision is that an offer notice must be served as soon as the landlord proposes to make a relevant disposal to a third party[4]. The offer notice must be served on the qualifying tenants[5] of the flats contained in the premises, 'the constituent flats'. It need not, indeed should not, be served on any other tenants or occupants. If there is any doubt that a particular person is a qualifying tenant, the notice should be served under cover of a letter explaining that it is served without prejudice to any contention that may later be made that the recipient is not a qualifying tenant.

1 LTA 1987, s 5(1).
2 See para **3.59** for the meaning of 'purposes'.
3 *Mainwaring v Henry Smith's Charity Trustees* [1998] QB 1, CA, per Sir Thomas Bingham MR at 20F.
4 *Mainwaring v Henry Smith's Charity Trustees* [1998] QB 1, CA.
5 See para **2.13**.

More than one building

4.02 If the proposed transaction involves the disposal of an estate or interest in more than one building – whether or not involving the same estate or interest – the landlord must sever the transaction so as to deal with each building separately[1]. If the landlord does not do so, he does not comply with the LTA 1987, s 5, and so will be treated as not having served a s 5 notice at all, thereby leading to possible prosecution[2], as well as entitling the tenants to proceed under s 11 onwards[3]. It is sometimes difficult to know whether premises are properly to be regarded as one or more buildings[4]; if there is any doubt, the landlord would be well advised to act on the safe side and sever the transaction. The LTA 1987 does not deal with the situation of a lease of more than one building held by 'the landlord' which includes a prohibition on the assignment of part[5].

1 LTA 1987, s 5(3). Cf *Kay Green v Twinsectra Ltd* [1996] 1 WLR 1587, where the Court of Appeal treated the tenants' s 12 purchase notice liberally as far as the description of property was concerned. The problem had been caused by the landlord's failure to sever the transaction and serve s 5 notices in respect of each building: [1996] 1 WLR 1587, per Aldous LJ at 1599C, per Staughton LJ at 1604D.
2 As to which, see para **10.09**.
3 As to which, see para **6.01**.
4 See the discussion of 'building' at para **2.03**.
5 LTA 1987, s 8E does not apply, as to which see para **5.15**.

Service on qualifying tenants

4.03 The obligation under the LTA 1987, s 5(1) is to serve the qualifying tenants, meaning all of them. However, it is possible that one or more will not be effectively served. The Act[1] treats the landlord as having complied with s 5 if he has served an offer notice on not less than 90% of the qualifying tenants on whom a notice is required to be served[2]. However, if the total number of qualifying tenants is less than ten, he will comply with the obligation by serving all but one of them[3]. In the most extreme case, where there are only two qualifying tenants[4] this means that service of a notice on only one of them would suffice. It might be thought acceptable for the landlord deliberately to omit serving 10% of the tenants, choosing to serve those he might believe to be the least interested in exercising their right to first refusal. However, it is considered that the better view is that s 5(1) of the LTA 1987 imposes an obligation to serve all the qualifying tenants[5], and that s 5(5) is a saving provision which only applies if service has been attempted on a particular tenant (or is impossible in practice) but is ineffective. If that view is correct, a landlord may be exposed to criminal prosecution if he deliberately omits to serve a qualifying tenant[6].

1 LTA 1987, s 5(5).
2 LTA 1987, s 5(5)(a).
3 LTA 1987, s 5(5)(b).
4 There must be at least two qualifying tenants for the LTA 1987 to apply to the premises under s 1(2)(b); see para **2.04**.
5 LTA 1987, s 5(1) says 'he shall serve a notice ... on the qualifying tenants'.
6 See para **10.09** for offences under the LTA 1987.

Form of notice

4.04 The LTA 1987 makes detailed provision as to the contents of s 5 notices. However, although there is power to make regulations prescribing the form of notice[1], that power has not been exercised to date, and there is no indication that it will be exercised in the future. The notice must be in writing[2]. Since the amendments made to the LTA 1987 by the Housing Act 1996, there are now different sections dealing with notices involving different types of disposal. Those sections, as we shall see, set out the requirements for the contents of s 5 notices; those contents are mandatory[3]. In Appendix I there are some suggested forms of s 5 notice reflecting those requirements[4]. Other works also set out suggested forms of notice. Some of these go beyond the statutory requirements and, for example, include warnings to the tenants, in bold letters, recommending them to seek independent legal advice. Since this is not required by the LTA 1987, there is no need to include such warnings and, indeed, it may not be in the landlord's interests to do so.

'Offer'

The offer contained in an offer notice under s 5 of the LTA 1987 is deemed to be made subject to contract[5]. Accordingly, it is not capable of acceptance so as to bring into being an enforceable contract. The remaining provisions of the Act deal with the consequences of acceptance.

1 LTA 1987, s 54(3).
2 LTA 1987, s 54(1)(a).
3 LTA 1987, s 5(2) uses the word 'must'.
4 Legal stationers sell forms of s 5 notice of their own composition.
5 LTA 1987, s 20(2)(a). In order to be bound to complete a sale, the parties would have to enter into a contract complying with the requirements of s 2 of the Law of Property (Miscellaneous Provisions) Act 1989.

Contract

4.05 Where the disposal consists of entering into a contract to create or transfer an estate or interest in land[1], the notice must set out the following matters:

(a) Particulars of the principal terms of the proposed disposal. This includes, in particular, the property, and the estate or interest to which the contract relates, and the principal terms of the contract, including the deposit and consideration required[2]. One way of ensuring that this requirement is met would be to enclose a copy of the draft contract with the notice. However, this may be burdensome if the contract is lengthy and there are many tenants to serve, and it is not necessary. If there is any doubt in the landlord's mind as to whether a term is properly described as 'principal', caution should be exercised and it should be referred to[3]. It is important that all the principal terms are referred to; if the tenants do not accept the offer and if the terms of a subsequent disposal by the landlord do not correspond with the s 5 notice, then the situation will be as if no s 5 notice at all had been served[4]. One situation which has arisen in practice is the proposed sale of the headlease of a building with the benefit of a notice of tenant's claim under the Leasehold Reform Act 1967[5]. It is considered that a s 5 notice must, in those circumstances, refer to the fact that the lease is being sold with the benefit of the 1967 Act notice.

(b) A statement that the notice constitutes an offer by the landlord to enter into a contract on the terms set out in the notice, which may be accepted by the requisite majority of qualifying tenants of the constituent flats[6]. There is no requirement to go beyond the statutory wording and, for example, to set out definitions of those terms.

(c) A period within which that offer may be accepted[7]. The period must be not less than two months beginning with the date of service of the notice. If as a result of the notice being served on different tenants on different dates, the period for acceptance would end on different dates, the notice has effect in relation to all the qualifying tenants as if it provided for the period to end on the latest of those dates[8]. Accordingly, if, for example, one tenant is served abroad long after the others, that later date will be the one which is used to calculate the subsequent timetable. There is no need to specify an actual date at least two months hence. The notice may say that the offer can be accepted within two months beginning with the date of service of the offer notice.

(d) A further period of not less than two months within which a person may be nominated by the tenants under s 6 of the LTA 1987[9]. Again, the notice may say that the person may be nominated within two months beginning with the date of acceptance.

1 See s 5A of the LTA 1987. For a discussion of such disposals, see paras **3.41, 3.57**. Section 5A does not apply to the grant of an option or right of pre-emption: LTA 1987, s 5A(6). Those disposals are dealt with by s 5C, as to which see paras **3.43, 3.44**.
2 LTA 1987, s 5A(2).
3 Cf *Michaels v Harley House (Marylebone) Ltd* [2000] Ch 104, CA, where Robert Walker LJ considered (at 122–124) the adequacy of information supplied pursuant to s 11 of the LTA 1987 (before it was amended by the Housing Act 1996). The transaction involved a complex disposal of shares in an associated company.
4 As occurred in *Staszewski v Maribella Ltd* [1998] 1 EGLR 34.
5 The vendor had satisfied the residence requirement under the Leasehold Reform Act 1967 by having occupied one of the flats in the building.
6 LTA 1987, s 5A(3).
7 LTA 1987, s 5A(4).
8 LTA 1987, s 5(4).
9 LTA 1987, s 5A(5). As to the nominated person under the LTA 1987, s 6, see para **5.04**.

Auction

4.06 Where the landlord proposes to make the disposal by means of a sale by public auction held in England and Wales, the offer notice must meet the following requirements[1]:

(a) It must contain particulars of the principal terms of the disposal proposed by the landlord, including the property to which it relates and the estate or interest in that property to be disposed of[2]. There is no express requirement that the reserve price must be mentioned in the offer notice and it is considered that it need not, indeed, should not, be. It is not one of the terms of the disposal, but rather confidential information which, if known, is likely to influence the bidding at the auction.

(b) It must state that the disposal is proposed to be made by means of a sale at a public auction[3].

(c) It must state that the notice constitutes an offer by the landlord, which may be accepted by the requisite majority of qualifying tenants of the constituent flats, for the contract (if any) entered into by the landlord at the auction to have effect as if their nominee, and not the purchaser, had entered into it[4].

(d) It must specify the same period for acceptance as under a s 5A notice (see para **4.05**, point (c))[5]. However, see also para **4.07**.

(e) It must specify a further period of 28 days within which a person or persons may be nominated under the LTA 1987, s 6[6]. It should be noted that this is less than the equivalent two-month period in respect of a s 5A notice.

(f) Unless the notice states the time and place of the auction, the landlord must serve a further notice stating those particulars not less than 28 days before the date of the auction[7]. The further notice must be served on the requisite majority of qualifying tenants of the constituent flats[8].

1 LTA 1987, s 5B(1).
2 LTA 1987, s 5B(2).
3 LTA 1987, s 5B(3).
4 LTA 1987, s 5B(4).
5 LTA 1987, s 5B(5).
6 LTA 1987, s 5B(6).
7 LTA 1987, s 5B(7).
8 See para **2.16** for 'requisite majority'.

Timing

4.07 There are special provisions concerning timing of an auction offer notice. First, it must be served not less than four months and not more than six months before the date of the auction[1]. Secondly, the period specified for acceptance of the offer must end not less than two months before the date of the auction[2]. Thirdly, the period specified for nominating a purchaser under the LTA 1987, s 6 must end not less than 28 days before the date of the auction[3]. These requirements have the effect of limiting the time for service of the offer notice on the qualifying tenants. It is considered that it may be preferable to specify dates for acceptance of the offer and appointment of the nominee so that these time limits are not inadvertently breached.

The property may not, in fact, be included in the originally specified auction for administrative or other reasons, in which case the landlord may wish to include it in a subsequent auction. The question could arise as to whether the offer notice procedure needs to be repeated in its entirety. It is considered that the property may be included in a later auction, provided (a) the qualifying tenants are given the required particulars of the later auction[4], and (b) the date of the later auction is not more than six months after the date on which the s 5B notice is served[5].

1 LTA 1987, s 5B(7).
2 LTA 1987, s 5B(7)(a).
3 LTA 1987, s 5B(7)(b).
4 In accordance with the LTA 1987, s 5B(8).
5 LTA 1987, s 5B(7).

Option

4.08 Where the disposal consists of the grant of an option or right of pre-emption, the following are the requirements of the offer notice[1]:

(a) It must contain particulars of the principal terms of the disposal proposed by the landlord, including in particular:
   (i) the property, and the estate or interest in that property, to which the option or right of pre-emption relates;
   (ii) the consideration required for the grant;
   (iii) the principal terms on which the option or right of pre-emption would be exercisable including the consideration payable on its exercise[2]. As with a contract (see para **4.05**, point (a)), it may be simpler to append a copy of the proposed option agreement to the offer notice.

(b) It must state that it constitutes an offer to grant an option or right of pre-emption on the terms set out, which may be accepted by the requisite majority of qualifying tenants of the constituent flats[3].

(c) The provisions as to the period for accepting the offer and appointing a nominee purchaser are the same as for contracts (as to which see para **4.05**, points (c) and (d))[4].

1 LTA 1987, s 5C(1).
2 LTA 1987, s 5C(2).
3 LTA 1987, s 5C(3).
4 LTA 1987, s 5C(4), (5).

Conveyance

4.09 Where the disposal is one proceeding straight to a conveyance and is not pursuant to a contract, option or right of pre-emption binding on the landlord, the offer notice has the following requirements[1]:

(a) it must contain particulars of the principal terms of the proposed disposal, including, in particular, the property to which it relates, the estate or interest to be disposed of and the consideration required[2];

(b) it must state that the notice constitutes an offer by the landlord to dispose of the property on those terms which may be accepted by the requisite majority of qualifying tenants of the constituent flats[3];

(c) the provisions as to the period for accepting the offer and appointing a nominee purchaser are the same as for contracts (as to which see para **4.05**, points (c) and (d))[4].

1 LTA 1987, s 5D(1).
2 LTA 1987, s 5D(2).
3 LTA 1987, s 5D(3).
4 LTA 1987, s 5D(4), (5).

Non-monetary disposal

4.10 There may be relevant disposals which are covered by the LTA 1987, s 5, but where the landlord does not require consideration consisting of money, or where the consideration does not wholly consist of money, there might, for example, be a proposed exchange of property or even a gift (other than to a family member or charity[1]). In such a case, the offer notice must contain the particulars relevant to the type of disposal under the LTA 1987, ss 5A–5D and, in addition, must state the following[2]:

(a) that an election may be made under the LTA 1987, s 8C[3] (explaining its effect);

(b) accordingly, the notice also constitutes an offer by the landlord, which may be accepted by the requisite majority of qualifying tenants of the constituent flats, for a person or persons nominated by them to acquire the property under the LTA 1987, ss 11–17.

It must specify a period within which that offer may be accepted, being not less than two months beginning with the date of service of the offer notice[4].

These rather convoluted provisions allow the tenants to acquire the property from the person acquiring it, as if no offer notice had been served; however, the tenants must pay the monetary equivalent of the property (to the extent that it was not disposed of for monetary consideration), which may be determined by a LVT[5].

1 Which would be excluded from being a relevant disposal by the LTA 1987, s 4(2)(e), as to which see para **3.28** ff.
2 LTA 1987, s 5E.
3 LTA 1987, s 5E(2)(a). Section 8C is discussed at para **5.13**.
4 LTA 1987, s 5E(3).
5 See the LTA 1987, s 8C, discussed at para **5.13**.

CHAPTER 5

Consequences of service of offer notice

5.01 As we have seen in Chapter 4, the various forms of offer notice all specify a period within which the tenants may accept the offer. It is open to the landlord and the requisite majority of qualifying tenants[1] to agree a longer period for acceptance of the offer. During the period for acceptance (whether the one specified in the offer notice or a longer agreed period), the landlord must not dispose of the protected interest except to a person or persons nominated by the tenants under the LTA 1987, s 6[2]. The 'protected interest' is defined[3] as the estate, interest or other subject-matter of an offer notice. Once an acceptance notice[4] is duly served[5], the landlord must not during the protected period[6] dispose of the protected interest except to a person duly nominated[7] by the requisite majority of qualifying tenants of the constituent flats. That person is called a 'nominated person'[8].

1 For the 'requisite majority', see paras **2.16, 2.17**.
2 LTA 1987, s 6(1). To do so is an offence under the LTA 1987, s 10A, as to which see para **10.09**.
3 In the LTA 1987, s 20(1).
4 See para **5.02**.
5 For the meaning of 'duly served', see the LTA 1987, s 6(3), discussed in para **5.03**.
6 Definited in the LTA 1987, s 6(4); see para **5.04**.
7 For the meaning of 'duly nominated', see the LTA 1987, s 6(5) discussed in para **5.04**.
8 LTA 1987, s 6(2).

Acceptance notice

5.02 An acceptance notice is a notice served on the landlord by the requisite majority of qualifying tenants[1] of the constituent flats informing him that the persons serving the notice accept the offer contained in his notice[2]. The notice must be in writing[3] and may be sent by post[4]. It must specify the names and addresses of all of the persons by whom it is served and the addresses of the flats of which they are qualifying tenants[5]. It should be remembered that all joint tenants constitute the 'qualifying tenant'[6]. In such a case, all their names must be included in respect of the flat in question. It is considered that a single notice must be served on behalf of all the tenants giving it; multiple notices are not permitted. Although words in the singular in an Act ('a notice') prima facie include the plural, that rule does not apply where the contrary intention appears[7]. The contrary intention appears in the LTA 1987, s 6(3) both by its emphasis on 'a notice' and the purpose of the acceptance notice, which is to inform the landlord clearly and speedily that there is a requisite majority of qualifying tenants wishing to accept the offer. If multiple notices were permissible, the landlord could not be sure that the tenants giving them were acting in concert as a majority, or even that they were aware that their neighbours had responded to the s 5 notice. There is no requirement that the notice should be signed by the tenants giving it; however, if any do not sign it, and there is later an issue as to whether they were participating in the acceptance of the offer, it will be necessary to provide evidence that they authorised the giving of the acceptance notice on their behalf. Accordingly, if it is possible to obtain the signatures of the tenants giving the notice, it would seem sensible to do so.

1 See para **2.16**.
2 LTA 1987, s 6(3). For a suggested form of notice, see Appendix I.
3 LTA 1987, s 54(1)(a).
4 LTA 1987, s 54(1)(b).
5 LTA 1987, s 54(2).
6 See para **2.13**.
7 Interpretation Act 1978, s 6(c).

5.03 The LTA 1987 does not give a tenant served with a s 5 notice the right to discover from the landlord details of the other tenants who have been served with such notices. Clearly, the landlord will have this information available, as he will be collecting rent and service charges from the tenants. This can present real problems in practice, particularly in large blocks, where many of the qualifying tenants may live abroad and may have sub-let their flats. The occupying sub-tenants may well not respond to a circular letter from tenants interested in acquiring the landlord's interest. It is open to the interested tenants to carry out a search at the Land Registry in respect of other flats, but the address of the lessee may well be out of date. One solution is for a qualifying tenant to serve notice on the landlord under s 11(3) of the Leasehold Reform, Housing and Urban Development Act 1993[1]. Such a notice requires the landlord to give him the name and address of a tenant of any separate set of premises contained in the relevant premises (ie the block of flats)[2]. The landlord has 28 days to comply with such a notice[3]. If the landlord does not respond in time, the tenant may use the default notice procedure under s 92 of the 1993 Act; however, that will inevitably prolong the provision of the necessary information beyond the time limit for serving an acceptance notice. Another problem for tenants is that they have no right to discover from the landlord the terms of other lettings or interests in the premises. Consequently, they may not be in a position to judge whether the terms of the disposal contained in the offer notice are attractive or not.

To be 'duly served' an acceptance notice must be served within the period specified in the offer notice for acceptance, or such longer period as is agreed between the landlord and the requisite majority of qualifying tenants of the constituent flats[4]. The LTA 1987 makes no provision for a negative response to be given to an offer notice. Accordingly, even if some expression of lack of interest is communicated to the landlord by some or all of the tenants[5], it is considered that this will not allow the landlord to proceed as if no acceptance notice has been given. The landlord must wait until the time limited for serving an acceptance notice has passed before he can be sure that none will be given.

1 A notice may also be served under the Leasehold Reform, Housing and Urban Development Act 1993, s 11(4) seeking information about interests derived out of the landlord's interest, where the information is reasonably required 'in connection with the making of a claim to exercise the right to collective enfranchisement'. It should be noted that a qualifying tenant under the 1993 Act is more restrictively defined, and must have a long lease at a low rent or a lease for a particularly long term (ie more than 35 years).
2 Leasehold Reform, Housing and Urban Development Act 1993, s 1(2).
3 Leasehold Reform, Housing and Urban Development Act 1993, s 11(7).
4 Leasehold Reform, Housing and Urban Development Act 1993, s 6(3).
5 It seems most unlikely that any kind of estoppel could arise, since the 1987 Act gives the tenants statutory rights, as in the case of the Rent Act (as to which see Woodfall on Landlord and Tenant, para. 23.007).

'Protected period'

5.04 This is the period beginning with the date of service of the acceptance notice and ending with the period for nominating a person under the LTA 1987, s 6, or such later period as may be agreed between the landlord and the requisite majority of qualifying tenants of the constituent flats[1].

'Duly nominated'

A person is duly nominated for the purposes of s 6 if he is nominated at the same time as the acceptance notice is served (usually in the acceptance notice itself) or afterwards, provided the nomination takes place before the end of the period for nomination specified in the offer notice (or such longer period as may be agreed between the landlord and the requisite majority of qualifying tenants)[2]. It seems that any legal 'person' may be nominated. It is not uncommon for the tenants to use the vehicle of a limited company to act as nominee purchaser, perhaps one specially formed for the task. It is important that the tenants agree from the outset how they are going to fund the purchase and how the price and legal costs are to be apportioned between them. Taking legal advice is strongly recommended. Otherwise between one and four[3] of the tenants (or other persons) may act as nominee purchaser.

1 LTA 1987, s 6(4). For the requisite majority, see para **2.16**.
2 LTA 1987, s 6(5).
3 Four is the maximum number that can hold the landlord's interest: Law of Property Act 1925, s 34(2).

Change of nominated person

5.05 A nominated person may be replaced by another person nominated by the requisite majority of qualifying tenants of constituent flats if, and only if, he has, for any reason, ceased to be able to act as a nominated person[1]. This would seem to be limited to cases where the nominated person, if an individual, dies or becomes physically or mentally incapable of acting as a nominee purchaser, or, if a limited company, is struck off the register. If two or more persons are nominated, and any of them ceases to act without being replaced, the remaining nominee(s) may continue to act[2].

1 LTA 1987, s 6(6).
2 LTA 1987, s 6(7).

Failure by tenants to give notice

5.06 Before turning to the position where the offer is accepted, it is convenient to consider what occurs if the tenants do not give the requisite notices. The plural 'notices' is used because the tenants must both duly serve an acceptance notice and nominate a person within the protected period[1]. If either of these steps in not carried out, the landlord may (subject to restrictions) dispose of the protected interest[2] to such person as he thinks fit[3]. He may do so during the period of 12 months beginning with the end of the protected period[4].

Example: Suppose a s 5 notice is served on the 1 June 2001, giving a date of the 1 October 2001 as the date for acceptance and the 15 December 2001 for a person to be nominated by the tenants. If the tenants do not accept the offer by the 1 October 2001, the landlord may dispose of the property to a third party by the 15 December 2002. If the tenants accept the offer, but do not nominate a person by the 15 December 2001, again the landlord may dispose of the property to a third party by the 15 December 2002.

There is nothing in the LTA 1987 which caters for the period between the date for acceptance and the date for nomination, in a case where the tenants have not accepted the offer.

1 For 'protected period' see para **5.04**.
2 For 'protected interest' see para **5.01**.
3 LTA 1987, s 7(1).
4 LTA 1987, s 7(1). It is considered that the suggestion in Dollar and Thompson-Copsey, *Tenants' Pre-Emption Rights*, para 4.3, that the 12-month period commences at the end of the acceptance period, is incorrect.

5.07 The restrictions which apply to the disposal depend on whether the offer notice proposed a sale by public auction (ie under the LTA 1987, s 5B) or not. If the offer notice was served under s 5B, the disposal must only be made by means of a sale at a public auction and the other terms must correspond to those specified in the offer notice[1]. The LTA 1987 does not permit a sale by private treaty immediately following an auction at which the particular property failed to sell under the hammer[2].

1 LTA 1987, s 7(2).

2 Such sales are not unusual in practice, but are outlawed under the LTA 1987. For an article describing this state of affairs as an 'anomaly', see a piece by Samantha Jenkins in the Estates Gazette (16 August 1997). The article refers to the need in one case to arrange a second auction shortly after the first. See para **4.07** for the timing in such a case.

5.08 In any other case, the landlord may only sell to a third party if the deposit and consideration required are not less than those specified in the offer notice and the other terms correspond to those specified in it[1]. There is, accordingly, nothing to stop the landlord from selling the property at a higher price than that offered to the tenants. Care must be taken to ensure that there is no variation in the other terms; in one case[2] a landlord fell foul of a similar provision under the LTA 1987[3] by failing to detail accurately the terms agreed between vendor and purchaser for payment of rent and service charges recoverable from the tenants.

The LTA 1987 emphasises[4] that it is only the disposal of the protected interest[5] which may be freely disposed of during the 12-month period. Any other disposal is subject to a fresh right of first refusal[6].

1 LTA 1987, s 7(3).
2 *Staszewski v Maribella Ltd* [1998] 1 EGLR 34, CA.
3 LTA 1987, s 11.
4 By the LTA 1987, s 7(4).
5 See para **5.01**.
6 See para **4.01**. This only applies, of course, to another disposal which is a relevant disposal.

Acceptance and nomination

5.09 Detailed provisions apply if, in response to an offer notice, the tenants both duly serve an acceptance notice and appoint a nominee[1]. The first is that, subject to the later provisions of the LTA 1987, the landlord may not dispose of the protected interest[2] except to the nominated person[3].

The landlord must make an immediate election. Within one month of the date of service of the notice of nomination, he must either serve notice on the nominated person indicating an intention not to proceed with the disposal of the protected interest[4], or be obliged to proceed[5].

These provisions do not prevent the landlord from serving a further offer notice on the qualifying tenants in respect of a different disposal[6]. Accordingly, it appears that there could, in theory, be several different proposed disposals pending at the same time. However, a multiplicity of offer notices might put in doubt the genuineness of the landlord, who can only serve an offer notice where he 'proposes' to make the relevant disposal in question[7].

1 LTA 1987, s 8(1).
2 See para **5.01**.
3 LTA 1987, s 8(2).
4 This is a notice of withdrawal for the purposes of s 9B(2)–(4) (s 8(4)), as to which see para **5.21**. For a form of notice see Appendix I.
5 LTA 1987, s 8(3).
6 LTA 1987, s 8(5).
7 See the LTA 1987, s 5(1); see also para **3.59**.

Landlord obliged to proceed

5.10 Special provisions apply where the landlord is obliged to proceed and the s 5 notice proposed a sale by auction[1]; these will be discussed below. In any other case, the landlord must, within one month of service of the notice of nomination, send a form of contract to the nominated person. The draft contract is for the acquisition of the protected interest and must contain the terms specified in the offer notice[2]. If the landlord fails to submit a draft contract in time (and there is no provision for extending the time limit) he is treated as having served a notice of withdrawal under s 9B of the LTA 1987 at the end of that period of one month[3].

If the landlord duly submits a draft contract, the nominated person has two months (or such longer period as may be agreed) to respond in one of two ways[4]. First, he may serve a notice on the landlord indicating an intention to no longer proceed with the acquisition. In such a case, he is treated as if he had served a notice of withdrawal under the LTA 1987, s 9A[5] at the same time as that notice[6]. Secondly, he may offer to exchange contracts, ie sign the contract and send it to the landlord with the requisite deposit. The 'requisite deposit' is the deposit specified in the contract, or 10% of the consideration, whichever is the less[7]. If the nominated person does not make either response in time (and there is no power to extend time other than with the landlord's agreement), he is treated as having served notice of intention not to proceed[8].

If the nominated person duly offers an exchange of contracts, but the landlord fails to complete the exchange within seven days of receiving the contract, he will be treated as having served a notice of withdrawal under the LTA 1987, s 9B at the end of the seven-day period[9].

1 LTA 1987, ss 8A(1), 8B.
2 LTA 1987, s 8A(2).
3 LTA 1987, s 8A(3). The effect of a notice of withdrawal, under the LTA 1987, s 9B, is considered in para **5.21**.
4 LTA 1987, s 8A(4).
5 As to which, see para **5.18**.
6 LTA 1987, s 9A(5). For a form of notice see Appendix I.
7 LTA 1987, s 8A(4).
8 LTA 1987, s 8A(5).
9 LTA 1987, s 8A(6). See para **5.21** for a discussion of a notice of withdrawal under the LTA 1987, s 9B.

5.11 One problem for which the LTA 1987 does not cater is a change in circumstances affecting the value of the property since the offer notice was served. An example would be the death of a statutory tenant leaving a flat vacant. The price quoted in the offer notice would reflect the existence of the statutory tenancy, but the nominated person would acquire the more valuable interest with vacant possession. Whereas such a change of circumstances is specifically catered for in the provisions dealing with a disposal in breach of the right of first refusal[1], paradoxically there is no such protection for a landlord who complies with his obligations. It would seem that the only solution is to withdraw from the instant disposal and start again – the drawback being the requirement to pay the tenants' costs[2].

1 See para **7.24** dealing with purchase notices.
2 See para **5.21** below.

Auction

5.12 Where the offer notice proposed a sale by auction[1] and the landlord is obliged to proceed, the nominated person may serve a notice electing that the provisions of the LTA 1987, s 8B shall apply[2]. The notice must be served on the landlord not less than 28 days before the date of the auction[3]. If no such notice is served, the nominated person is treated as having served a notice of withdrawal under the LTA 1987, s 9A[4] at the end of the 28-day period[5].

If a contract is entered into at the auction[6], the landlord must, within seven days of the auction, send a copy of the contract to the nominated person[7]. The nominated person then has 28 days to serve notice on the landlord accepting the terms of the contract and fulfilling the purchaser's conditions under it[8], such as paying a deposit. If he does so, the contract has effect as if the nominated person, and not the purchaser, has entered the contract[9]. Unless otherwise agreed, any time limit in the contract starts to run again from the date of the nominated purchaser's notice of acceptance. Moreover, the nominated person has at least 28 days to complete regardless of the terms of the contract[10]. If the nominated person does not, within the 28-day period, serve notice of acceptance and fulfil the conditions, he is again treated as having served notice of withdrawal under the LTA 1987, s 9A[11] at the end of that period[12].

The provision substituting the nominated person for the contractual purchaser may well create unfairness to the purchaser, particularly one who has spent time and effort researching the property before the auction. The LTA 1987 makes no provision for him to be compensated for wasted expenditure, and he has no recourse to an action for breach of contract against the landlord, since his removal from the contract is effected by statute[13]. On the other hand, many auction catalogues either refer to the fact that a particular property is subject to LTA 1987 rights, or give a general warning that the Act may apply to the lots being sold. Most buyers of reversions to multiply occupied residential buildings can be expected to be familiar with the LTA 1987 and can make their own inquiries.

1 Ie it was served under the LTA 1987, s 5B.
2 LTA 1987, s 8B(2).
3 LTA 1987, s 8B(2).
4 As to which, see para **5.18**.
5 LTA 1987, s 8B(6).
6 It is considered that this means that the property is sold at the auction sale, by being knocked down to the highest bidder, and would not include a private treaty sale concluded in the auction room. See also para **5.07**.
7 LTA 1987, s 8B(3).
8 LTA 1987, s 8B(4).
9 LTA 1987, s 8B(4).
10 LTA 1987, s 8B(5).
11 As to which, see para **5.08**.
12 LTA 1987, s 8B(6).
13 It is considered that the contract would be regarded as frustrated.

Non-monetary disposal

5.13 As we have seen[1], the landlord may be proposing to dispose of property, at least in part, for non-monetary consideration. This might involve the grant to the landlord of rights over other property owned by the person to whom he proposes to dispose of the premises containing the qualifying tenant's flats, or a swap of properties. Clearly, the qualifying tenants would be in no position to offer the landlord the same consideration as the proposed 'purchaser'. In such a case, the LTA 1987 provides for the qualifying tenants to elect to pay an equivalent monetary consideration to the purchaser[2]. The statutory provisions are rather convoluted. Following acceptance of the s 5E offer notice, the requisite majority of qualifying tenants[3] of the constituent flats may serve notice on the landlord electing that the LTA 1987, s 8C should apply[4]. The notice must be served within the period specified in the s 5E offer notice for nominating a person to act for them under s 6[5] of the LTA 1987, or such longer period as may be agreed with the landlord[6].

Once such an election is made, the LTA 1987 assumes that the landlord will proceed to dispose of the protected interest on terms corresponding to those specified in his offer notice under ss 5A, 5B, 5C or 5D[7]. This would, prima facie, be a breach of the Act. However, the LTA 1987 provides that ss 11–17, which deal with the enforcement of the tenants' rights against subsequent purchasers[8], apply with certain modifications. Section 8C does not state that s 10A, which creates a criminal offence of failing to comply with Part I of the LTA 1987[9], applies to such a disposal. The only sensible conclusion is that that criminal sanction does not apply in these circumstances. It is assumed that no s 5 notice has been served and the time limits for the procedures for enforcement against the purchaser are reduced[10].

In calculating the price that the tenants must pay to the purchaser, the value of the consideration which did not consist of money must be assessed. It will be equivalent to the monetary value received by the landlord. Either the landlord or the nominated person may apply to the LVT to determine the amount of the consideration payable to the purchaser[11]. It is considered that it is the open market value of the actual consideration received by the landlord which must be assessed. Suppose the landlord exchanges the reversion to a block of flats for a piece of development land. Expert valuation evidence concludes that the market value of the reversion was £50,000 and the value of the development land was £40,000. In those circumstances, the tenants would only have to pay £40,000, although the asset they are acquiring is worth £50,000.

1 See para **4.10**.
2 LTA 1987, s 8C. The provisions of s 8C must be explained in an offer notice under s 5E: LTA 1987, s 5E(2)(a).
3 See para **2.16**.
4 LTA 1987, s 8C(2). For a form of notice, see Appendix I.
5 Ie the nominated person.
6 LTA 1987, s 8C(2).
7 LTA 1987, s 8C(3).
8 As to which, see Chapters 6, 7 and 8.
9 See para **10.09**.

10 The period under the LTA 1987, s 11A(3) for serving notice requiring information from the new landlord is reduced from four months to 28 days, and the periods under the LTA 1987, ss 12A(2) and 12B(3) for the exercise of the tenants' rights against the purchaser are reduced from six months to two months.
11 For the procedure see para **10.18**.

Option or right of pre-emption

5.14 We have seen that it is the grant of an option or right of pre-emption that is the relevant disposal, rather than the subsequent disposal of the land pursuant to it[1]. However, where, pursuant to the option or right, the landlord makes another, later, disposal affecting the premises before a specified period, the tenants' rights against the purchaser take effect as if the later disposal were the relevant disposal[2]. The period is four months from the date when the requisite majority of qualifying tenants[3] are served with notices under s 3A of the Landlord and Tenant Act 1985[4], or other documents indicating the original disposal has taken place and alerting them to their rights under the LTA 1987 Act and the time within those rights must be exercised[5].

1 See paras **3.42-3.45**.
2 LTA 1987, s 8D(1). This is plainly sensible. In such a case, the tenants will (like the purchaser) acquire the premises and not just an option over it.
3 See para **2.16**.
4 Section 3A is set out in Appendix II.
5 LTA 1987, s 8D(2). See paras **3.45** and **3.46** for a more detailed discussion.

Covenant affecting disposal

5.15 Where the landlord is obliged to proceed[1] but is precluded by a covenant, condition or other obligation from disposing of the protected interest[2] to the nominated person without obtaining the consent of another person, he must use his best endeavours to secure that consent[3]. If it appears to the landlord that the other person is obliged not to withhold his consent unreasonably, but has withheld it, the landlord must institute proceedings for a declaration to that effect[4]. This situation is likely to arise only where the landlord is disposing of an intermediate lease, and the consent of the superior lessor is required. In such a case, the superior landlord is under a statutory duty not to withhold consent unreasonably[5]. It is considered that it will be a very rare case where a landlord will be able to establish reasonable grounds to object to an assignment of an intermediate lease to the nominee of occupational underlessees[6].

The duty of the landlord to obtain consent ceases if either party withdraws from the transaction[7] or the landlord's offer lapses because the Act ceases to apply to the premises[8].

1 See paras **5.09, 5.10**.
2 See para **5.01**.
3 LTA 1987, s 8E(1).
4 LTA 1987, s 8E(1)(b).

5 Landlord and Tenant Act 1988.
6 For the law on reasonableness, see *Woodfall on Landlord and Tenant*, vol 1, para 11.138 ff.
7 Under the LTA 1987, ss 9A or 9B, as to which see paras **5.18, 5.21**.
8 Under the LTA 1987, s 10; see para **5.22**.

5.16 Where the landlord has discharged his duty[1], but no consent is given and no declaration made by the court, the landlord may serve a notice on the nominated person stating that to be the case[2]. Where such a notice has been served the landlord may, during the following 12 months, dispose of the protected interest[3] to anyone he wishes subject to certain restrictions[4]. If the original offer notice was under the LTA 1987, s 5B (sale by auction), the disposal must be by public auction on the terms set out in the offer notice[5]. In any other case, the deposit and consideration must be not less than those specified in the offer notice or, if higher, those agreed (subject to contract) between the landlord and the nominated person, and the other terms must correspond with the offer notice[6].

Where the landlord gives notice under the LTA 1987, s 8E(3), he may recover any costs reasonably incurred between the end of the first four weeks of the nomination period[7] and the date of giving the notice. The costs may be recovered from the nominated person[8] and the qualifying tenants who served the acceptance notice, who are jointly and severally liable[9].

1 Ie to use best endeavours to obtain consent and, if appropriate, apply for a declaration.
2 For a suggested form of notice, see Appendix I.
3 See para **5.01**.
4 LTA 1987, s 8E(3).
5 LTA 1987, s 8E(4).
6 LTA 1987, s 8E(5).
7 This is apparently a printing error in the statute, since 'nomination period' is not a defined term. It was presumably intended to refer to 'protected period', as to which see para **5.04**.
8 Incorrectly described as 'the nominated party' in the LTA 1987, s 8E(6); another printing error.
9 LTA 1987, s 8E(6).

Withdrawal

5.17 The LTA 1987 makes provision for both the nominated person and the landlord to withdraw from the proposed transaction by serving notice on the other party. The provisions do not apply after a binding contract has been entered into or otherwise comes into existence under the LTA 1987 between the landlord and the nominated person[1]. We will start by considering withdrawal by the nominated person.

1 LTA 1987, ss 9A(8) and 9B(5).

Nominated person

5.18 There are two situations where the nominated person serves a notice of withdrawal. The first is where he (obviously on the instructions of the tenants who nominated him) does not wish to proceed. Where the landlord is obliged to proceed[1], the nominated person may serve a notice on him, called a 'notice of withdrawal'[2], indicating his intention to no longer proceed with the acquisition of the protected interest[3].

The second situation arises where, at any time, the nominated person becomes aware that the number of qualifying tenants of the constituent flats desiring to proceed with the acquisition is less than the requisite majority of qualifying tenants of those flats[4]. In such a case, he must forthwith serve a notice of withdrawal[5]. In practice, it is likely to be a reluctant landlord who will wish to invoke this provision to require the tenants to withdraw. It is not unheard of for landlords (themselves or through a nominee) to purchase the leases of participating qualifying tenants in order to reduce their number to below the minimum required to form the requisite majority. The landlord will then inform the nominated person that the tenant of the flat in question no longer desired to proceed, and thereby he 'becomes aware' that the requisite majority is no longer supporting the acquisition. This, in turn, may lead the tenants to try to encourage others, who were not previously participating, to join in to make up a majority again. There is no requirement of notice to be given to the nominated person, and no method is prescribed for making him 'aware', but it is obviously in the interest of any tenant who no longer wishes to participate to inform the nominated person in writing to avoid any later argument. It is possible that the identity of the participating tenants may alter from time to time, as long as there is always a requisite majority[6]. However, it is considered that as soon as there is not a requisite majority, and the nominated person is so aware, he must serve a notice of withdrawal and cannot delay, even for a short time, while trying to obtain extra support from other tenants. Any extra tenants must therefore be 'on board' before the nominated person receives notification that a sufficient number have dropped out to destroy the requisite majority.

1 See paras **5.09** and **5.10**.
2 See Appendix I for a suggested form of notice.
3 LTA 1987, s 9A(1).
4 For the requisite majority see para **2.16**.
5 LTA 1987, s 9A(2).
6 See the LTA 1987, s 18A(4). 'The persons constituting the requisite majority of qualifying tenants for one purpose may be different from the persons constituting such a majority for another purpose.' For discussion of the requisite majority, see para **2.16**.

5.19 Where the nominated person serves notice of withdrawal, the landlord has 12 months to dispose of the protected interest to such person as he thinks fit, subject to restrictions[1]. In the case of a s 5B offer notice (sale by auction) the disposal must be by sale at a public auction and the other terms must correspond with those specified in the offer notice[2]. In any other case, the deposit and consideration must not be less than as specified in the offer notice or, if higher, not less than as agreed (subject to contract) between the landlord and the nominated person, and the other terms must correspond with the offer notice[3].

1 LTA 1987, s 9A(3).

2 LTA 1987, s 9A(4).
3 LTA 1987, s 9A(5).

Costs of landlord

5.20 If notice of withdrawal is served before the end of the first four weeks of the nomination period specified in the offer notice, neither the nominated person nor the qualifying tenants who served the acceptance notice are liable for any of the landlord's costs incurred in connection with the disposal[1]. In the case of a notice of withdrawal served later, the landlord may recover any costs reasonably incurred by him in connection with the disposal between the end of those four weeks and the date of service of the notice of withdrawal. The nominated person and the qualifying tenants who served the acceptance notice are jointly and severally liable for the costs[2]. The LTA 1987 does not make provision as to how the costs are to be recovered, if disputed[3].

1 LTA 1987, s 9A(6).
2 LTA 1987, s 9A(7).
3 Cf the LTA 1987, s 14(4) discussed at para **9.06**.

Landlord

5.21 Where the landlord is obliged to proceed[1], he may serve notice on the nominated person, a 'notice of withdrawal'[2], indicating his intention to no longer proceed with the disposal of the protected interest[3]. He does not have to have a particular reason for serving notice of withdrawal. Once such a notice is given, the landlord is not entitled to dispose of the protected interest[4] during the period of 12 months beginning with the date of service[5].

Costs of nominated person/qualifying tenants

If a notice of withdrawal is served before the end of the first four weeks of the nomination period specified in the offer notice, the landlord is not liable for any costs incurred by the nominated person or tenants serving the acceptance notice[6]. In the case of a later notice of withdrawal, the nominated person and the qualifying tenants who served the acceptance notice may recover from the landlord any costs reasonably incurred by them in connection with the disposal between the end of those four weeks and the date of service of the notice of withdrawal[7].

1 See paras **5.09, 5.10**.
2 For a suggested form of notice, see Appendix I.
3 LTA 1987, s 9B(1).
4 See para **5.01**.
5 LTA 1987, s 9B(2).
6 LTA 1987, s 9B(3).
7 LTA 1987, s 9B(4).

Lapse of landlord's offer

5.22 It may happen that the premises which are the subject of an offer notice cease to fall within Part I of the LTA 1987. We have seen[1] that s 1(2) of the Act defines premises to which Part I applies. The most likely change of circumstances would seem to be if the number of flats held by qualifying tenants fell below the 50% threshold. If, after an offer notice has been served, Part I ceases to apply to the premises, the landlord may serve a notice on the qualifying tenants of the constituent flats[2] stating that the premises have ceased to be premises to which Part I applies and that the offer notice and anything done in pursuance of it is to be treated as not having been served or done[3]. It appears from the use of the word 'may' that the landlord is not obliged to serve such a notice, and would be entitled therefore to disregard the change of circumstances. In such a case, the LTA 1987 continues to apply as before[4].

1 See para **2.02**.
2 A landlord is treated as having duly served notice if he has served notice on not less than 90% or, where there are less on all but one: LTA 1987, s 10(2). This saving provision would not seem to absolve the landlord from the duty to attempt service on all of the tenants: see para **4.03**.
3 LTA 1987, s 10(1). For a suggested form of notice, see Appendix I.
4 LTA 1987, s 10(3).

5.23 Where notice is served, the provisions of Part I of the LTA 1987 cease to have effect in relation to the disposal referred to in the offer notice[1]. These provisions do not apply after a binding contract has been entered into between the landlord and the nominated person[2]. Where a binding contract has been entered into but lawfully rescinded by the landlord (eg for failure to complete), the landlord may dispose of the protected interest as he wishes (at whatever price) for 12 months from the date of rescission[3]. It is important, therefore, that the tenants do not give the landlord any cause to rescind the contract once it is entered into.

1 LTA 1987, s 10(1).
2 LTA 1987, s 10(4).
3 LTA 1987, s 10(5).

Chapter 6

Information notices

Information: s 11A notices

The right to serve notice

6.01 Where a landlord has made a relevant disposal affecting premises to which, at the time of the disposal, Part I of the LTA 1987 applied ('the original disposal') and no notice was served by the landlord under s 5 of the LTA 1987 with respect to that disposal, or the disposal was made in contravention of any provision of ss 6–10[1] of the Act, then, so long as the premises are still premises to which Part I of the Act applies, the requisite majority of the qualifying tenants have various rights conferred by ss 11A 12A, 12B and 12C of the LTA 1987. These sections enable the requisite majority of qualifying tenants to serve notice on the purchaser[2] requiring the purchaser to:

(a) inform the tenant of the terms of the original disposal[3];
(b) elect, where the original disposal consisted of entering into a contract, that the contract shall have effect as if entered into not with the purchaser but with the person or persons nominated by the requisite majority of qualifying tenants of the constituent flats[4];
(c) require, by service of a notice ('a purchase notice') on the purchaser requiring him, to dispose of the estate or interest which was the subject matter of the original disposal, on the terms on which it was made (including those relating to the consideration payable) to a person nominated by such majority of qualifying tenants of those flats[5];
(d) where the original disposal consisted of a surrender by the landlord of a tenancy held by him ('the relevant tenancy'), to grant a new tenancy of the premises which were the subject matter of the relevant tenancy, on the same terms as those of the relevant tenancy and so as to expire on the same date as that tenancy would have expired to a person or persons nominated by any such majority of qualifying tenants of those flats[6].

1 As to which, see Chapter 5.

2 This being the transferee (or, in the case of a surrender of a tenancy, the superior landlord) under the original disposal: LTA 1987, s 11(3). References in this part of the text to the 'purchaser' are to the transferee under the original disposal.
3 LTA 1987, s 11A, discussed in this Chapter.
4 LTA 1987, s 12A(1).
5 LTA 1987, s 12B(2).
6 LTA 1987, s 12C. There are time limits for service of these various notices which are set out in the LTA 1987, in s 11A(3) for the purposes of a notice under s 11A; s 12A(2) in the case of a notice under s 12A; s 12B(3) in the case of a notice under s 12B and s 12C(3) in the case of a notice under s 12C. As to the time limits, see para **6.04**.

Information which may be requested

6.02 In order to take advantage of the rights conferred by ss 12A, 12B or 12C[1], the LTA 1987 enables the requisite majority of qualifying tenants to serve notice pursuant to s 11A on the purchaser requiring the purchaser to:

(a) serve notice providing particulars of the terms on which the original disposal was made (including the deposit and consideration required and the date on which it was made)[2];

(b) where the original disposal consisted of entering into a contract, to provide, in addition, a copy of the contract[3];

It has been said that the s 11A notice is intended to provide the qualifying tenants with the information which they need in order to decide whether to exercise their rights under ss 12A,12B and 12C[4].

1 As summarised in para **6.01**.
2 LTA 1987, s 11A(1)(a).
3 LTA 1987, s 11A(1)(b). As to the time for compliance, see para **6.10**.
4 *Michaels v Harley House (Marylebone) Ltd* [2000] Ch 104, CA, per Robert Walker LJ at 122.

By whom served

6.03 The s 11A notice is to be served by 'the requisite majority of the qualifying tenants of the constituent flats'. This means the qualifying tenants of constituent flats with more than 50% of the available votes. There is one vote per qualifying tenant of each flat[1]. The date for determining the requisite majority is the date of service of the s 11A notice[2].

1 LTA 1987, s 18(3). See also para **2.16**.
2 LTA 1987, s 18A(2)(b), in circumstances where no notice under s 5 has been served.

Time for service

6.04 The notice is required to be served upon the purchaser before the end of period of four months beginning with the date by which:

(a) notices under s 3A of the Landlord and Tenant Act 1985[1] relating to the original disposal; or
(b) where that section does not apply, documents of any other description:
   (i) indicating that the original disposal has taken place, and
   (ii) alerting the tenants to the existence of their rights under Part I of the LTA 1987 and the time within which any such rights must be exercised,

have been served on the requisite majority of qualifying tenants of the constituent flats.

1 As to which see para **6.05**.

Section 3A of the Landlord and Tenant Act 1985

6.05 A notice pursuant to s 3A of the Landlord and Tenant Act 1985 is required to be served if the purchaser of the landlord's interest is required to give a notice pursuant to s 3 of the 1985 Act. Section 3 of the 1985 Act provides that if the interest of the landlord under a tenancy of premises which consist of or include a dwelling is assigned, the new landlord should give notice in writing of the assignment, and of his name and address, to the tenant not later than the next day on which rent is payable under the tenancy or, if that is within two months of the assignment, the end of that period of two months. A number of points need to be noted:

(1) There is no definition of 'new landlord' but clearly it refers to the person who has acquired the interest of a landlord under the relevant tenancy[1].
(2) The heading of s 3(1) of the Landlord and Tenant Act 1985 refers to 'the assignment' of the landlord's interest under the tenancy. An assignment of the landlord's interest includes any conveyance other than a mortgage or charge[2]. No guidance is given as to when the landlord's interest is assigned where the landlord's interest is the subject of registration at HM Land Registry. The legal estate in registered land passes only upon registration, that is when the purchaser's name is entered on the proprietorship register[3]. As there is an interval of time between the date of application for the registration and the actual date of registration, the Land Registration Rules provide that the legal estate is deemed to have passed retrospectively on the date on which the application for registration was deemed delivered[4]. It has been held that in the context of registered land a legal estate in the tenant's lease was not assigned until it was registered so that, in that particular case, the assignor was entitled to exercise a break clause personal to the assignor notwithstanding that the assignor had done all that he could to assign the lease[5].
(3) Section 3(1) of the Landlord and Tenant Act 1985 makes it clear that the notification is to be given no later than the 'next day on which rent is payable under the tenancy'. Three points arise. First, if the rent day is before the expiry of a period of two months, two months is substituted for the next rent

day as the last day by which compliance with a s 3(1) notice is required. Secondly, if the rent is payable annually or half yearly, then it would appear that (assuming the assignment occurred shortly after the last rent day) a period of nearly 12 or some six months respectively is given for compliance. Thirdly, there is no definition of 'rent'. What if, for instance, the insurance or service charge is reserved as 'rent'? It has been said that there is no reason why this should not be viewed as 'rent' properly so called, the parties having decided to confer upon the debt in question the attributes of 'rent'[6]. Thus if a lease reserves the service charge payments as rent the date of the next payment of the quarterly interim service charge will be the 'next day on which rent is payable'[7].

(4) 'Tenancy' includes a statutory tenancy[8].

(5) The notice under s 3 of the Landlord and Tenant Act 1985 need only be given where the landlord's interest has been assigned. Thus it is not every case of a 'relevant disposal' for the purposes of s 4 that a notice pursuant to s 3(1) of the 1985 Act is required to be given. Such a notice would not, for instance, be required to be given where the relevant disposal consisted of the entry into a contract to dispose of the landlord's estate or interest, was the grant of an option or was a surrender of the landlord's tenancy to the superior landlord. In such cases it would not appear that the landlord's interest has been assigned[9].

1 Arguably this could apply to the grantee of a long lease from the freehold owner on the basis that '... the interest of the landlord' under the relevant tenancy is the immediate reversion and it is that interest which has been assigned by the grant of the intermediate lease albeit that there has been no disposition of the freehold: see *Belvedere Court Management Ltd v Frogmore Developments Ltd* [1997] QB 858, CA in respect of the wording of the LTA 1987, s 16 prior to its amendment by the Housing Act 1996, and the court's consideration of the words 'the person to whom he has disposed of that estate or interest'.

2 Landlord and Tenant Act 1985, s 3(4).

3 Land Registration Act 1925, ss 19(1) and 22(1).

4 Land Registration Rules 1925, SI 1925/1093, rr 83, 85.

5 *Brown & Root Technology Ltd v Sun Alliance and London Assurance Co Ltd* [2000] 2 WLR 566, CA.

6 *Escalus Properties Ltd v Robinson* [1996] QB 231, CA.

7 An interesting question arises where the payment is reserved as rent and is payable on demand. Often the tenant's contribution to the premium payable for insurance is to be paid on demand. In these circumstances, when is the next day on which the rent is payable? If it is the date of the demand it means that, subject to any earlier dates arising in the interim in respect of other payments of rent, the landlord may delay notification under s 3(1) of the Landlord and Tenant Act 1985 by delaying the demand.

8 Landlord and Tenant Act 1985, s 3(4). A statutory tenant is expressly included as a qualifying tenant for the purposes of the 1987 Act: LTA 1987, s 60(1).

9 As to the meaning of 'assignment', see point (2) in para **6.05**. In these circumstances, no notice under s 3(1) of the Landlord and Tenant Act 1985 is required to be served, and accordingly no notice under s 3A of the 1985 Act is required to be served. The time for serving the s 11A notice will, therefore, expire at the end of the period of four months beginning with the date by which documents of the class referred to in s 11A(3) have been served on the requisite majority of qualifying tenants of the constituent flats.

6.06 Where a new landlord is required by the Landlord and Tenant Act 1985, s 3(1) to give notice to a tenant of an assignment to him, then the new landlord may be required to serve, in addition to that notice, a notice pursuant to s 3A of the Landlord and Tenant Act 1985. He is required to do so if:

(a) the tenant is a qualifying tenant within the meaning of Part I of the LTA 1987; and

(b) the assignment was a relevant disposal at a time when Part I of the 1987 Act applied to the premises.

The s 3A notice must be in writing and must notify the tenant:

(a) that the disposal was one to which Part I of the LTA1987[1] applied;

(b) that the tenant (together with other qualifying tenants) may have the right under Part I:

   (i) to obtain information about the disposal, and

   (ii) to acquire the purchaser's interest in the whole or part of the premises in which the tenant's flat is situated;

   (iii) of the time within which any such right must be exercised, and the fact that the time would run from the date of receipt of notice under s 3A of the LTA 1987 by the requisite majority of qualifying tenants[2].

1 Landlord and Tenant Act 1985, s 3A(2). It is to be noted that the wording refers to 'disposal to the landlord' whereas the amended provisions of the LTA 1987 refer to 'purchaser'.
2 Landlord and Tenant Act 1985, s 3A(2)(c).

6.07 There are criminal sanctions for a failure to comply with the duty imposed by s 3A of the Landlord and Tenant Act 1985[1]. A notice under s 3A of the 1985 Act is required to be served albeit the relevant disposal has been effected in compliance with the provisions of Part I of the LTA 1987. Even though the tenants will have no right to acquire the estate or interest so disposed of, nevertheless the 'new landlord' for the purposes of s 3A of the 1985 Act is still required to serve the notice informing the tenant of the matters referred to in s 3A(2) of the 1985 Act. It is not considered, however, that the requisite majority of qualifying tenants of the constituent flats could then serve a s 11A notice, for it would appear clear from a consideration of sub-ss (1) and (2) of the LTA 1987, s 11 that the right to serve a s 11A notice arises only where there has been a contravention of the provisions of the Act (either by a failure to serve a s 5 notice or a contravention of any provision of the LTA 1987, ss 6–10).

1 Landlord and Tenant Act 1985, s 3A(3).

6.08 As noted in para **6.06** above, s 3A(2)(c) of the Landlord and Tenant Act 1985 refers to the new landlord notifying the tenants of the time for exercising the right to obtain information (ie the time for serving the s 11A notice) as running 'from the date of receipt of notice under this section [3A] by the requisite majority of qualifying tenants'[1]. Section 11A(3) of the LTA 1987, however, refers to the date by which a s 11A notice should be served as the date by which, inter alia, a notice under s 3A of the 1985 Act has 'been served on the requisite majority of qualifying tenants of the constituent flats'. Thus s 11A of the LTA 1987 refers to 'service' on the requisite majority as commencing the time for exercising the right to request information, whereas s 3A refers to the time running from the 'date of receipt of notice' under s 3A. It may be that there is little difference in point of time between the service and receipt of a notice under s 3A[2].

1 Landlord and Tenant Act 1985, s 3A(2)(c).
2 In the context of Pt II of the Landlord and Tenant Act 1954, it has been held that there is no difference in point of time between the 'giving' of a notice under s 25 of that Act and the receiving of such a notice: *Sun Alliance Assurance Co v Hayman* [1975] 1 WLR 248, CA. But this would still appear, however, not to answer the question whether the notice is served when received or received when served.

Form of s 11A notice

6.09 There is no prescribed form for a s 11A notice[1]. It must, however:

(a) be in writing[2];

(b) specify the names of all of the persons by whom it is served[3]; and

(c) specify the addresses of the flats of which the persons by whom it is served are qualifying tenants[4].

1 A suggested form of notice is at Appendix I.
2 LTA 1987, s 54(1)(a).
3 LTA 1987, s 54(2).
4 LTA 1987, s 54(2).

Compliance with s 11A – notice in response

6.10 The importance of the LTA 1987, s 11A is that compliance with it enables the purchaser to start time running against the tenants for service of a purchaser notice. In all cases for service of a purchase notice[1], whether under the LTA 1987, ss 12A, 12B or 12C, the time for serving such a notice expires at the end of a period of six months beginning with, inter alia, compliance by the purchaser with a notice served upon him under s 11A[2]. A person served with a s 11A notice must comply with it within the period of one month beginning with the date on which it is served on him[3]. There is no prescribed form of reply. Although the form of reply by the purchaser is not referred to as a 'notice'[4], one would ordinarily expect the particulars which are to be provided[5] to be in writing.

1 Although the LTA 1987 defines only a notice under s 12B as a purchase notice, it is convenient to refer to all such notices as purchase notices.
2 LTA 1987, ss 12A(2)(a), 12B(3)(a) and 12C(3)(a).

3 LTA 1987, s 11(4).
4 Notices required or authorised to be served under the LTA 1987 are to be in writing.: LTA 1987, s 54(1).
5 As to which see para **6.02**.

6.11 It has been held by the Court of Appeal[1] in respect of the pre-1996 provisions that :

(a) a notice served under the LTA 1987, s 11(1)[2] need not be contained in a single document or given upon the same date. Provided the requisite particulars of the terms on which the original disposal is made are furnished within the period stipulated then, prima facie, the purchaser complies with his obligation;
(b) the words 'the terms on which the original disposal was made (including those relating to the consideration payable)'[3] were apt to include all terms which, whether contained in the contract prior to the conveyance or provided for collaterally and operating at the time of the conveyance, amount to an agreement or arrangement between the parties as to the amount of money paid or payable or yet to be ascertained as payable by a purchaser in connection with the acquisition of the interest disposed of;
(c) an arrangement between a vendor and the purchaser varying the terms for the payment of a sum of £10,000 so as to provide for it to be held to the order of the vendor pending ascertainment of the sum payable in the light of subsequent calculation and/or investigation by the purchaser's accountants, was a term of the disposal which was required to be brought to the attention of the tenants;
(d) letters served by the landlord were not sufficient compliance with the s 11 notice if they were patently directed to persuading the tenant that she was not entitled to serve a s 11 notice at all and the purpose of enclosing the contract was simply to demonstrate that the consideration for the s 5 offer notice had been lower than that originally required of the tenants and that the landlord was paying more. A letter which did not purport to comply with the LTA 1987, s 11(3) but denied that compliance was required, and which did not state expressly that the disposal (ie the conveyance) had taken place on terms provided in the contract, could not be said to be one which left the informed recipient clear as to its effect.

1 *Staszewski v Maribella Ltd* [1998] 1 EGLR 34, CA. Section 11(1) of the LTA 1987 in its pre-1996 form required particulars to be provided of 'the terms on which the original disposal was made (including those relating to the consideration payable) and the date on which it was made'.
2 There appears to be no reason why this conclusion is not equally applicable to a notice under the LTA 1987, s 11A having regard to the terms of the pre-1996 s 11(1).
3 Section 11A of the LTA 1987 refers to 'particulars of the terms on which the original disposal was made (including the deposit and consideration required) and the date on which it was made': LTA 1987, s 11A(1)(a).

CHAPTER 7

Purchase notices

Section 12A notices: right of qualifying tenants to take the benefit of the contract

7.01 Where the original disposal consists of entry into a contract, the requisite majority of qualifying tenants of constituent flats have an opportunity of either having recourse to the landlord, so as to treat the contract as if it had been entered into with a person or persons nominated by the requisite majority of qualifying tenants[1], or to have recourse to the purchaser under such contract and acquire the benefit of the contract from the purchaser[2]. The LTA 1987 confers upon the qualifying tenants of constituent flats a right, by service of notice to the landlord, to elect that where the original disposal consists of entering into a contract, 'the contract shall have effect as if entered into not with the purchaser but with a person or persons nominated ... by the requisite majority of the qualifying tenants of constituent flats'[3].

1 LTA 1987, s 12A.
2 LTA 1987, s 12B, discussed in para **7.10** ff.
3 LTA 1987, s 12A(1).

By whom must notice be served?

7.02 The election to treat the contract as having been made with the nominated person or persons is to be made by notice. The notice is to be served by the 'requisite majority of qualifying tenants of the constituent flats'[1]. Accordingly, the notice must specify the names of all of the persons by whom it is served and the addresses of the flats of which they are qualifying tenants[2]. The requisite majority[3] is to be determined as at the date of the service of the s 12A notice[4]. This is the case if no s 5 or s 11A notice has been served. However, if, as is likely, a s 11A notice has been served then the date for determining the requisite majority of qualifying tenants of constituent flats is the date of the s 11A notice[5]. The nominated person must be nominated for the purposes of the s 12A notice in the notice itself[6]. The person is nominated by the requisite majority of qualifying tenants. Once nominated he can only be replaced by the requisite majority of qualifying tenants if, and only if, he has, for any reason, ceased to be able to act as a nominated person[7].

1 LTA 1987, s 12A(1).
2 LTA 1987, s 54(2). If a flat is let to joint tenants, all of them are jointly the 'qualifying tenant' (see para **2.13**) and must be named.
3 Which is determined in accordance with the provisions of the LTA 1987, s 18A, as to which see para **2.16**..
4 LTA 1987, s 18A(2)(c).
5 LTA 1987, s 18A(2)(b).
6 LTA 1987, s 12D(1).
7 LTA 1987, s 12D(2). As to the meaning of 'ceased to be able to act', see para **5.05**.

Form of s 12A notice

7.03 There is no prescribed form of notice. The notice must, however, be in writing[1]. It has been said in respect of the pre-1996 provisions, in the context of the service of a purchase notice[2], that its purpose was to give to the new landlord adequate notice that the qualifying tenants of the building wish to acquire the freehold upon the terms of the original disposal or upon terms to be decided by the LVT[3]. Subject to such a notice being sufficient to give adequate notice to the new landlord of the qualifying tenants' desire to purchase the estate or interest that they should have been offered by the original landlord, the other requirements of the purchase notice would appear to be only directory[4].

1 LTA 1987, s 54(1)(a). For a suggested form of notice, see Appendix I.
2 A notice under the LTA 1987, s 12A is not defined as a purchase notice. It is a notice to treat the contract entered into as one made with the nominated person. It is only a notice under s 12B that is defined by the LTA 1987 as a purchase notice.
3 *Kay-Green v Twinsectra* [1996] 1 WLR 1587, CA, per Aldous LJ. In *Denetower Ltd v Toop* [1991] 1 WLR 945, CA, which was a case where it was alleged that the purchase notice was invalid as it failed to define the property adequately, Browne-Wilkinson V-C said at 953H:

> 'Given the complexity of the Act, a draftsman of a notice would be presented with an impossible task in seeking to specify in detail the exact property to be acquired. A notice in terms such as those contained in the present notice gives to the new landlords adequate notice of the claim. Details of the property to be acquired and the terms of the acquisition can in default of agreement be sorted out by the rent assessment committee on an application under section 13(1).'

4 *Kay-Green v Twinsectra* [1996] 1 WLR 1587, CA.

Time for serving notice

7.04 The notice under the LTA 1987, s 12A to be served by the requisite majority of qualifying tenants of constituent flats is to be served before the end of the period of six months beginning:

(a) if a notice was served on the purchaser under the LTA 1987, s 11A, with the date on which the purchaser complies with that notice;
(b) in any other case, with the date by which documents of any description:
    (i) indicating that the original disposal has taken place, and

(ii) alerting the tenants to the existence of their rights under this Part and the time within which any such rights must be exercised,

have been served on the requisite majority of qualifying tenants of the constituent flats[1].

1 LTA 1987, s 12A(2). As to service of s 11A notices, see para **6.04**.

Compliance with terms of contract

7.05 The s 12A notice has no effect unless the nominated person pays any deposit which was required to be paid upon entry into the contract and fulfils any other conditions required to be fulfilled by the purchaser on entering into the contract[1]. Although no express period of time is provided for by the LTA 1987 for paying the deposit or fulfilling any condition, it would appear that the period of time specified by the contract applies, for it is provided that unless otherwise agreed any time limit in the contract starts to run again on the service of the s 12A notice[2]. Ordinarily one would expect the deposit to be paid upon entry into the contract. Thus there would appear to be no 'time limit in the contract' which runs again by virtue of the service of the s 12A notice. If the deposit is not paid the 'penalty' seems to be simply that the s 12A notice does not take effect[3].

The 'conditions' required to be fulfilled by the purchaser may be more difficult for the nominated person to satisfy. One can envisage circumstances, for instance, where the contract is conditional upon, say, an application made by the purchaser[4] for a change in use, eg by converting part of the business premises of a building into further residential accommodation[5]. It may involve the nominated person having to incur substantial expense in preparing plans, etc[6]. It is also unclear what is to happen if, for instance, the condition is one which only the purchaser can fulfil, eg where the contract is conditional upon, say, repayment of a debt[7] within a specified period of time.

1 LTA 1987, s 12A(3)(a), (b).
2 LTA 1987, s 12A(4).
3 LTA 1987, s 12(3). If the nominated person simply does not pay, eventually the purchaser could serve a termination notice in accordance with the LTA 1987, s 17(3). See para **9.11**.
4 With the purchaser being under an obligation to make an application and to use reasonable endeavours thereafter to pursue it.
5 The provisions of the LTA 1987 apply to conditional contracts: LTA 1987, s 4A(1).
6 The purchaser would own and probably have copyright in the plans prepared for him and is unlikely to be keen to transfer these to the nominated person.
7 It may be the redemption of a charge. The jurisdiction of the LVT to modify the terms of the disposal arises only where the original disposal includes 'other property': see para **7.07**. See also paras **7.19–7.23** as to the LVT's approach to the matters to be determined under the s 12A notice.

Completion of the contract

7.06 The nominated person is given a period of not less than 28 days[1], beginning with the day on which he is deemed to have entered into the contract, to complete the contract. Presumably if the completion date has passed and the landlord has served a completion notice upon the purchaser by the time that the s 12A notice is served upon the landlord, the completion notice served upon the purchaser is simply of no effect. What is the date on which the nominated person 'is deemed to have entered into the contract'? No mention is made of the date upon which the nominated person is so deemed but, presumably, the date can be no earlier than the date of service of a s 12A notice and no later than the date upon which a nominated person fulfils any requirements as to the deposit to be paid upon entering into the contract and any other conditions required to be fulfilled by the purchaser on entering into the contract.

1 The contract may, of course, specify a longer period.

Original disposal including 'other property'

7.07 If the contract entered into by the landlord relates to other property as well as the premises to which Part I of the LTA 1987 applied at the time of the disposal, the notice served under s 12A takes effect only in relation to the premises to which Part I applied at the time of the original disposal and the terms of the contract have effect with any necessary modification[1]. The severance in the notice of the 'other property' from the premises to which Part I applied at the time of the landlord's entry into the contract with the purchaser is not essential. The severance would appear[2] to be automatic whether or not the nominated person is aware of or desires to take the 'other property'. The LTA 1987 provides that where there is 'other property' the notice 'has effect only in relation to' the Part I premises[3]. This wording is different from that under the LTA 1987, ss 12B and 12C which provide that the 'notice … shall require the purchaser only to make a disposal' relating to the Part I premises[4]. Under the pre-1996 provisions[5] it was provided, in respect of the service of a purchase notice, that the notice should require the new landlord to dispose of the estate or interest 'only' so far as relating to the particular premises and upon terms of the original disposal subject to such modifications as were necessary or expedient. A purchase notice which referred to the entirety of an estate which consisted of several buildings, containing houses or bungalows, was nevertheless valid. It was said that the requirements as to the contents of the purchase notice were only directory. Albeit the purchase notice included extra property, that did not invalidate the notice as a whole. It gave adequate notice of the requirement of the qualifying tenants that the landlord should transfer the buildings to which the LTA 1987 applied. Further, the notice also stated that in the alternative to disposal to the nominated person on the original terms, the terms were to be determined by a LVT. Thus the landlord was given adequate notice that the qualifying tenants of such of the buildings to which the LTA 1987 applied wished to acquire the freehold interest in them. That was sufficient[6].

Where the contract is to be modified so as to remove references to 'other property', there is, equally, to be a modification of the terms on which the disposal is to be made including the apportionment of any consideration. Any new terms or the apportioned consideration may be specified in the notice[7]. Alternatively, the modified terms and the apportionment of the consideration can be left to be determined by a LVT[8]. Where a purchase notice referred to several buildings, some of which were unaffected by the LTA 1987, it was held[9], under the pre-1996 provisions[10], that the purchase notice was not required to state that the terms upon which the original disposal were to be modified. The notice expressly required the purchaser to 'dispose of the said estate or interest to them on (i) the same terms on which the said estate or interest was disposed of to [the purchaser]; or (ii) alternatively on such terms as may be determined by a Rent Assessment Committee pursuant to section 12(3)(b) of the above-mentioned enactment'. Although the notice could have been worded so as to refer to the words of the relevant section of the LTA 1987, there was no need for it to do so. It was sufficient to make it clear to the landlord that the qualifying tenants wished to have the estate conveyed to them upon the same terms with such appropriate modifications as would be agreed or settled by a LVT. For practical purposes the purchaser could have been in no doubt, after receipt of the notice, that the terms would have to be settled, in default of agreement, by a LVT.

If the requisite majority of qualifying tenants of the constituent flats make provision in their notice for the modifications of the terms on which the disposal is to be made this does not bind the landlord in the sense that any questions arising in relation to any matter specified in the notice is to be determined by the LVT[11].

1 LTA 1987, s 12A(5).
2 The sub-section goes on to state, however, that 'In such a case [ie where the contract refers to other property] the notice under this section may specify the subject matter of the disposal and the terms on which the disposal is to be made (whether doing so expressly or by reference to the original disposal), or may provide for that estate or interest, or any such terms, to be determined by a leasehold valuation tribunal'.
3 LTA 1987, s 12A(5)(a).
4 See the LTA 1987, ss 12B(4)(a) and 12C(5)(a).
5 See the LTA 1987, s 12(3) of the pre-1996 provisions. The terms of the current provisions are not too dissimilar. See fn 2 above.
6 *Kay-Green v Twinsectra* [1996] 1 WLR 1587, CA.
7 LTA 1987, s 12(4).
8 LTA 1987, ss 12(4), 13(1)(b).
9 *Kay-Green v Twinsectra* [1996] 1 WLR 1587, CA.
10 LTA 1987, s 12(3)(a)(ii).
11 LTA 1987, s 13(1).

Incumbrances/changes in value of property since original disposal

7.08 It will be seen[1] that if, since the original disposal, the property becomes subject to an incumbrance, then, unless the court otherwise orders, the property will be transferred to the nominated person with a reduction in purchase price. Similarly, if, since the original disposal, the property increases in monetary value owing to a change in circumstances (other than a change in the value of money) the change is to be reflected in the price to be paid[2]. However, no express provision is made by the LTA 1987 for these changes in value to be reflected in the price to be paid under the contract, where the original disposal consists of entering into a contract and the qualifying tenants have served notice under s 12A of the LTA 1987 to treat the contract as if entered into with the nominated person. In relation to incumbrances the reasoning was, presumably, that the contract would identify that which was being acquired by the nominated person and any subsequent incumbrance created by the landlord would give rise to a breach of contract. Thus, for instance, if the landlord entered into a contract for the disposal of the freehold of a block of, say, 16 flats, two of which were vacant, the contract would ordinarily provide that the freehold would be with vacant possession only in respect of two flats. The landlord would be unable to create a lease of either or both of the flats without giving rise to the increase being dealt with by the terms of the contract. For instance, in the example given, if all 16 flats were subject to leases, and, after the date of the original disposal, one of the flats became vacant, unless the contract were to make express provision for a variation of the contract price upon any flat becoming vacant, it would seem that the price specified in the contract is the price to be paid by the nominated person, albeit there has been an increase in value of the property as a result of vacant possession of one of the flats being available. The nominated person is not going to complain about the value increasing. The jurisdiction of the LVT to modify the terms of the disposal arises only where the original disposal includes 'other property'.

1 See para **7.17**.
2 See para **7.24**.
3 See para **7.07** in relation to s 12B notices, and para **7.32** in relation so s 12C notices.

Original disposal including 'other buildings' to which Part I of the LTA 1987 applies

7.09 The LTA 1987 makes express provision for the landlord, when he serves an offer notice[1] on the qualifying tenants of the constituent flats, where the transaction involves the disposal of an estate or interest in more than one building, to sever the transactions so as to deal with each building separately[2]. There is nothing in the LTA 1987, s 12A providing for the qualifying tenants to sever the transaction where the original disposal involves the disposal of an estate or interest in more than one building. It has been said that a purchase notice is adequate if it gives notice of the desire of the qualifying tenants to have the estate or interest in the premises to which Part I of the LTA 1987 applies transferred to a nominated person[3]. There is no problem if there is only one building to which Part I of the Act applies, as the Act contains provision for dealing with disposals which contain 'other property'[4]. There would also appear to be little difficulty if the tenants of several buildings to which Part I applied, and which formed the subject matter of the original disposal, together wish to purchase them in their entirety. A notice served on behalf of the qualifying tenants of the buildings would probably be valid[5]. But what if, say, in respect of three buildings to which Part I applied and which formed the subject matter of the original disposal, only the qualifying tenants of one desired to exercise their rights under the LTA 1987 and acquire only one of the buildings? It is considered that, notwithstanding the absence of any express provision enabling the qualifying tenants to sever the transaction, a notice pursuant to s 12A severing the transaction, so as to limit the notice to one only of the buildings, will be a valid notice[6]. But what if the purchase price has not been apportioned? The disposal may have been sold as one lot at one price. Again, where there is 'other property' the LVT may carry out an apportionment[7]. But there are no provisions for apportionment of the price where the disposal consists of several buildings all of which qualify and, therefore, there is no 'other property'.

1 Pursuant to the LTA 1987, s 5(1).
2 LTA 1987, s 5(3); see para **4.02**.
3 *Kay-Green v Twinsectra* [1996] 1 WLR 1587, CA, per Aldous LJ. See also paras **7.03** and **7.07**.
4 LTA 1987, s 12A(5).
5 This seems to be implicit in *Kay-Green v Twinsectra* [1996] 1 WLR 1587, CA, as to which see also fn 11 below.
6 In *Kay-Green v Twinsectra* [1996] 1 WLR 1587, CA the disposal consisted of a total of six buildings of which only three were qualifying premises. The s 12 notice (pre-1996 amendments) referred to only five of them. Only two of the five buildings referred to were qualifying premises. The Court of Appeal upheld the notice as to the two qualifying buildings. This was a case of 'other property': three of the six buildings did not qualify. However, the tenants did not sever the five buildings as they were required to do so by the then LTA 1987, s 12(3). The severance provisions were treated as directory only. What was imperative was that the notice should refer to the qualifying tenants' desire to purchase the estate or interest that ought to have been offered. It did this in relation to two of the buildings which ought to have been offered.
7 See para **7.21**. This was undertaken in the *Kay-Green* case by the LVT: *Kay-Green v Twinsectra* [1997] 1 EGLR 219. A single price was determined for the two qualifying buildings.

Right of qualifying tenants to compel re-sale by purchaser: s 12B notices

7.10 Rather than serving notice upon the landlord so as to treat the contract entered into by the landlord with the purchaser as being one entered into with the person nominated by the qualifying tenants, the requisite majority of qualifying tenants of the constituent flats may instead serve a notice (a 'purchase notice') on the purchaser requiring him to dispose of the estate or interest that was the subject matter of the original disposal on the terms on which it was made (including those relating to the consideration payable) to a nominated person[1]. The section applies so long as no notice has been served under the LTA 1987, s 12A.

1 LTA 1987, s 12B(2).

7.11 These provisions, which compel the purchaser to resell to the nominated person, apply not only to where the original disposal consists of entry into a contract[1] but also where the original disposal does not consist of entry into a contract[2]. Thus the provisions apply equally to the situation where the relevant disposal consists of a transfer of the landlord's interest without any preceding contract, ie the parties have gone straight to transfer.

1 LTA 1987, s 12B(1)(a).
2 LTA 1987, s 12B(1)(b).

By whom must notice be served?

7.12 The notice is to be served by the 'requisite majority of qualifying tenants of the constituent flats'[1]. If no s 5 notice or s 11A notice has been served, the total number of constituent flats for ascertaining the majority is determined on the date of service of the s 12B notice[2]. If a s 11A notice is served, the total number of available votes for determining the requisite majority is determined by reference to the date of service of the s 11A notice[3].

1 LTA 1987, s 12B(2). See para **2.16**.
2 LTA 1987, s 18A(2)(c).
3 LTA 1987, s 18A(2)(b).

Form of s 12B notice

7.13 A purchase notice must give adequate notice to the new landlord of the qualifying tenants' desire to purchase the estate or interest that they should have been offered by the original landlord. That it has been said is imperative, in the sense that it must be followed to the letter, but the other requirements of the purchase notice would appear to be only directory[1]. A failure to refer to all of the flats within the building did not invalidate the purchase notice where albeit one of the seven flats within the building was not referred to in the notice. The notice was valid, as it required the purchaser to dispose of the freehold interest that the purchaser held in 'the above-mentioned premises'. Given that what was being referred to was a freehold interest in the building in which the seven flats were situated, it was said that it would be absurd to understand the notice as only requiring part of that freehold interest to be transferred. Further, if there was doubt a letter sent with the notice made it clear that what was being referred to was the whole of the freehold interest in the building[2].

1 *Kay-Green v Twinsectra* [1996] 1 WLR 1587, CA. See also para **7.07**. For a suggested form of notice, see Appendix I.
2 *Kay-Green v Twinsectra* [1996] 1 WLR 1587, CA. As to the court's willingness to refer to a covering letter to make clear the terms of the notice, see *Germax Securities Ltd v Spiegal* (1978) 37 P & CR 204, CA.

Time for serving notice

7.14 The notice is to be served no later than the end of the period of six months beginning with:

(a) the date on which a notice under the Landlord and Tenant Act 1985, s 3A relating to the original disposal has been served on the requisite majority of qualifying tenants of the constituent flats; or

(b) where s 3A of the 1985 Act does not apply, documents of any other description indicating that the original disposal has taken place and alerting the tenants to the existence of their rights under Part I of the LTA 1987 and the time within which such rights must be exercised, have been served on the requisite majority of qualifying tenants to the constituent flats[1].

If, however, a notice pursuant to the LTA 1987, s 11A has been served on the purchaser then the notice must be served before the end of the period of six months beginning with the date on which the purchaser complies with the s 11A notice[2].

1 LTA 1987, s 12B(3)(b)(i), (ii).
2 LTA 1987, s 12B(3)(a).

7.15 The effect of these time provisions is that the requisite majority of qualifying tenants can seek to extend time for serving a s 12B notice by ensuring that a s 11A notice is served. The s 11A notice is required to be served before the end of the period of four months beginning with the date by which notices under s 3A of the Landlord and Tenant Act 1985 relating to the original disposal, or where that section does not apply, documents of any other description indicating that the original disposal has taken place, and alerting the tenants to the existence of their rights under the LTA 1987, Part I and the time within which any such rights must be exercised, have been served on the requisite majority of qualifying tenants of the constituent flats[1]. Accordingly if, say, the purchaser serves a s 3A notice on the requisite majority of qualifying tenants, the tenants have four months within which to serve a s 11A notice, and after due compliance by the purchaser with the s 11A notice the tenants will have six months within which to serve a purchase notice under s 12B.

1 LTA 1987, s 11A(3).

Original disposal including 'other property'

7.16 It is sometimes the case that the relevant disposal is not the disposition of a single estate comprising the landlord's freehold or long leasehold interest. In practice, contracts/transfers sometimes tend to be complex documents involving 'other property'. Where the relevant disposal includes 'other property' in addition to premises to which the LTA 1987, Part I applied at the time of the disposal, the purchase notice *shall* require the purchaser only to make a disposal relating to those premises, and will require him to do so on the terms on which it was made (including those relating to the consideration payable) with any necessary modification[1]. The purchase notice may specify the subject matter of the disposal and the terms on which the disposal is to be made (whether doing so expressly or by reference to the original disposal), or may provide for those matters to be determined by a LVT[2]. A notice has been held to be valid notwithstanding the fact that it referred to the registered title of the property which included property other than the premises to which Part I applied, and required the purchaser to dispose of the terms of the original disposal subject to such modifications as were necessary or expedient. It was held that it was unnecessary for the notice to define precisely the property to be acquired[3]. Similarly, a purchase notice which referred to the entirety of an estate without severing those parts to Part I did not apply, and which consisted of several buildings containing houses or bungalows, has been held to be valid. It was said that the requirements as to the contents of the purchase notice were only directory. Albeit the purchase notice included extra property, that did not invalidate the notice as a whole as it gave adequate notice of the requirement of the qualifying tenants that the landlord should transfer the buildings to which the LTA 1987 applied[4].

The tenants have no right to compel the sale of other property, eg garages held under separate leases[5], or of chattels, such as building materials, bought by the purchaser for work on flats which have not yet been incorporated into the building[6].

1 LTA 1987, s 12B(4). There is an interesting contrast here between this sub-section and the LTA 1987, s 12A(5). In a case where the original disposal consists of entry into a contract and the requisite majority of qualifying tenants seek to exercise their rights against the landlord, then if the contract relates to 'other property' there is no mandatory requirement for the notice to sever the 'other property'. However, sub-s (4) of s 12B of the LTA 1987 uses the word 'shall' which, by reference to the contrast, would appear to be a mandatory requirement. Thus where the original disposal consists of entry into a contract and the tenants seek to exercise their right against the *purchaser* rather than the landlord and the contract relates to 'other property', the purchase notice must be one which deals only with the premises to which Pt I applied at the time of the disposal. In light of the decision in *Kay-Green v Twinsectra* [1996] 1 WLR 1587, CA, it is probably the case that notwithstanding the apparent mandatory wording the current requirement to sever is directory only.
2 LTA 1987, s 12B(4).
3 *Denetower Ltd v Toop* [1991] 1 WLR 945.
4 *Kay-Green v Twinsectra* [1996] 1 WLR 1587, CA.
5 *Denetower Ltd v Toop* [1991] 1 WLR 945.
6 *30 Upperton Gardens Management Ltd v Akano* [1990] 2 EGLR 232.

Charges or incumbrances since the original disposal

Charges

7.17 The purchaser may have charged the subject matter of the original disposal since the original disposal. In those circumstances, unless the court otherwise directs, the charge[1] to secure the payment of money or performance of any other obligation is discharged on the re-disposal of the premises to the nominated person, subject to the detailed provisions of Part I of Sch 1 of the LTA 1987[2].

1 Which includes a mortgage or lien but not a rentcharge: LTA 1987, s 12B(6).
2 LTA 1987, s 12B(5)(a). See para **7.33**.

Incumbrances

7.18 If, since the original disposal, the property which the purchaser is required to dispose of becomes subject to an 'other incumbrance' then, unless the court otherwise directs, the property shall be disposed of subject to the incumbrance but with a reduction in the consideration payable to the purchaser corresponding to the amount by which the existence of the incumbrance reduces the value of the property[1]. There is no definition of 'incumbrance' within the LTA 1987. It is considered that it would, accordingly, be given its ordinary meaning of subsisting third party rights. Thus the grant of a lease of a single flat has been held to be an incumbrance[2]. The grant of a reversionary lease has been held not to be an incumbrance[3].

1 LTA 1987, s 12B(5)(b). The date for valuing the reduction is not specified: see para **7.25**.
2 *Belvedere Court Management Ltd v Frogmore Developments Ltd* [1997] QB 858, CA.
3 *Belvedere Court Management Ltd v Frogmore Developments Ltd* [1997] QB 858, CA. However, a lease of roof space not previously demised to the tenants and granted to the husband of the purchaser (who had purchased in breach of the LTA 1987) was held to be an incumbrance: *Englefield Court Tenants v Skeels* [1990] 2 EGLR 230, LVT. In *Nolan v Eagle Wharf Developments Ltd* [1992] 2 EGLR 223, LVT the new landlord of a purpose-built block of flats comprising three floors of 12 one-bedroom flats granted a 999-year lease of the loft space and a similar lease of the car park to the block. It was held that the nominated person took free of the leases. It was considered that as the leases themselves constituted relevant disposals under s 4 of the LTA 1987, the leases fell outside the meaning of 'incumbrance'. However, this reasoning was criticised by Sir Thomas Bingham MR in *Belvedere Court Management Ltd v Frogmore Developments Ltd* [1997] QB 858, CA. It was said that: 'If a further lease is a "relevant disposal", that disposal may give rise to a fresh right of first refusal as against the new landlord (and the person who has taken the lease). It is not material to the question under section 12(4) [which corresponds to s 12B(5) of the LTA 1987] which relates to the rights of the tenants arising from the original landlord's disposal; for that purpose it is still necessary to ask whether the lease granted by the new landlord is an "incumbrance".' A repairs notice served under the provisions of the Housing Act 1985 has been held to constitute an 'incumbrance' for the purposes of the LTA 1987: *Gregory v Saddiq* [1991] 1 EGLR 237, LVT (where the notice was in fact served before the s 12 notice and thus was held not to affect the price); *Saga Properties Ltd v Palmeira Square Nos 2–6 Ltd* [1995] 1 EGLR 199 (various notices served by Hove Borough Council under the provisions of the Town and Country Planning Act 1990, the Housing Act 1985 and the Building Act 1983 after acquisition by the new landlord treated as incumbrances reducing the price to be paid).

Approach of LVT to 'matters to be determined' under the purchase notice

Price where no 'other property'

7.19 The terms of the purchase notice should require the purchaser to dispose of the estate or interest that was the subject matter of the disposal 'on the terms on which it was made (including those relating to the consideration payable)'[1]. Whether or not the price agreed between the landlord and the purchaser represents a market price, the nominated person is required to pay that price; there is no general power to re-determine the price[2]. Thus where the consideration for the disposal was nil, that was the 'price' which the nominated person was required to pay[3]. If the consideration for the original disposal was a non-monetary consideration then the LTA 1987 makes express provision as to the monetary value which is to be paid by the nominated person[4].

1 LTA 1987, s 12B(2).
2 *Cousins v Metropolitan Guarantee Ltd* [1989] 2 EGLR 223, LVT; *Sullivan v Safeland Investments Ltd* [1990] 2 EGLR 227, LVT; *Venus v Khan* [1990] 2 EGLR 237, LVT.
3 *Woodridge Ltd v Downie* (1997) 76 P & CR 239, LT.
4 LTA 1987, s 8C. See para **5.13**.

7.20 In one case[1] where the property actually sold to the original purchaser was the same as the property sold to the nominated person, the LVT departed from the valuation of that of the parties to the original disposal on the basis that there had been a misdescription between the property offered for sale at auction and the property which was the subject matter of the original disposal and formed the subject matter of the sale to the nominated person[2].

1 *Cousins v Metropolitan Guarantee Ltd* [1989] 2 EGLR 223, LVT.
2 The authors would agree with the view expressed in *Woodfall on Landlord and Tenant*, vol 4, para 28.027 that in this respect this decision must be considered to be wrong. As is stated by the learned authors, 'the estate or interest does not change merely because someone wrongly describes it, particularly where, as in that case, the error was simply a statement that the property had more rooms that it in fact had, which could no doubt have been verified on inspection'.

Price where 'other property'

7.21 Where the original disposal included 'other property', the LVT may have to undertake the task of apportioning the consideration under the original disposal so as to ascertain the amount which the nominated person is required to pay upon the redisposal to him. Where the landlord and the purchaser have effected an apportionment, albeit that apportionment was purely arbitrary, the LVT has refused to interfere with the apportionment[1]. The LVT is not bound to adopt the landlord's apportionment, but can and will carry out its own valuation exercise to determine the proper apportionment.Where the price has not been apportioned the LVT will, again, not value the subject property de novo. It is the price paid under the original disposal which must be apportioned[2].

1 *Venus v Khan* [1990] 2 EGLR 237, LVT.
2 *Sullivan v Safeland Investments Ltd* [1990] 2 EGLR 227; *Groundpremium Property Management Ltd v Longmint* [1998] 1 EGLR 131, LVT.

Additional sums

7.22 It would appear that where there is an agreement between the landlord and the purchaser for the letter to pay arrears of rent and service charges in addition to the purchase price, such sums are to be paid by the nominated purchaser, as it reflects the consideration for the subject matter of the original disposal[1]. Other terms which require payment of money, eg payment of the landlord's conveyancing costs, ought equally to be paid by the nominated person, as they form part of the terms of the original disposal and form the basis on which the nominated purchaser is required to purchase[2]. Where the purchaser paid the landlord a sum to extend the time for compliance with a notice to complete the contract, it was held that this formed part of the consideration for the original disposal and was thus a sum required to be paid by the nominated person[3].

1 *Linkproud Ltd v Ballard* [1997] 1 EGLR 181; *Stazewski v Maribella Ltd* [1998] 1 EGLR 34 where the whole case was premised on the basis that the arrears of rent and service charges were part of the purchase price and, therefore, was a 'term of the original disposal' and was required to be referred to in response to the notice served by the tenants pursuant to what is now the LTA 1987, s 11A.

2 *Woodridge Ltd v Downie* (1997) 76 P & CR 239, LT. In fact in that case the landlord's conveyancing costs were not required to be paid by the nominated person. The agreement to pay the costs was contained in the collateral agreement and, in fact, was an oral agreement unenforceable under s 2 of the Law of Property (Miscellaneous Provisions) Act 1989. The basis for the decision was the fact that the agreement was void under the 1989 Act.
3 *Wilkins v Horrowitz* [1990] 2 EGLR 217.

Other terms

7.23 The basic right conferred by the LTA 1987 is for the tenant to acquire the whole of the property transferred. As has been seen, where the disposal includes 'other property' the LTA 1987 makes express provision for the modification of the terms of the disposal[1]. The purchase notice may provide that the modification of those terms may be left to the determination of the LVT[2]. However, it has been said, in a case which involved no 'other property', that there is no doubt they have a discretion to modify the terms of the original disposal[3]. It was said that the Act enabled the Tribunal to exercise a wide discretion as to terms and did not require them to incorporate verbatim into the conveyance to the nominated person the terms of the original disposal. Accordingly, it was held that where the original disposal contained an option in favour of the landlord to re-purchase, the Tribunal had power to exclude it from the terms of the disposal to the nominated person[4]. The difficulty with this decision is that it was made under the pre-1996 wording. Under that wording the purchase notice could (albeit the disposal did not include other property) provide for the estate or interest to be disposed of and the terms of the disposal to the nominated person to be determined by a LVT[5]. It has been held that the Tribunal may grant as a term of the disposal to the nominated person perpetual rights over roadways and paths rather than the freehold[6]. This decision has been applied to gardens and amenity land[7]. Both of these decisions were again on the old wording.

1 LTA 1987, ss 12A(5), 12B(4) and 12C(5). Appurtenances of the building go with the building: *Denetower Ltd v Toop* [1991] 1 WLR 945, CA.
2 LTA 1987, ss 12A(5), 12B(4), 12C(6).
3 *Newman v Kay* [1991] 2 EGLR 237, LVT. It may be that it is under this discretion that the LVT can deal with conditions to be fulfilled by the purchaser under the contract with which the nominated person would have difficulty with complying: see para **7.05** in relation to the conditions of the contract where a s 12A notice is to be served.
4 *Newman v Kay* [1991] 2 EGLR 237, LVT. The incorporation into the terms of the original disposal of an option to the landlord to re-purchase may be used as a means of deterring the qualifying tenants from proceeding with the acquisition. The option, which could be by way of a call option, could provide for the purchase price to be, say, 25% lower than that paid by the purchaser. A disposal back to the landlord after acquisition by the nominated person pursuant to the option would be an exempt disposal.
5 LTA 1987, ss 12(3)(b) and 13(1) prior to the 1996 amendments. The opportunity to require the LVT to determine the terms of the disposal has not been repeated in the new wording of ss 12A, 12B, 12C and 13 save for where modification is required to accommodate the fact that the disposal includes other property in addition to that to which Pt I of the LTA 1987 applies: see ss 12A(5), 12B(4). Interestingly, sub-ss (5) and (6) of s 12C do not appear to limit the right to require the Tribunal to determine the terms of the disposal to the nominated person to a disposal of a relevant tenancy where the relevant tenancy included premises other than premises to which the LTA 1987 applied. However, s 13 (as amended), when dealing with the Tribunal's jurisdiction to determine matters in the purchase notice as being matters left for determination by the Tribunal, fails to refer to s 12C(5), (6).

6 *Denetower Ltd v Toop* [1991] 1 WLR 945, CA. In that case it was held that the tenants' right to acquire the freehold in the building included the gardens and other appurtenances of the flats which were expressly or impliedly included in the demises of the flats to the tenants. It was said that 'building' in the LTA 1987 included the appurtenances of the building. It was said that 'As roadways and paths over which the tenants have express or prescriptive rights of ways ... they are appurtenances of the building. However, it may well be that a rent assessment committee acting under section 13(1) may reach the conclusion that the appropriate provision should be that the tenants should not acquire the freehold in the land of the roadway and paths, but be granted perpetual rights of way over them'.

7 *Twinsectra Ltd v Jones* [1998] 2 EGLR 129, LT.

Increase in monetary value of the property required to be disposed of in pursuance of a purchase notice

7.24 Where the property which the purchaser is required to dispose of in pursuance of the purchase notice has since the original disposal increased in monetary value owing to any change in circumstances (other than a change in the value of money), the amount of the consideration payable to the purchaser for the disposal by him of the property in pursuance of the purchase notice should be the amount that might reasonably have been obtained on a corresponding disposal made on the open market at the time of the original disposal if the change in circumstances had already taken place[1]. Thus, for instance, if the purchaser has obtained vacant possession of one or more flats of the building which has formed the subject matter of the original disposal, that may be reflected in the price to be paid by the nominated person[2]. Vacant possession may, for instance, also be obtained by forfeiture. However, in these circumstances if relief from forfeiture is likely to be granted the price will not be increased[3]. Similarly, if repairs or other works have been carried out then these must be taken into account[4].

1 LTA 1987, s 12B(7).

2 *Twinsectra Ltd v Jones* [1998] 2 EGLR 129, LT (death of regulated tenant).

3 *Crumpton v Unifox Properties Ltd* [1992] 2 EGLR 82, CA.

4 *Saga Properties Ltd v Palmeira Square Nos 2–6 Ltd* [1995] 1 EGLR 199; cf *Crumpton v Unifox Properties Ltd* [1992] 2 EGLR 82, CA, where the expenditure on the improvements did not add value.

7.25 The provisions of the LTA 1987 identify the valuation date for determining any increase, namely the date of the original disposal, assuming the change in circumstances had taken place[1]. No corresponding provision is made in respect of valuing the property which the purchaser is required to dispose of in pursuance of the purchase notice where is has, since the date of the original disposal, become subject to an incumbrance[2]. No guidance is given by the LTA 1987 as to what is the date of valuation. Candidate dates would appear to be the date of the original disposal; the date of the making of the incumbrance, or the date upon which the matter is being considered by the LVT.

1 LTA 1987, s 12B(7).

2 The LTA 1987 simply refers, in the case of an incumbrance, to there being a 'reduction in the consideration payable corresponding to the amount by which the existence of the incumbrance reduces the value of the property'.

Change in the value of money

7.26 This would appear to refer to general inflation (eg the Retail Prices Index) rather than increases or decreases in the property market, which have often fluctuated more strongly. That is borne out by the statement of the minister as the Bill was being debated in committee[1].

1 House of Commons Standing Committee A, 23 April 1987, Cols 42–44. The opposition spokesman, Mr Nick Raynsford (proposing an amendment to leave out this expression), argued that new landlords 'should not be able to receive a windfall gain because property prices increase at a rate that is way ahead of inflation. The clause [if left unamended] will allow them to benefit from such increases'. The Minister, Mr Mark Robinson, rejecting the amendment, replied 'If the value of the property has increased relative to prices generally, the tenants would pay a higher price, but they would be obtaining a more valuable asset'.

Original disposal including 'other buildings' to which Part I of the LTA 1987 applies.

7.27 Where the original disposal included more than one building to which Part I of the LTA 1987 applies, LTA 1987, s 12B makes no express provision for severance of the transaction by the qualifying tenants when serving the purchase notice. As to the approach to be taken by the qualifying tenants, see the discussion of this problem in the context of the LTA 1987, s 12A[1]. One of the difficulties, as mentioned in that discussion, is how an apportionment is to be undertaken where no apportionment is made in respect of the consideration referred to, and the consideration is simply a global sum for all the buildings included within the disposal.

1 See para **7.09**.

Right of qualifying tenants to compel grant of new tenancy by a superior landlord: s 12C notices

7.28 If the original disposal consisted of the surrender by the landlord of a tenancy held by him ('the relevant tenancy') then the requisite majority of qualifying tenants of the constituent flats may serve a notice on the purchaser requiring him to grant a new tenancy of the premises which were subject to the relevant tenancy. The terms upon which the new tenancy is to be granted are the same terms as those of the relevant tenancy. The duration of the term to be granted is one which is to expire on the same date as the relevant tenancy would have expired. The new tenancy is to be granted to a person or persons nominated by the requisite majority of qualifying tenants of the constituent flats[1].

1 As to the definition of 'requisite majority of qualifying tenants of the constituent flats', see para **2.16**.

Form of s 12C notice

7.29 There is no prescribed form of notice. It must, however, be in writing[1].

1 LTA 1987, s 54(1). See also paras **7.03** and **7.13** for further discussion as to the form of the notice. For a suggested form of notice, see Appendix I.

Time for serving notice

7.30 The time for serving the notice is a period which expires at the end of six months beginning with the same dates as are required for a notice under the LTA 1987, s 12B[1].

1 See para **7.14**.

Consideration to be paid

7.31 It may be that a surrender of the lease would have involved a reverse premium. Any amount paid to the landlord as consideration for the surrender is to be paid by the nominated person to the purchaser[1]. The LTA 1987 makes provision only for payment back to the purchaser of an amount paid to the landlord as consideration for the surrender. If other consideration was given then it would appear that the purchaser does not recover the consideration given for the surrender. For instance, assume that in consideration of the surrender the purchaser granted to the landlord shares in the purchaser or assigned to the landlord shares in another company in which the purchaser had invested. The landlord appears, in those circumstances, to retain the consideration. Any difficulties in relation to consideration other than monetary payments can easily be avoided by the appropriate drafting of the contract as between landlord and purchaser.

1 LTA 1987, s 12C(4). There would appear to be no provision for the payment of interest on this sum.

Where the relevant tenancy included premises other than premises to which the LTA 1987, Part I applied at the time of the disposal

7.32 It may be that the relevant tenancy included not only premises to which Part I of the LTA 1987 applied but other premises to which the Act did not apply. In these circumstances the requisite majority of qualifying tenants of the constituent flats can, by their purchase notice under s 12C, require the purchaser to grant a new tenancy relating only to the premises to which Part I applied at the date of the disposal[1]. The purchase notice may specify the subject matter of the disposal and the terms on which the disposal is to be made (whether doing so expressly or by reference to the original disposal), or may provide for those matters to be determined by a LVT[2].

1 LTA 1987, s 12C(5)(a). See also the discussion in respect of ss 12A and 12B notices at paras **7.07** and **7.16**.

2 LTA 1987, s 12C(6).

Discharge of charges

7.33 Part I of Sch 1 to the LTA 1987 contains detailed provisions dealing with the discharge of a charge to secure the payment of money or performance of any other obligation by the purchaser or any other person, where that charge has been created since the original disposal[1]. The general position is that the nominated person is to apply the consideration payable, in the first instance, in or towards the redemption of any charge (or if there is more than one of them, then according to their priorities)[2].

If the totality of the consideration payable is applied in discharge of the charge but is insufficient to redeem the charge or charges in its or their entirety, then, nevertheless, the effect of so applying the consideration payable is to discharge the property from the charge[3].

If there is a debenture-holders' charge, that is to say, a charge (whether a floating charge or not) in favour of the holders of a series of debentures issued by a company or other body of persons, or in favour of trustees for such debenture-holders, then the charge will not be discharged upon the transfer to the nominated person[4]. However, the exemption from discharge does not apply in favour of a debenture-holders' charge which, at the date of the instrument by virtue of which the property is disposed of by the purchaser, is (as regards that property) a specific and not a floating charge[5].

1 LTA 1987, s 12B(5)(a) and Sch 1, Pt 1.
2 LTA 1987, Sch 1, para 2(1). The wording in para 2(1) is slightly odd as it refers to the duty of the nominated person to apply 'the consideration payable' towards redemption. 'The consideration payable' is defined in the LTA 1987, Sch 1, para 1 as meaning 'the consideration payable to the purchaser for the disposal by him of the property referred to in section 12B(7)'. Section 12b(7) deals with the situation where the value of the property increased after the original disposal. Presumably the intention was that the consideration payable was to be that provided for by s 12B(7). Schedule 1 does not, however, express this intention in these terms.
3 LTA 1987, Sch 1, Pt I, para 2(2).
4 LTA 1987, Sch 1, para 2(3).
5 LTA 1987, Sch 1, para 2(4).

7.34 In considering the amount payable under the charge, one is to disregard the right of the chargee to consolidate the charge with a separate charge on other property[1]. The LTA 1987, further, provides for payment of interest only to the date of payment, notwithstanding that the terms of the security make other provision or no provision as to the time and manner of payment[2].

1 LTA 1987, Sch 1, para 3(1).
2 LTA 1987, Sch 1, para 3(2).

7.35 The payment by the nominated person would ordinarily be made to the chargee. However, the nominated person may pay such part of the consideration that is required to be applied to redeem the charge into court if:

(a) for any reason difficulty arises in ascertaining how much is payable in respect of the charge[1];

(b) effecting payment is diffcult because:

(i) a person who is or may be entitled to receive payment cannot be found or ascertained;

(ii) any such person refuses or fails to make out a title, or to accept payment and give a proper discharge, or to take any steps reasonably required of him to enable the sum payable to be ascertained and paid; or

(iii) a tender of the sum payable cannot, by reason of complications in the title to it or the want of two or more trustees, or for other reasons, be effected, or not without incurring or involving unreasonable costs or delay[2].

1 LTA 1987, Sch 1, para 4(1)(a).
2 LTA 1987, Sch 1, para 4(1)(b), (ii).

7.36 Where any property is discharged[1] from a charge (without the obligation secured by the charge being satisfied by the receipt of the whole or part of the consideration payable), the discharge of the property transferred to the nominated person from the charge shall not prejudice any right or remedy for the enforcement of those obligations against other property comprised in the same or any other security, nor prejudice any personal liability as principal or otherwise of the purchaser or any other person[2].

1 By the LTA 1987, s 12B(5)(a.
2 LTA 1987, Sch 1, para 5.

CHAPTER 8

Subsequent purchasers

LTA 1987, s 16: rights of qualifying tenants against subsequent purchaser

General

8.01 The LTA 1987 contains provisions to enable the qualifying tenants, in effect, to trace the estate or interest which was the subject matter of the original disposal where the purchaser to whom the disposal was originally effected (in non-compliance with the provisions of the LTA 1987), has himself effected a transfer of the estate or interest of that which was the subject matter of the original disposal[1]. While the original disposal by the original landlord must have been a 'relevant' disposal, the same does not apply to a disposal by the purchaser. Section 16 the LTA 1987 applies to *any* disposal by the purchaser and preserves the tenants' rights of first refusal arising from the original (relevant) disposal by the original landlord[2]. If the disposal to the subsequent purchaser is also a relevant disposal under the Act, the qualifying tenants will be entitled in relation to it to rely on the provisions of the Act on the basis that it (the subsequent disposal) is an original disposal[3] or rely on their rights under s 16.

1 LTA 1987, s 16.
2 *Belvedere Court Management Ltd v Frogmore Developments Ltd* [1997] QB 858, CA.
3 In which case the 'subsequent purchaser' is the 'purchaser' for the purposes of the LTA 1987.

Obligation of purchaser in case of notice served under s 11A (right to information as to terms of disposal) by qualifying tenants where there has been a subsequent disposal

8.02 Where the original disposal has been made by the landlord in contravention of the provisions of the LTA 1987 (whether it be a failure to serve an offer notice pursuant to the LTA 1987, s 5 or by failing to comply with any one of the provisions contained in ss 6–10[1] of the LTA 1987), the requisite majority of qualifying tenants of the flats contained in the premises affected by the relevant disposal ('the constituent flats') may, if the premises are still premises to which the Act applies, serve a notice on the purchaser requiring particulars as to the terms of the original disposal[2].

1 The provisions of the LTA 1987 which restrict a landlord once he has served an offer notice.
2 See para **6.01**.

8.03 The purchaser upon whom a notice under the LTA 1987, s 11A has been served is required to comply with it within the period of one month beginning with the date on which it is served on him. If, at the date that the purchaser receives that notice served under s 11A he no longer holds the estate or interest that was the subject matter of the original disposal, the purchaser shall, within the one-month period for complying with the s 11A notice:

(a) serve notice on the person specified in the notice as the person to whom particulars are to be provided of the name and address of the person to whom he has disposed of the estate or interest ('the subsequent purchaser'); and
(b) serve on the subsequent purchaser a copy of the notice received under the LTA 1987, s 11A and of the particulars given by him in response to it[1].

1 LTA 1987, s 16(2)(a), (b).

8.04 A number of points need to be noted:

(1) first, under the terms of the original disposal the purchaser is, notwithstanding the fact that he no longer holds the estate or interest which was the subject matter of the original disposal at the time that the notice under the LTA 1987, s 11A is served upon him, required to comply with the notice served pursuant to s 11A; ie he is required to give, in addition to the information required by s 16(2), the appropriate particulars as required by the LTA 1987, s 11A. In other words, s 16(2) is imposing additional obligations upon the purchaser rather than substituting the obligations under that section for those under s 11A;
(2) secondly, compliance by the purchaser with the s 11A notice determines the date by which the requisite majority of qualifying tenants of the constituent flats may serve notices under the LTA 1987, ss 12A, 12B or 12C on the subsequent purchaser as if he were the transferee under the original disposal. Ordinarily, in the case of service of such notices on the original transferee where no subsequent disposal has been effected, the notice, whether under ss 12A, 12B or 12C, must be served before the end of the period of six months beginning with, if a notice under s 11A is served, the date on which the purchaser complies with that notice[1]. However, where at the time when the notice is served on the purchaser under s 11A he no longer holds the estate or interest which was the subject matter of the original disposal, it would appear that the period for serving notice under ss 12A, 12B or 12C, commences from the *later* of:

(a) six months from the date that the purchaser provides particulars in response to the s 11A notice; and

(b) the date on which the purchaser served a notice on the requisite majority of qualifying tenants of the constituent flats pursuant to s 16(2)(a), ie gives notice that there has been a transfer to the subsequent purchaser[2].

The view that the date for service of the relevant s 12A, s 12B or s 12C notice is capable of indefinite extension upon a failure by the purchaser to comply with s 16(2)(a) derives from the provisions of s 16(4). This provides that:

> 'Once the purchaser serves a notice in accordance with sub-section (2)(a) or (3)(b), sections 12A to 14 shall, instead of applying to the purchaser, apply to the subsequent purchaser as if he were the transferee under the original disposal.'

1 LTA 1987, s 16(2)(a), (b).
2 LTA 1987, ss 12A(2)(a), 12C(3)(a). If the notice is not served by the requisite majority of qualifying tenants of the constituent flats under the LTA 1987, s 11A, the date ends with the period of six months beginning with the date by which documents of any description indicating that the original disposal has taken place and alerting the tenants to the existence of their rights under Pt I, and the time within which any such rights are to be exercised, have been served on the requisite majority of qualifying tenants of the constituent flats: LTA 1987, ss 12A(2)(b), 12B(3)(b), 12C(3)(b).

8.05 It has been held under the terms of the earlier wording of the LTA 1987, s 16[1] that unless and until the purchaser serves notice pursuant to the terms of s 16(2)(a), the rights of the qualifying tenants against the subsequent purchaser remain in abeyance; in the absence of any notice pursuant to s 16(2)(a), the condition for the application of ss 12A–14 to the subsequent purchaser instead of the purchaser has not been fulfilled. It remains the continuing duty of the purchaser to serve a notice under s 16(2)(a). If it does not do so it can be compelled to do so[2].

1 *Belvedere Court Management Ltd v Frogmore Developments Ltd* [1997] QB 858, CA. The earlier wording in *Belvedere* considered by the Court of Appeal was: 'If the new landlord serves a notice in accordance with sub-section (1)(a)(ii) or (b)(ii) above, section 12 to 14 shall, instead of applying to the new landlord, apply to the subsequent purchaser as if he were the transferee under the original disposal'. The current s 16 was substituted by the Housing Act 1996, Sch 6.
2 By injunction: LTA 1987, s 19.

8.06 There is no prescribed form for the notice that is required to be served in compliance by the purchaser with the LTA 1987, s 16(2) upon the persons to whom particulars are to be provided in response to the notice served under the LTA 1987, s 11A. The Court of Appeal, on not dissimilar wording of the pre-1996 provisions of s 16[1], held that the purchaser is required to serve a notice which will leave the tenants or their nominee in no doubt that it is a s 16(2)(a) notice which is intended[2]. This is most easily done by reference to the section itself, but an express reference to the section is not essential if the purport of the notice is quite clear[3]. In one case a notice was served by the purchaser in response to a purchase notice pursuant to the LTA 1987, s 12 served by the qualifying tenants where the purchaser had acquired a long leasehold interest and, therefore, the immediate reversion to the tenants' interests. The notice informed the tenants that, in fact, the purchaser had granted long leases of each flat and that, accordingly, the s 12 purchase notice was to be subject to and with the benefit of the leases granted to the third party, a wholly owned subsidiary of the purchaser. It was held that the notice was not sufficient for the purposes of the then provisions of s 16, as not only did it fail to refer to s 16 but it was not clearly to be understood as giving notice under that section[4]. This was so notwithstanding the fact that the tenants responded to the letter by serving a purchase notice under the then s 16(3). The notice must be in writing[5]. It may be sent by post[6].

1 Prior to the substitution of the LTA 1987, s 16 by the Housing Act 1996, Sch 6.
2 There is no reason to think that a similar requirement will be unnecessary in the case of the new wording.
3 *Belvedere Court Management Ltd v Frogmore Developments Ltd* [1997] QB 858, CA, per Sir Thomas Bingham MR.
4 *Belvedere Court Management Ltd v Frogmore Developments Ltd* [1997] QB 858, CA.
5 LTA 1987, s 54(1)(a).
6 LTA 1987, s 54(1)(b). See also para **10.14**.

What happens if the purchaser disposes of the estate or interest that was the subject matter of the original disposal after receiving notice under the LTA 1987, s 11A?

8.07 There is nothing in the LTA 1987, s 16 which provides for the situation in which the purchaser disposes of his estate or interest after receipt of a s 11 or s 12A, s 12B, or s 12C notice, nor is there any apparent sanction if he does so[1]. Sir Thomas Bingham MR[2] was of the view that it was a continuing duty of the purchaser to perform a mandatory duty laid on the purchaser by the LTA 1987 and this took effect as soon as the purchaser disposes of his estate or interest after service of a relevant notice. Although there is no warrant in the language of the LTA 1987 for this suggestion, 'constructive judicial legislation' was called for, and such a construction would act to promote the object of the Act. Hobhouse LJ has said:

> 'Is it an essential part of a scheme that the new landlord[3] must have already disposed of the reversion before the section 12 notice is served? Obviously the draftsman had not anticipated that the new landlord will act in defiance of a section 12 notice and this has led him to draft section 16(1) as he has. But is one to construe the sub-section as if it can only apply where the further disposal has preceded the section 12 notice? No reason has been suggested why this should be the intent of the statute. It would merely create a lacuna in the scheme of the statute. If a subsequent purchaser has bought a reversion in respect of which the tenants have already served a purchase notice, why should he be any less under an obligation to transfer it to the tenants than if he had purchased the reversion before they had done so? The mechanisms of section 16

can still work in this additional situation. The new landlord can serve the section 16(1) notices. The tenants can then acquire the statutory right against the subsequent purchaser. There is no reason why the substantive provisions in sections 16(2) and (3)[4] should not take effect. ... It follows that I answer this question by saying that the new landlord cannot by disposing of the reversion after service of a section 12 notice upon him avoid his legal obligation under section 12 (though he may have put it out of his power to perform it himself) nor does it relieve him from the obligation under section 16 to serve the requisite notices. The tenants therefore remain entitled to require the new landlord to perform the obligations set out in section 16(1) and to insist on the statutory machinery being followed by the new landlord[5].'

1 This omission was referred to by Sir Thomas Bingham MR in *Belvedere Court Management Ltd v Frogmore Developments Ltd* [1997] QB 858, CA. Notwithstanding these comments, the substituted provisions of the LTA 1987, s 16 and the offences set out in s 10A of the LTA 1987 (both substituted by the Housing Act 1996, Sch 6) still make no provision for this situation.

2 In *Belvedere Court Management Ltd v Frogmore Developments Ltd* [1997] QB 858.

3 Hobhouse LJ was considering the pre-1996 wording rather than 'purchaser' as in the substituted wording.

4 LTA 1987, s 16(2), (3) as before the court were worded as follows:

'(2) If the new landlord serves a notice in accordance with sub-s (1)(a)(ii) or (b)(ii) above, sections 12 to 14 shall, instead of applying to the new landlord, apply to the subsequent purchaser as if he were the transferee under the original disposal.

(3) Sub-sections (1) and (2) above shall have effect, with any necessary modifications, in a case where, instead of disposing of the whole of the estate or interest referred to in sub-section (1) to another person, the new landlord has disposed of it in part or in parts to one or more other persons and accordingly sections 12 to 14 shall:

(a) in relation to any part of that estate or interest retained by the new landlord, apply to the new landlord, and

(b) in relation to any part of that estate or interest disposed of to any other person, apply to that other person instead as if he were (as respects that part) the transferee under the original disposal.'

5 *Belvedere Court Management Ltd v Frogmore Developments Ltd* [1997] QB 858.

Notices under the LTA 1987, ss 12A, 12B or 12C

8.08 Where, at the time when a notice is served on the purchaser under the LTA 1987, ss 12A, 12B or 12C, the purchaser no longer holds the estate or interest that was the subject matter of the original disposal, the purchaser is required forthwith to:

(a) forward the notice to the subsequent purchaser; and

(b) serve on the nominated person notice of the name and address of the subsequent purchaser[1].

Once the purchaser serves such a notice then the LTA 1987, ss 12A–14 shall, instead of applying to the purchaser, apply to the subsequent purchaser as if he was the transferee under the original disposal[2].

1 LTA 1987, s 16(3).
2 LTA 1987, s 16(4).

8.09 Until the purchaser has complied with the requirement of the LTA 1987, s 16(3)(b)[1] the provisions of ss 12A–14 remain in abeyance. This would appear to follow on from a consideration of the provisions of s 16(2)(a)[2].

1 That is to say serving notice on the nominated person of the name and address of the subsequent purchaser.
2 See paras **8.04** and **8.05**.

8.10 The modification of the application of the LTA 1987, s 16 where the purchaser, instead of disposing of the whole of the estate or interest that was the subject matter of the original disposal, disposes of it in part or in parts to one or more other persons, is discussed below[1].

1 See para **8.12**.

The estate or interest which is the subject matter of the original disposal

8.11 Section 16(1) of the LTA 1987 applies only where, at the date when notice is served on the purchaser under ss 11A, 12A, 12B and 12C, the purchaser no longer holds the estate or interest which is the subject matter of the original disposal. Where the purchaser has acquired the freehold, the grant of an intermediate headlease has the effect of transferring the reversion of the tenants' leases from himself to another immediate landlord, the head lessee. In those circumstances the purchaser must be regarded as no longer holding the estate or interest that had been the subject matter of the original disposal. The estate or interest is the immediate reversion to the tenants' leases. The grant of a lease which has the effect of transferring the reversion of the tenants' leases has the effect that the purchaser no longer has the reversion. Thus where the landlord transferred to the purchaser a long leasehold interest and the purchaser thereafter granted individual leases of the tenants' flats, it was held that the grant of the long leasehold fell within s 16(1)[1].

1 *Belvedere Court Management Ltd v Frogmore Developments Ltd* [1997] QB 858, CA.

Disposal by purchaser of part of the estate or interest that was the subject matter of the original disposal

8.12 It is provided that the provisions relating to the rights of qualifying tenants against a subsequent purchaser have effect, with necessary modifications, in a case where instead of disposing of the whole of the estate or interest which was the subject matter of the original disposal to another person, the purchaser has disposed of it in part or parts to one or more other persons. In such a case the LTA 1987, ss 12A–14 apply to the purchaser in relation to any part of that estate or interest retained by him and in relation to any part of that estate or interest disposed of to any other person, apply to that other person instead as if he were (as respects that part) the transferee under the original disposal[1]. Thus where L transfers to the purchaser the reversion and the purchaser disposes of the reversion of individual flats retaining the common parts, the structure and exterior of the building, ss 12A–14 continue to apply to the purchaser in relation to the common parts, the structure and exterior[2].

1 LTA 1987, s 16(5).
2 This example is taken from the facts of *Belvedere Court Management Ltd v Frogmore Developments Ltd* [1997] QB 858, CA.

CHAPTER 9

Termination of rights against purchaser or subsequent purchaser

Introduction

9.01 Section 17 of the LTA 1987 contains provisions enabling the purchaser or subsequent purchaser to serve notice on the qualifying tenants of the constituent flats so as to bring an end to the application of the right of first refusal insofar as it may apply to the original disposal. The right to serve such a notice of termination arises in a number of differing circumstances. Section 14 of the LTA 1987 contains provisions for the withdrawal of notices served by the requisite majority of qualifying tenants. These are considered in the paragraphs below.

Premises affected by the original disposal ceasing to be premises to which the LTA 1987, Part I applies: s 17(1) notices

9.02 If the premises affected by the original disposal have ceased to be premises to which the LTA 1987, Part I applies[1], the purchaser, or subsequent purchaser as the case may be[2], may serve notice on the qualifying tenants of the constituent flats so stating and that any notice served on him pursuant to the LTA 1987, ss 11A, 12A, 12B or 12C and any thing done in pursuance of it, is to be treated as not having been served or done[3]. The notice need not be served on all of the qualifying tenants of the constituent flats. It is sufficient that the landlord serves such a notice on not less than 90% of those tenants or, where the qualifying tenants number less than ten, if he has served such a notice on all but one of them[4]. The date for determining the total number of constituent flats is presumably the date at which the notice is served. Although the provisions of the LTA 1987, s 18A identify the dates for determining the total number of constituent flats of qualifying tenants in respect of notices served under the LTA 1987, ss 5, 11A 12A,12B and 12C, no mention is made of s 17 of the LTA 1987.

1 As to the meaning of 'ceased to be premises to which this Part applies', see para **5.22**.

2 References in the LTA 1987, s 17 to 'purchaser' include a subsequent purchaser to whom ss 12A–14 apply by virtue of s 16(4) or (5): LTA 1987, s 17(7). It would seem that where the purchaser has failed to serve a notice in accordance with the LTA 1987, s 16(2)(a) or (3)(b), a

notice under s 17(1) cannot be served, for until the purchaser has served the appropriate notice ss 12A–14 remain inapplicable: see para **8.09**.

3 LTA 1987, s 17(1).

4 LTA 1987, s 17(2)(a), (b). Oddly this section refers to 'a landlord' serving the s 17(1) notice, whereas all other sub-sections of s 17 refer to the 'purchaser' (which definition includes a subsequent purchaser). The purchaser need not of course be the landlord, eg where the nature of the disposal consists of entry into a contract to acquire the reversion. It would seem therefore that the reference to 'landlord' is a mistake.

9.03 An example illustrates the circumstances in which notice under the LTA 1987, s 17(1) may be served. Let us assume a block of four flats, each of which is let to qualifying tenants. Let us also assume that the tenancies of the qualifying tenants are statutory tenants under the Rent Act 1977 and that a s 12B notice is served by only three of the tenants, T4 not wishing to participate. If T3's and T4's statutory tenancies come to an end by, for instance, vacating their respective flats and serving notices under s 3(3) of the Rent Act 1977[1], only two of the four flats are held by qualifying tenants and the total number of flats held by such tenants does not exceed 50% of the total number of flats contained in the premises[2]. Thus a notice under s 17(1) can then be served: the premises are no longer premises to which the Act applies because not more than 50% of the flats are held by qualifying tenants. The notice under s 17(1) need be served only on 90% of the qualifying tenants of constituent flats[3]. As the qualifying tenants number less than ten it is sufficient to serve the s 17(1) notice 'on all but one of them'[4]. In those circumstances only one of the two remaining tenants need be served with the s 17(1) notice.

1 Which enables that statutory tenant to terminate it on giving not less than three months' notice.

2 See the LTA 1987, s 1(2)(b)(c). Two is 50%; it does not *exceed* 50%.

3 LTA 1987, s 17(2)(a).

4 LTA 1987, s 17(2)(b). For a suggested form of notice, see Appendix I. But see para **4.03** for the number to be served.

9.04 There is no prescribed form of notice, but any notice authorised or required to be served under the LTA 1987 shall be in writing and may be sent by post[1]. Where a notice under s 17(1) is served, Part I shall cease to have effect in relation to the purchaser in connection with the original disposal. However, the notice has no effect upon the consequences of the landlord's failure to comply with the LTA 1987.

1 LTA 1987, s 54(1).

9.05 There is no time limit for service of a notice under the LTA 1987, s 17(1). However, it would appear from the terms of s 17(1) that there should be a coincidence between the service of a notice pursuant to it and the circumstances enabling the purchaser to serve such a notice. Section 17(1)(a) refers to the present tense ('have ceased to be premises to which this Part applies') rather than including the past tense (eg 'have or had ceased'). It would seem therefore that if the purchaser fails to serve a notice under s 17(1) when he had the opportunity and the premises again become premises to which the LTA 1987 applies it will be too late to serve the notice. If the purchaser is entitled to serve a notice under s 17(1) but does not do so, Part 1 continues to apply in relation to the original disposal as if the premises were still premises to which Part I applies[1].

1 LTA 1987, s 17(6). It has been suggested that it is curious that this sub-section applies only to sub-s (1) and not to sub-ss (3) and (4), and that, therefore, it may be that somehow the LTA 1987 ceases to apply even if the landlord does not take the opportunity which he may have to serve such notices. It is considered that the reason that express reference was required to the LTA 1987 continuing to apply where no notice under sub-s (1) is served, is that the circumstances in which a notice under that sub-section may be served are where the premises are no longer caught by the LTA 1987. This is not the case with notices under sub-ss (3) and (4), the service of which are not dependent on or related to the premises ceasing to be premises to which the LTA 1987 applies. Sub-section (6) is merely intended to make clear the position which would otherwise be left uncertain in the absence of express provision. It is considered that if the circumstances have arisen entitling a landlord to serve a notice under sub-ss (3) or (4), the LTA 1987 continues to apply notwithstanding the non-service of such a notice. As to sub-ss (3) and (4), see paras **9.11–9.15**.

Withdrawal by nominated person: s 14(2) notices

9.06 It is the duty of the nominated person, if he becomes aware that the number of qualifying tenants of the constituent flats who desire to proceed with the disposal to the qualifying tenants, pursuant to a notice served under the LTA 1987, ss 12B or 12C, is less than the requisite majority of those tenants, forthwith to serve a notice of withdrawal[1]. If a notice of withdrawal is served by the nominated person upon becoming aware that the number of qualifying tenants of the constituent flats is less than the requisite majority, the purchaser may recover from the nominated person any costs reasonably incurred by him in connection with the disposal to the qualifying tenants down to the time when the notice of withdrawal is served upon him[2]. If the notice of withdrawal is served at a time when proceedings arising under or by virtue of the LTA 1987, Part I are pending before the court or the Lands Tribunal, the liability of the nominated persons for any costs incurred by the purchaser shall be such as may be determined by the court or (as the case may be) by the Tribunal[3]. The costs that may be recovered by the purchaser, however, do not include any costs incurred by him in connection with an application to the LVT[4].

1 LTA 1987, s 14(2).
2 LTA 1987, s 14(3).
3 LTA 1987, s 14(4).
4 LTA 1987, s 14(5).

Comparison of s 17(1) and s 14(2) notices

9.07 There is an important difference between premises ceasing to be premises to which the LTA 1987 applies and there ceasing to be a requisite majority of qualifying tenants who wish to proceed with the acquisition. The fact that there ceases to be a requisite majority desiring to proceed with the acquisition does not lead to the premises ceasing to be premises to which the LTA 1987 applies. Let us assume a block of four flats where a notice under the LTA 1987, s 12B has been served. The definition of 'the requisite majority of qualifying tenants of the constituent flats' requires there to be qualifying tenants of constituent flats with more than 50% of the available votes[1]. Assume that at the date of the service of the s 12B notice there were four qualifying tenants[2]. In those circumstances the requisite majority will be three[3]. Three of the tenants wished to participate and the three served a s 12B notice. If later one of the three, let us call him T3, no longer wishes to proceed with the acquisition because he is proposing to sell his lease[4], there ceases to be a requisite majority of qualifying tenants of the constituent flats and a s 14(2) notice should be served if the nominated person becomes aware of the fact that a requisite majority no longer subsists. No notice could, however, be served under the LTA 1987, s 17(1) by the purchaser. The reason is that the premises have *not* ceased to be premises to which Part I of the LTA 1987 applies. Part I still applies as the premises still contain two or more flats held by qualifying tenants[5] and the number of flats held by such tenants exceeds 50% of the total number of flats contained in the premises[6]. It is considered that in these circumstances the right of the tenants who wish to proceed continues. The nominated person, let us assume, is not aware that the number of qualifying tenants has fallen below the requisite majority. No obligation, therefore, to serve a notice under the LTA 1987, s 14(2) arises. If after the assignment by T3 of his lease, the assignee wishes to proceed with the disposal there is again a requisite majority of qualifying tenants of the constituent flats, for there is more than 50% of the available votes[7] who wish to proceed.

1 LTA 1987, s 18A(1). As to the date for determining the total number of qualifying tenants of constituent flats, see para **2.17**.

2 LTA 1987, s 18A(2)(c) provides that in determining the number of available votes, in order to be able to determine whether or not there is a requisite majority of more than 50% of the available votes, the available votes are to be determined, where a notice is served under the LTA 1987, ss 12A, 12B or 12C, without having previously been served under the LTA 1987, ss 5 or 11A, as equal to the total number of constituent flats let to qualifying tenants on the date of service of the notice under ss 12A, 12B or 12C as the case may be: LTA 1987, s 18A(2)(c). In other words, there is one vote per constituent flat let to a qualifying tenant.

3 Two is not 'more than 50% of the available votes' within the meaning of the LTA 1987, s 18A(1); three is.

4 The assignment of a lease by a participating tenant gives rise to an interesting question as to what constitutes an intention no longer to proceed. See further para **9.08**.

5 The fact that a tenant does not wish to participate does not stop the tenant from being a qualifying tenant.

6 LTA 1987, s 1(2)(c). There are still four flats held by qualifying tenants, albeit the tenant of flat 4 never participated and the tenant of flat 3 subsequently changed his mind having previously participated.

7 Those votes being equal to the number of constituent flats let to qualifying tenants on the date of service of the notice under the LTA 1987, s 12B: LTA 1987, s 18A(2)(c).

9.08 The example given highlights a difficulty for the nominated person, particularly in relation to small blocks of flats where any fluctuation in the tenant population may give rise to a falling below the requisite majority. Let us assume, for instance, in the example given, that the nominated person is aware of T3's desire to assign his leasehold interest and his wish no longer to proceed with the acquisition of the freehold. However, let us also assume that the nominated person is equally aware that the prospective purchaser of T3's lease, the assignee, is equally keen to proceed with the acquisition of the freehold. It would seem on a literal interpretation of the LTA 1987, s 14(2) that a notice of withdrawal should be served. However, there appears to be no good reason in those circumstances why a notice of withdrawal is required when there will continue to be, after the assignment, a requisite majority of qualifying tenants of constituent flats. After the assignment, the assignee can stand in T3's shoes[1].

1 LTA 1987, s 20(3).

9.09 A notice of withdrawal under the LTA 1987, s 14(2) is required to be served if the nominated person becomes aware *before contracts are exchanged with the purchaser*[1] that the number of qualifying tenants of the constituent flats desiring to proceed with the disposal is less than the requisite majority of those tenants. Thus after exchange it would appear not to matter that there ceases to be a requisite majority desiring to proceed; both the nominated person and the landlord are bound by the contract entered into. However, there is no qualification in the LTA 1987, s 17(1) to the effect that a notice of termination must be served before contracts are exchanged with the nominated person. Thus if the premises cease to be premises to which the LTA 1987 applies, albeit after exchange of contracts with the purchaser, the purchaser may arguably still serve a notice of termination under s 17(1)[2]. The entry into any contract by the nominated person with the purchaser would not appear to offer protection, as upon service of a s 17(1) notice it is provided that anything done by the purchaser in pursuance of a notice under ss 11A, 12A, 12B or 12C '... shall be treated as not having been ... done'[3].

1 LTA 1987, s 14(2) refers to: 'If at any such time ... ', which is a reference to the time in section 14(1), namely, ' ... before a binding contract is entered into in pursuance of the notice [served under the LTA 1987, ss 12B or 12C]'.
2 Contrast the provisions of the LTA 1987, s 10(4), dealing with the landlord's right to serve a notice withdrawing the offer notice, which makes it clear that the right of withdrawal does not apply once a binding contract for the disposal of the protected interest has been entered into between the landlord and the nominated person.
3 LTA 1987, s 17(1)(b).

9.10 The notice under the LTA 1987, s 17(1) is required to be served upon the qualifying tenants of the constituent flats. A notice under s 14(2) of the LTA 1987 is to be served by the nominated person.

No binding contract having been entered into: s 17(3) and (4) notices

9.11 Section 17(3) of the LTA 1987 provides that, where a period of three months beginning with the date of service of a notice under the LTA 1987, ss 12A, 12B or 12C on the purchaser has expired, without any binding contract having been entered into between the purchaser and the nominated person and without there having been made any application in connection with the notice to the court or to a LVT, the purchaser may serve on the nominated person a notice stating that the notice, and anything done in pursuance of it, is to be treated as not having been served or done[1]. If the matter is referred to the court or to the LVT and a period of two months beginning with the date of the determination of that application has expired, and no binding contract has been entered into between the purchaser and the nominated person and no further application has been made to the court or to a LVT, the purchaser may serve on a nominated person a notice stating that any notice served on him under ss 12A, 12B or 12C, and anything done in pursuance of such notice, is to be treated as not having been served or done[2]. Where the purchaser serves a notice in accordance with the LTA 1987, s 17(3) or (4), Part 1 shall cease to have effect in relation to the purchaser in connection with the original disposal[3]. However, the notice does not relieve the *landlord* from a failure to comply with the provisions of the LTA 1987.

1 LTA 1987, s 17(3).
2 LTA 1986, s 17(4).
3 LTA 1987, s 17(5).

9.12 The premise of the LTA 1987, s 17(3) is that the service of a s 12A, s 12B or s 12C notice is not of itself sufficient to enable the qualifying tenants to acquire the estate or interest that was the subject matter of the original disposal unless a binding contract is entered into subsequent to the service of the s 12A, 12B or 12C notice. Two points, however, ought to be noted.

9.13 First, it is unclear why s 17(3) provides for termination where no binding contract has been entered into between the purchaser and the nominated person in the context of a s 12A notice. A s 12A notice is served where the original disposal consists of entry into a contract, and the requisite majority of qualifying tenants of the constituent flats serve notice to elect that the contract should have effect as if entered into not with the purchaser but with the person or persons nominated by the requisite majority of qualifying tenants of the constituent flats. No new contract would appear to be required to be entered into upon service of a s 12A notice, for the effect is that the nominated person is, in effect, being substituted for the purchaser in the original contract which formed the subject matter of the original disposal. Support for this view is to be derived from the provisions of s 12A(4) which provides that 'nothing in the contract as it has effect by virtue of a notice under this section shall require the nominated person to complete the purchase before the end of the period of 28 days beginning with the day on which he is deemed to have entered into the contract'. Thus the reference in sub-s (1) of s 12A to the contract having 'effect as if entered into not with the purchaser but with the [nominated person] ... ' and sub-s (4) referring to the date 'on which he is deemed to have entered into the contract' suggests that no further contract need be entered into between the nominated person and the purchaser, contrary to the assumption in sub-s (3) of s 17[1].

1 The fact that no new contract needs to be entered into appears to be recognised by the LTA 1987, s 14(1). This section, which refers to the nominated person's right/obligation to withdraw, does so in the context of notices under the LTA 1987, ss 12B and 12C only. The section deals with the right/obligation to withdraw 'before a binding contract is entered into in pursuance of the notice' under ss 12B or 12C. No reference is made to s 12A, dealing with the right of the qualifying tenants to take the benefit of a contract entered into by the landlord without complying with the LTA 1987.

9.14 Secondly, from a practical point of view, this right of termination can be avoided by a tenant by ensuring that steps are taken either by referring the matter to court or to the LVT. In the simple case where the qualifying tenants wish to take over the estate or interest that forms the subject matter of the original disposal, no application needs to be made to the LVT to determine any question arising in relation to any matters specified in the notice served under the LTA 1987, ss 12A, 12B or 12C. The nominated person can, however, prior to the expiry of the three-month period provided for by s 17(3), make an application pursuant to s 19 of the LTA 1987 for an order requiring the purchaser to comply with his duty to transfer the estate or interest that formed the subject matter of the original disposal to the nominated person. Section 19 is dependent upon establishing default of a statutory obligation[1]. No time limit is in fact specified in either ss 12A, 12B or 12C after service of the relevant notice, as to the time within which the purchaser should transfer to the nominated person the estate or interest that formed the subject matter of the original disposal. The default is, by way of example, in the context of a 12B notice, the failure of the purchaser to dispose of the estate or interest that was the subject matter of the original disposal. The s 12B notice requires the purchaser to so transfer the estate or interest and where there is nothing to be referred to the LVT one would certainly expect that interest to be transferred to the nominated person within the three-month period contemplated by the LTA 1987, s 17(3).

1 However, it should be noted that the application under the LTA 1987, s 19 for an order is to be made only after service of a default notice has been given and 14 days have elapsed since the date of service of that notice without the default having been remedied: LTA 1987, s 19(2).

Subsequent purchasers and s 17(3) notices

9.15 The right of termination provided for by the LTA 1987, s 17(3) may be particularly troublesome where there has been a subsequent purchaser. Where the relevant notice pursuant to ss 12A, 12B or 12C of the LTA 1987 has been served upon the purchaser at a time when he no longer holds the estate or interest which was the subject matter of the original disposal, the purchaser is required, as has been seen[1], to forward the notice to the subsequent purchaser and serve on the nominated person notice of the name and address of the subsequent purchaser[2]. Once the purchaser has complied with that obligation, ss 12A–14 of the LTA 1987, instead of applying to the purchaser, apply to the subsequent purchaser as if he were the transferee under the original disposal[3]. Section 17(3) refers to the three-month period as commencing from '... the date of service of a notice under section 12A, 12B, or 12C on the purchaser ... '. However, it is considered that notwithstanding service of a s 12A, s 12B, or s 12C notice on 'the purchaser', where, at the date of service the purchaser no longer holds the estate or interest that was the subject matter of the original disposal there is a reasonable argument for contending that the three-month period begins on the date that the notice is served on the subsequent purchaser. Although s 17(3) refers to 'the purchaser' it is clear that references to 'the purchaser' include a subsequent purchaser to whom ss 12A–14 apply by virtue of the LTA 1987, s 16(4) : LTA 1987, s 17(7). It would be odd if the three-month period began upon service on the purchaser. If this were the correct date the purchaser could hold on to the s12A, s 12B or s 12C notice until shortly before or even after the expiry of the three-month period. The nominated person has no reason to know of the transfer to the subsequent purchaser and thus has no reason to consider making an application under s 19 of the LTA 1987 to require the purchaser to serve a notice in accordance with the LTA 1987, s 16(3)(b). Immediately the s 12A, s 12B or s 12C notice is forwarded by the purchaser to the subsequent purchaser the latter will be in, or shortly be in, a position to serve a s 17(3) notice.

1 See para **8.08**.
2 LTA 1987, s 16(3).
3 LTA 1987, s 16(4).

CHAPTER 10

Miscellaneous

Avoidance

10.01 The introduction of the LTA 1987 involved a major interference with the thriving market in buying and selling freeholds – indeed that was its intention. Not surprisingly, property dealers immediately sought ways around it. One of the easiest loopholes to exploit was the use of an associated company[1]. The freehold (or head leasehold) interest would be transferred to an associated company specially formed for the task. The shares in the associated company would then be sold to the purchaser. There was no relevant disposal since what was being sold was a block of shares, not an interest in property. Another course of action would be simply to ignore the LTA 1987. There were no criminal or civil sanctions for breach of its provisions. At worst, the tenants could serve a purchase notice under the LTA 1987, s 12 and acquire the interest at the same price. Admittedly the costs of the transaction would be lost. However, many tenants would not have the inclination or organisation to compel a sale on to them by using a purchase notice, and some purchasers were prepared to take the risk.

The perceived lack of teeth in the legislation was remedied by the wholesale amendments brought in by the Housing Act 1996. There are now criminal penalties for failing to observe the requirements of the LTA 1987. The associated company loophole has been tightened by excluding from the definition of relevant disposal a transfer to a company which has been an associated company of the landlord for at least two years[2]. The entry into a conditional contract is a relevant disposal[3].

1 See the discussion in para **3.53** on relevant disposals. For a discussion of the device, see articles in the Estates Gazette on May 14 1998 by Stuart Lightman and on August 13 1988 by Prof J Adams.
2 See para **3.53** ff
3 See para **3.57**.

10.02 There are now only very limited opportunities for avoidance. The first only applies where the landlord is contemplating the long term, perhaps at the beginning of a new development. The landlord (a company) thinks it may wish to dispose of the freehold in due course (other than to the tenants), having granted long leases of most, if not all, of the flats. Provided the eventual disposal is going to be two years in the future, the landlord can create a subsidiary at the outset. When he wishes to sell his interest, he transfers it to the associated company and then the shares in the associated company are sold to the purchaser.

10.03 The landlord may find a purchaser and wish to enter into some kind of agreement with him conditional on the tenants not accepting the offer contained in the s 5 notice. Since it is now impossible lawfully to (i) enter into a conditional contract (since that is itself a relevant disposal[1]), or (ii) grant an option, in either case exercisable if the tenants do not accept the offer, there is seemingly nothing that can be done which involves the landlord committing himself. However, the LTA 1987 does not prevent the potential purchaser unilaterally committing himself to buying the property if the tenants do not accept the offer in the s 5 notice. The commitment would have to be by deed executed by the potential purchaser, since no consideration may pass.

1 LTA 1987, 4A(1).

10.04 It would seem that a method of avoidance would be to have as a term of the original disposal an option in favour of the landlord entitling the landlord to call for a re-disposal of the property forming the subject matter of the original disposal if the same were to be acquired by qualifying tenants of the constituent flats within the building pursuant to their rights under Part I of the LTA 1987. The option could provide, for instance, that the price to be paid by the landlord is, say, only a percentage of that which was payable by the purchaser, eg, say, 50%. The disposal pursuant to the option would not be a relevant disposal[1].

1 LTA 1987, s 4(2)(i).

10.05 A possible means of avoidance may be to utilise the exemption provided by the LTA 1987 for disposals made in connection with 'the appointment of a new trustee or in connection with the discharge of any trustee'[1]. Assume that the landlord's interest is vested jointly in two companies, L1 and L2, on trust for L1. L1 may dispose of his entire beneficial interest to P without having to serve an offer notice[2]. His retirement as a trustee and the appointment of P in his place, together with the transfer of the legal estate to P and L2, would appear to be an exempt disposal.

1 LTA 1987, s 4(2)(g); see para **3.33** ff.
2 See para **3.05**.

10.06 Another tactic (though not avoiding the LTA 1987 at the outset of a transaction) which has been employed by landlords or purchasers is to acquire enough of the qualifying tenants' flats to ensure that the numbers wishing to proceed falls below the requisite majority. Once that happens, the nominated person must serve a notice of withdrawal[1]. The length of the process under the LTA 1987 is usually sufficient to give the landlord or purchaser an opportunity to make attractive offers to one or more of the tenants, and there is nothing in the LTA 1987 to prevent approaches being made. The tenants are obviously most vulnerable to such a manoeuvre if their majority is small. If any tenant wishes to withdraw from the majority, he cannot be prevented from doing so[2].

1 LTA 1987, s 14(2).
2 *Mainwaring v Henry Smith's Charity Trustees (No 2)* [1997] 1 EGLR 93.

10.07 Although not strictly avoidance, one course of action which could be carried out by a landlord is to grant a lease superior to the qualifying tenant's interests for just over seven years. The grant of that lease is a relevant disposal, in respect of which an offer notice must be served. Having put in place the intermediate lease, the landlord is free to sell the freehold, subject of course to the intermediate lease[1]. That will only be of interest to a purchaser who does not mind waiting for over seven years to become a direct reversioner.

1 See also paras **2.11, 2.12**.

Enforcement

10.08 It was one of the major defects in the LTA 1987 as originally drafted that there was no sanction for violation of the duties imposed on the landlord[1]. The only remedy was an application to the court under the LTA 1987, s 19 requiring compliance with the statute following a default notice[2]. The situation was remedied by the Housing Act 1966, which introduced criminal penalties against defaulting landlords[3].

1 See *Belvedere Court Management Ltd v Frogmore Developments Ltd* [1997] QB 858, per Sir Thomas Bingham MR at 866 for a trenchant comment on that state of affairs.
2 See further para **10.12**. In *Michaels v Taylor Woodrow Developments Ltd* [2000] 4 All ER 645, Jacob J held that a tenant could not establish the tort of conspiracy against a landlord and its purchaser where the contract was made so as to prevent the tenants from exercising rights under the LTA 1987. Permission to appeal was granted.
3 In s 10A inserted into the LTA 1987.

10.09 It is now a criminal offence for a landlord, without reasonable excuse, to make a relevant disposal affecting premises to which the LTA 1987, Part I applies without serving an offer notice, or in contravention of any prohibition or restriction imposed by the LTA 1987, ss 6–10[1]. It is important to note, however, that the fact that a disposal might involve a criminal offence does not affect the validity of the disposal[2]. So far as the authors are aware, there have been no prosecutions, let alone convictions, under s 10A. Accordingly, it would seem that either the introduction of a criminal penalty has proved to be an effective deterrent, or local housing authorities[3] have not had the resources or inclination to prosecute.

1 LTA 1987, s 10A(1).
2 LTA 1987, s 10A(5).
3 Who are the bodies responsible for bringing prosecutions: LTA 1987, s 10A(4).

Reasonable excuse

10.10 There is no guidance in the LTA 1987 as to what might be a reasonable excuse. There are a large number of reported cases on the meaning of this expression in a variety of different statutes, all creating markedly different offences from this one[1]. Many landlords take legal advice before pursuing a scheme which is designed to avoid the provisions of the LTA 1987. One can imagine a prosecution arising in a case where some such scheme is held not to have been effective, and the landlord is held to have made a relevant disposal without serving an offer notice. Could the landlord rely upon the fact that he acted on legal advice to the effect that the scheme would be effective? It is considered that the answer is likely to depend on the actual advice given and by whom. If the advice was unequivocal, and was given by someone with expertise in this area of the law, it would seem that a landlord would be entitled to have relied on it without question. If, however, the advice was anything less than unequivocal and/or was not given by a lawyer with landlord and tenant expertise, it is likely to be regarded as not amounting to a reasonable excuse.

1 See *Stroud's Judicial Dictionary* (6th edn), pp 2192–2196.

10.11 The offence created is summary, and the penalty is a fine not exceeding level 5 on the standard scale[1]. If the offender is a body corporate, an individual may also be convicted if the offence was committed with his consent or connivance (or was due to his neglect) and he is a director, manager, or secretary or other similar officer, or a person purporting to act in such capacity[2]. Where the affairs of a body corporate are managed by its members, this provision applies to the acts or defaults of a member in connection with his functions of management as if he were a director of the body corporate[3].

1 LTA 1987, s 10A(2). The current maximum fine is £5,000.
2 LTA 1987, s 10A(3).
3 LTA 1987, s 10A(3).

Other remedies

10.12 The LTA 1987 provides no other sanction than service of a default notice[1] and an application, if necessary, for an injunction to procure compliance with the landlord's statutory duty[2]. The tenant(s) must act quickly, otherwise they risk being estopped from relying on their rights under the LTA 1987, and will be refused an order by the court[3]. There is no right to claim damages for breach of statutory duty[4], nor for the same reason can a tenant found a tortious claim on the basis of an unlawful means conspiracy, where the landlord and purchaser have been parties to a scheme to evade the provisions of the LTA 1987[5].

1 Under the LTA 1987, s 19. For a form of default notice, see Appendix I.
2 *Belvedere Court Management Ltd v Frogmore Developments Ltd* [1997] QB 858, per Sir Thomas Bingham MR at 866D.
3 As occurred in *Michaels v Harley House (Marylebone) Ltd* [2000] Ch 104, CA.
4 *Michaels v Taylor Woodrow Developments Ltd* [2000] 4 All ER 645, per Laddie J at 651.
5 *Michaels v Taylor Woodrow Developments Ltd* [2000] 4 All ER 645, where such a claim was struck out as disclosing no arguable cause of action. Permission to appeal was granted and it is understood that an appeal is pending.

Notices

10.13 Any notice required or authorised to be served under the LTA 1987 must be in writing and may be sent by post[1]. Although there is power to prescribe forms of notice (inter alia) under Part I[2], that power has not been exercised to date.

1 LTA 1987, s 54(1).
2 LTA 1987, s 54(3).

Service

10.14 Apart from the fact that service by post is permitted, there are no other requirements as to service. Consequently, any method of service is permissible, the important factor being whether the notice is actually received. Section 7 of the Interpretation Act 1978 applies to service by post. Accordingly, unless the contrary intention appears, service is deemed to be effected by properly addressing, pre-paying and posting a letter containing the document, and, unless the contrary is proved, to have been effected at the time at which the letter would be delivered in the ordinary course of post. In addition, the following points on service should be noted:

(a) evidence that the letter was returned undelivered is sufficient to 'prove the contrary'[1];

(b) evidence of a temporary absence of the addressee from his usual address is not sufficient to prove the contrary, even if the sender knows of his absence[2];

(c) to be properly addressed, the address must not be one where the addressee no longer resides[3], or has never lived[4];

(d) a notice may be served on a company by leaving it at, or sending it by post to, the company's registered office[5].

There is no equivalent to s 23 of the Landlord and Tenant Act 1927.

1 *R v County of London Quarter Sessions Appeal Committee, ex p Rossi* [1956] 1 QB 682.
2 *Layton v Shires* [1960] 2 QB 294; *Hosier v Goodall* [1962] 2 QB 401; *Cooper v Scott-Farnell* [1969] 1 WLR 120.
3 *White v Weston* [1968] 2 QB 647.
4 *Willowgreen Ltd v Smithers* [1994] 1 WLR 832.
5 Companies Act 1985, s 725(1).

10.15 Special provision is made in respect of any notice purporting to be served under any provision of the LTA 1987, Part I by the requisite majority of qualifying tenants[1]. Such a notice must specify the names of all the tenants by whom it is served and the addresses of the flats of which they are qualifying tenants[2]. There is no compliance with this requirement by simply setting out the names of all the leaseholders, even though it may contain the names of tenants who have authorised its service sufficient to constitute the requisite majority. The notice must identify those on whose behalf it is given; the landlord cannot be expected to inquire which of the persons named in a comprehensive list claim to be members of the requisite majority[3].

1 Defined in the LTA 1987, s 18A, as to which see para **2.16**.
2 LTA 1987, s 54(2). If more than one person constitute the qualifying tenant, all must be named: see para **2.13**.
3 *Elnaschie v Pitt Place (Epsom) Ltd* (1988) 31 HLR 278, CA, a case in which it was held that a s 11 notice was invalid for the reasons set out in the text. The House of Lords refused permission to appeal.

Inaccuracies

10.16 Part I of the LTA 1987 contains no saving provision whereby defects or inaccuracies in notices can be treated as immaterial[1]. However, the well known principles in *Mannai Investment Co Ltd v Eagle Star Life Assurance Co Ltd*[2] will apply to notices under the LTA 1987, as they apply to contractual and other statutory notices[3]. Accordingly, a notice will not be invalidated if it contains an obvious or evident error and, notwithstanding the error, the notice read in its context is sufficiently clear to leave a reasonable recipient in no reasonable doubt as to its terms. Moreover, the recipient of the notice will be presumed to be familiar with the provisions of the LTA 1987[4].

1 Cf Sch 3, para 15(1) of the Leasehold Reform, Housing and Urban Development Act 1993.
2 [1997] AC 749, HL.
3 In *York v Casey* [1998] 2 EGLR 25, the Court of Appeal held that the *Mannai* principle applied to statutory notices. See also *Keepers and Governors of John Lyon Grammar School v Secchi* [1999] 3 EGLR 49, CA.
4 *Mannai Investment Co Ltd v Eagle Star Life Assurance Co Ltd* [1997] AC 749, HL.

Proceedings

10.17 Jurisdiction under the LTA 1987 is divided between the courts and the LVT. The county court is given jurisdiction to determine any question arising under any provision of Part I of the LTA 1987, other than a question falling within the jurisdiction of a LVT by virtue of s 13(1) of the LTA 1987[1]. There is now no longer any specific reference to proceedings taken in the High Court[2], which retains its inherent jurisdiction. It is plainly anticipated that proceedings will generally be started in the county court, though where issues of complexity or high value are involved, it may be appropriate to bring a claim in the High Court[3]. On 15 October 2001, Part 56 of the Civil Procedure Rules ('CPR') 1998 will come into force[4]. A claim under the LTA 1987 is a 'landlord and tenant claim' within Part 56[5]. Procedural rules will be set out in a Practice Direction[6] which, at the time of writing, has not been published. Under Part 56 of the CPR 1998, a claim must be started in the county court for the district in which the land is situated unless the claimant certifies the reasons for bringing the claim in the High Court[7]; the Practice Direction will set out circumstances which may justify such a course of action[8]. At present, and until 15 October 2001, the pre-CPR relating to Part I of the LTA 1987 have been preserved[9]. A Part 8 claim form must be used, since the LTA 1987 proceedings are listed in the Practice Direction–Part 8 (Section A–High Court, and Section B–county court). In respect of county court proceedings, the Part 8B Practice Direction sets out an alternative procedure to be followed than that normally applied under Part 8. It is considered best to reply by filing and serving a defence[10]. The procedural rules are rather unclear and appear to have been hurriedly drafted without being thought through.

1 LTA 1987, s 52(1), (2).
2 LTA 1987, s 52(4), (5), having been repealed by the Courts and Legal Services Act 1990.
3 For example, in *Michaels v Harley House (Marylebone) Ltd* [1997] 1 WLR 967, proceedings which involved complex questions of company law were commenced by originating summons in the Chancery Division of the High Court.
4 Civil Procedure (Amendment) Rules 2001, rr 1(d), 17.
5 CPR 56.1(1)(e).
6 CPR 56.1(2).
7 CPR 56.2(1), (2).
8 CPR 56.2(3).
9 CPR Sch 1, RSC Ord 97, rr 1(1), 2, 3, 14, 18 and Sch 2, CCR Ord 43, rr 1(1), 2, 17, 21.
10 See paras B2–B15. This Practice Direction has been described by Professor I R Scott as 'very difficult to follow' (Civil Procedure News 2/99), a view with which the authors agree. It certainly involves some contradictions: eg CCR Ord 43, r 2(1) requires an answer to be served, though an 'answer' is no part of the CPR. On the other hand, PD8B, para B14 refers to the case where the defendant has filed a defence to the Pt 8 claim form, although no other rule or Practice Direction provides for a defence to a Pt 8 claim form.

LVT

10.18 A LVT[1] has jurisdiction to hear the following matters[2]:

(1) any question arising in relation to matters specified in a notice under the LTA 1987, s 12A (where the qualifying tenants take the benefit of a contract), s 12B (where the tenants can compel a sale to them by the purchaser[3]) or s 12C (where the tenants can compel the grant of a new tenancy by a superior landlord[4]). It is the terms of the purchase notice which defines the scope of the LVT's jurisdiction[5];

(2) any question arising for determination as mentioned in the LTA 1987, s 8C(4) (assessment of non-monetary consideration[6]), s 12A(5) (terms of benefit of contract where severance required[7]) and s 12B(4) (terms of acquisition where purchase requires severance[8]).

In relation to the LTA 1987 as originally enacted, it was held that whilst the LVT had jurisdiction to determine questions arising under a s 12 purchase notice, it could not determine the validity of such a notice, which was a matter for the court[9]. It is considered that the same distinction applies to the current provisions.

1 A LVT is a rent assessment committee by another name: LTA 1987, s 52A(1).
2 LTA 1987, s 13(1).
3 See para **7.19**.
4 See para **7.32**.
5 *134 Shirland Road Management Co Ltd v Lester* [1997] 2 EGLR 207.
6 See para **5.13**.
7 See para **7.07**.
8 See para **7.16**.
9 *Denetower Ltd v Toop* [1991] 1 WLR 945, per Sir Nicholas Browne-Wilkinson V-C at 954D.

10.19 There have been a number of LVT decisions as to their jurisdiction under the original LTA 1987, s 13. The first[1], controversially[2], held that the property had been sold at auction on the basis of an incorrect description. Since the property accurately described was said to amount to a different estate or interest, the LVT felt able to adjust the price the tenants had to pay. In fact, the misdescription in that case, namely the number of rooms, did not amount to change of the estate or interest, and it is considered that the LVT were not entitled to decide the case as they did.

1 *Cousins v Metropolitan Guarantee Ltd* [1989] 2 EGLR 223.
2 *Woodfall on Landlord and Tenant* considers it as having been decided incorrectly; see para 28.027(c).

10.20 In other cases, the LVT has properly determined that it cannot go behind the original sale price[1]. However, if the landlord has failed to comply with its obligation to deal with each building separately[2], requiring a global price to be apportioned, the LVT can make its own apportionment and is not bound to accept the old or new landlord's figures[3]. In one case[4], no consideration was specified in the transfer, but the purchaser agreed orally to pay the landlord's conveyancing costs. The Lands Tribunal held that the tenants' nominee purchaser was entitled to acquire the property for nil consideration; the arrangement to pay the conveyancing costs was not a term of the original disposal.

1 *30 Upperton Gardens Management Ltd v Akano* [1990] 2 EGLR 232; *Venus v Khan* [1990] 2 EGLR 237; *Gregory v Saddiq* [1991] 1 EGLR 237.
2 See the LTA 1987, s 5(3) (previously s 5(5)).
3 *Sullivan v Safeland Investments Ltd* [1990] 2 EGLR 227; *Groundpremium Property Management Ltd v Longmint Ltd* [1998] 1 EGLR 131.
4 *Woodridge Ltd v Downie* (1997) 76 P & CR 239, LT.

10.21 Where the new landlord had paid a sum, in addition to the purchase price, representing the right to collect outstanding arrears of rent and services charges, the extra sum was held by the Lands Tribunal to be payable by the tenants' nominee purchaser[1]. The LVT cannot, however, decide a dispute as to whether service charges are owing[2].

1 *Linkproud Ltd v Ballard* [1997] 1 EGLR 181. An earlier decision of the LVT on similar facts, but to the opposite effect (*Davis v Stone* [1992 2 EGLR 222) is considered to have been incorrectly decided.
2 *Venus v Khan* [1990] 2 EGLR 237, LVT.

10.22 Where the estate to be disposed of by the new landlord has been incumbered since the original disposal[1], the LVT must determine any alteration in value, unless the property is to be transferred free of the incumbrance[2]. Any increase in value since the original disposal[3] must also be taken into account by the Tribunal. Examples where this has been done are repairs carried out by the landlord or purchaser[4], and the death of a regulated tenant giving vacant possession of one of the flats[5].

In relation to the other terms of the transfer, the LVT has held[6] it has a wide (though not roving) discretion, taking the terms of the original disposal as the starting point. It is not limited to leaving the nominated person to stand in the shoes of the purchaser.

1 In *Gregory v Saddiq* [1991] 1 EGLR 237, LVT a repairs notice under the Housing Act 1985 was held capable of constituting an incumbrance but was not taken into account in that case because the notice had been served prior to the original disposal.
2 See para **7.18** dealing with incumbrances. For LVT decisions on these provisions, see *Englefield Court Tenants v Skeels* [1990] 2 EGLR 230, LVT and *Nolan v Eagle Wharf Developments Ltd* [1992] 2 EGLR 223, LVT, [1992] 46 EG 113. Both these decisions were considered by the Court of Appeal in *Belvedere Court Management Ltd v Frogmore Developments Ltd* [1997] QB 858 at 877.
3 See para **7.24** ff.
4 *Saga Properties Ltd v Palmeira Square Nos 2–6 Ltd* [1995] 1 EGLR 199, LT.
5 *Twinsectra Ltd v Jones* [1998] 2 EGLR 129, LT.
6 *Newman v Kay* [1991] 2 EGLR 237. It should be noted that the landlord did not appear at the hearing. See also the discussion at para **7.23** where it is noted that this discretion may not now be available in light of the post-1996 wording.

Constitution

10.23 At least one of the members of the LVT must be a person who has experience in the valuation of land[1], and generally they will be chaired by a legally qualified member. Traditionally, they have relied upon their own knowledge and experience, whatever the evidence or representations submitted by the parties. It is considered that if evidence is given by experienced surveyors on each side, a Tribunal should be slow to depart from the limits of their evidence or to arrive at its decision by a method not adopted by either valuer; and it should certainly not do so without giving the parties an opportunity to address the Tribunal on such a proposal.

1 Housing Act 1980, Sch 22, para 1, applied by the LTA 1987, s 52A(5).

Procedure

10.24 Regulations have been made which govern the procedure before the LVT[1]. There is no prescribed form of application but it must contain the information set out in Sch 1 to the Regulations[2].

Where a matter is referred to the LVT, it may, by notice in writing served on the tenant or landlord or any superior landlord, require him to give to the Tribunal, within such period (being not less than 14 days from service of the notice) as may be specified in the notice, such information as the LVT may reasonably require[3].

1 The Rent Assessment Committee (England and Wales) (Leasehold Valuation Tribunal) Regulations 1993, SI 1993/2408, made under the LTA 1987, s 52A(2), which are set out Appendix II.
2 The Rent Assessment Committee (England and Wales) (Leasehold Valuation Tribunal) Regulations 1993, reg 3(1).
3 Housing Act 1980, Sch 22, para 7(1), applied by s 52A(5) of the LTA 1987. If any person fails without reasonable cause to comply with such a notice, he is liable on summary conviction to a fine not exceeding level 3 on the standard scale: Housing Act 1980, para 7(2).

10.25 The Tribunal may, whether of their own motion or on a party's application, hold a pre-trial review[1]. At the review, any direction can be given which appears necessary or desirable for the just, expeditious and economical disposal of the proceedings. This will usually include an order for the exchange of evidence well before the hearing. If that does not take place, the Tribunal must take all reasonable steps to ensure that each party has a copy of the other side's documents and the results of any enquiries made by the Tribunal[2]. If a party does not have such documents in advance of the hearing, the Tribunal should adjourn the hearing to give them an opportunity to deal with the documents[3]. In the absence of any pre-hearing directions the parties will often arrange to exchange their evidence in advance, which is obviously sensible. Many hearings are prolonged by the Tribunal's requirement for the witnesses to read their evidence aloud.

Hearings are held in public in the absence of special reasons[4]. Parties can act in person, or by a representative such as counsel or a solicitor[5]. The parties must be given at least 21 days' notice of the hearing[6]. If a party does not appear, the Tribunal may hear the case in their absence provided they have been duly notified[7].

Proceedings are generally less formal than at a court hearing and the rules of evidence are sometimes ignored. However, 'the Rules of Natural Justice demand that not only must a Tribunal act judicially and fairly but also that it must be seen to act judicially and fairly'[8]. The Tribunal's decision must be recorded in a signed document containing the reasons for the decision, and a copy must be sent to each party[9]. At present the LVT has no power to award costs, but the Commonhold and Leasehold Reform Bill introduced in December 2000 contains provisions for a costs order to be made in limited circumstances.

1 The Rent Assessment Committee (England and Wales) (Leasehold Valuation Tribunal) Regulations 1993, reg 4G.
2 The Rent Assessment Committee (England and Wales) (Leasehold Valuation Tribunal) Regulations 1993, reg 9(1).
3 The Rent Assessment Committee (England and Wales) (Leasehold Valuation Tribunal) Regulations 1993, reg 9(2).
4 The Rent Assessment Committee (England and Wales) (Leasehold Valuation Tribunal) Regulations 1993, reg 5(5).
5 The Rent Assessment Committee (England and Wales) (Leasehold Valuation Tribunal) Regulations 1993, reg 6(b).
6 The Rent Assessment Committee (England and Wales) (Leasehold Valuation Tribunal) Regulations 1993, reg 5(2).

7 The Rent Assessment Committee (England and Wales) (Leasehold Valuation Tribunal) Regulations 1993, reg 7.
8 *Huff v The Trustees of the Sloane Stanley Estate* (1997, unreported, LVT).
9 The Rent Assessment Committee (England and Wales) (Leasehold Valuation Tribunal) Regulations 1993, reg 11(1), (3).

Appeals

10.26 An appeal from the High Court or county court requires permission, and is governed by the CPR Part 52. An appeal from the High Court lies to the Court of Appeal, as does an appeal from a county court judge in a case allocated to the multi-track. In any other county court appeal, the appeal lies to a High Court judge.

An appeal from the LVT lies to the Lands Tribunal by a person dissatisfied with the LVT's decision[1]. At present there is no requirement for permission to appeal to be obtained in relation to an appeal under Part I of the LTA 1987, but the Commonhold and Leasehold Reform Bill introduced in December 2000 includes provisions requiring permission to be obtained (from either the LVT or Lands Tribunal) in respect of all appeals from the LVT. The appeal takes effect as a complete rehearing[2]. It is determined upon the evidence before it, rather than that adduced before the LVT. The LVT's decision must be shown to be wrong, in which case the appeal must be allowed. The jurisdiction of the Lands Tribunal is not limited to matters of law or valuation, but includes matters of fact or value[3]. There have been only three reported cases of appeals to the Lands Tribunal under Part I of the LTA 1987[4]. There is a further right to appeal to the Court of Appeal with permission of the Lands Tribunal or the Court of Appeal[5].

There is a right to appeal from the Court of Appeal to the House of Lords with the permission of either. There have been no such appeals under Part I of the LTA 1987[6].

1 Housing Act 1990, Sch 22, para 2, applied by the LTA 1987, s 52A(5).
2 *Wellcome Trust Ltd v Romines* [1999] 3 EGLR 229, per Mr P H Clarke FRICS, in which the Lands Tribunal comprehensively reviewed the authorities under the Leasehold Reform Acts dealing with appeals pursuant to Sch 22, para 2 of the Housing Act 1980.
3 *Wellcome Trust Ltd v Romines* [1999] 3 EGLR 229.
4 *Saga Properties Ltd v Palmeira Square Nos 2–6 Ltd* [1995] 1 EGLR 199; *Linkproud Ltd v Ballard* [1997] 1 EGLR 181; *Twinsectra Ltd v Jones* [1998] 2 EGLR 129; *Woodridge Ltd v Downie* (1997) 76 P & CR 239.
5 There have been no such appeals to date.
6 However, in *Belvedere Court Management Ltd v Frogmore Developments Ltd* [1997] QB 858, the Court of Appeal would have given leave to either party had they applied; see the report in [1996] 1 EGLR at 68K–L.

CHAPTER 11

Prospective purchasers: section 18

11.01 The LTA 1987 contains a special provision[1] to give protection to a prospective purchaser. It arises where two conditions apply, the first being where a disposal of an estate or interest in any premises consisting of the whole or part of a building 'is proposed to be made by a landlord'[2]. The second condition is that it appears to the proposed transferee, 'the purchaser', that the disposal would, or might, be a relevant disposal to which the LTA 1987 applies[3]. In such circumstances the purchaser may serve notices on the tenants of the flats contained in the premises 'the flats affected'. It should be noted that the notices can be served on any tenants – there is no need for the purchaser to establish that they are qualifying tenants.

1 LTA 1987, s 18.
2 LTA 1987, s18(1)(a).
3 LTA 1987, s 18(1)(b).

Form of notice

11.02 As with other notices referred to in the LTA 1987, it must be in writing[1], and there is no prescribed form, though there is power to prescribe one[2]. The notice must:

(a) inform the recipient of the general nature of the principal terms of the proposed disposal, including, in particular, the property to which it would relate, the estate or interest in that property proposed to be disposed of by the landlord, and the consideration required by the landlord for making the disposal[3];

(b) invite the recipient to serve a notice on the purchaser stating:

  (i) whether the landlord has served a s 5 notice[4] in respect to the disposal;

  (ii) if not, whether he is aware of any reason why he is not entitled to be served with a section 5 notice; and

(iii) if he is not so aware, whether he would wish to avail himself of the right of first refusal if a s 5 notice were served[5];

(c) inform the recipient of the remaining provisions of the LTA 1987, s 18[6].

1 LTA 1987, s 54(1)(a). For service, see para **10.14**.
2 LTA 1987, s 54(3). A suggested form of notice is in Appendix I.
3 LTA 1987, s 18(2)(a).
4 On him or any predecessor in title. For s 5 notices, see Chapter 4.
5 LTA 1987, s 18(2)(b).
6 LTA 1987, s 18(2)(c).

11.03 Where the purchaser has served s 18 notices on at least 80% of the tenants of the flats affected, then the premises affected by the disposal are treated as if Part I of the LTA 1987 does not apply if one of two conditions is fulfilled[1]. The first alternative is where not more than 50% of the tenants on whom those notices have been served by the purchaser have served notices on him under the LTA 1987, s 18(2)(b)[2] by the end of the period of two months beginning with the date when the *last* of them was served with a s 18 notice. The second alternative is where more than 50% of the tenants on whom s 18 notices have been served by the purchaser have served notices on him under s 18(2)(b), but those notices indicate (in each case) that the tenant does not regard himself as being entitled to be served with a s 5 notice, or would not wish to avail himself of the right of first refusal if a s 5 notice was served.

In calculating the 50% and 80% each flat affected is regarded as having one tenant, who counts towards the percentage in question whether or not he is a qualifying tenant[3].

1 LTA 1987, s 18(3).
2 Referred to in para **11.02**.
3 LTA 1987, s 18(4).

11.04 The s 18 procedure is intended to be a protection for an intended purchaser[1]. In contrast to the requirement to serve s 5 notices, s 18 is permissive[2]. It is not a substitute for service of s 5 notices. 'Section 18 plainly envisages that a section 5 notice should have been served by the time that a prospective purchaser may, if he wishes to protect himself, serve a notice under section 18[3]'. However, the purchaser has no right to obtain details of the tenants or tenancies, and may well be dependant upon information provided by the existing landlord. A Land Registry search of the landlord's registered title will reveal details of the registered proprietors of long leases of any flats which are carved out of that title, but will not reveal anything about other tenancies.

1 *Mainwaring v Henry Smith's Charity Trustees* [1998] QB 1, CA. The judgment of the Court of Appeal is a cautionary tale for landlords seeking to deprive tenants of the right of first refusal. Moreover, at the time of the transaction the subject of that case, criminal penalties had not been introduced. Reference should also be made to para **3.59** discussing the meaning of 'proposes'.

2 *Mainwaring v Henry Smith's Charity Trustees* [1998] QB 1, CA at 9D.
3 *Mainwaring v Henry Smith's Charity Trustees* [1998] QB 1, CA at 20G.

11.05 It should be noted, finally, that the LTA 1987 gives no right to a purchaser of the landlord's interest to obtain information from the landlord about the nature of the premises or tenancies of flats in the building being acquired. It is, therefore, prudent to seek information about such tenancies in pre-contract enquiries. Legal stationers produce printed forms of pre-contract enquiries; a recommended example, dealing with the LTA 1987, is in Appendix II. The vendor can be asked, if appropriate, to confirm and/or warrant that the LTA 1987 does not apply to the sale.

Appendix I

List of appendices

Notices under the Landlord and Tenant Act 1987

(1) Notice under section 5A

To [AB Name (if known–otherwise 'the tenant') and address of tenant of flat]

1. CD [the landlord, or EF his agent on behalf of the CD landlord] of [address] proposes to dispose of his [freehold/leasehold] interest in [address of the building] in which the flat of which you are the tenant is situated.

2. The proposed disposal consists of entering into a contract to [eg create a headlease in respect or transfer the freehold] of the building.

3. The principal terms of the proposed disposal are as follows:
   - (i) the property is ...
   - (ii) the estate or interest in that property to which the contract relates is ...
   - (iii) the principal terms of the contract, including the deposit and consideration required, are [or, a copy of the proposed contract is attached hereto].

4. This notice constitutes an offer by CD to enter into a contract on the above terms which may be accepted by the requisite majority of qualifying tenants of the flats contained in the premises.

5. This offer may be so accepted by [insert date], or the date two months after service of this notice or (if later) the date of service of this form of notice on the last of the qualifying tenants.

6. You and the other qualifying tenants have a further period of two months from the date of such acceptance to nominate a person or persons under section 6 of the Landlord and Tenant Act 1987.

7. Any notice accepting this offer or other communication concerning this notice should be sent to me [or to EF] at [address].

Dated ...

(2) Notice under section 5B

To [AB Name (if known–otherwise 'the tenant') and address of tenant of flat]

1. CD [the landlord, or EF his agent on behalf of the CD landlord] of [address] proposes to dispose of his [freehold/leasehold] interest in [address of the building] in which the flat of which you are the tenant is situated.

2. The proposed disposal is by means of a sale at a public auction.

3. The principal terms of the proposed disposal are as follows:

   (i) the property is ...

   (ii) the estate or interest in that property to which the contract relates is ...

   [(iii) insert any others]

4. This notice constitutes an offer by CD which may be accepted by the requisite majority of qualifying tenants of the flats contained in the premises for the contract (if any) entered into by CD at the auction to have effect as if a person or persons nominated by such majority of qualifying tenants, and not the purchaser, had entered into it.

5. This offer may be so accepted by [insert date], or the date two months after service of this notice or (if later) the date of service of this form of notice on the last of the qualifying tenants. This date must by not less than two months before the date of the auction.

6. You and the other qualifying tenants have a further period of 28 days from the date of such acceptance to nominate a person or persons under section 6 of the Landlord and Tenant Act 1987. This date must be not less than 28 days before the date of the auction.

7. The auction will take place on [insert time and date] at the premises of [name and address of auctioneers]. [NB if this paragraph is not included, a further notice containing the time and place of the auction and the name of the auctioneers must be served on the requisite majority of qualifying tenants not less than 28 days before the auction.]

8. Any notice accepting this offer or other communication concerning this notice should be sent to me [or to EF] at [address].

Dated [not less than four months and not more than six months before the date of the auction].

(3) Notice under section 5C

To [AB Name (if known–otherwise 'the tenant') and address of tenant of flat]

1. CD the landlord, or EF his agent on behalf of the CD landlord] of [address] proposes to dispose of his [freehold/leasehold] interest in [address of the building] in which the flat of which you are the tenant is situated.

2. The proposed disposal consists of the grant of an [option or right of pre-emption].

3. The principal terms of the proposed disposal are as follows:
   (i) the property is ...
   (ii) the estate or interest in that property to which the contract relates is ...
   (iii) the consideration required by CD for granting the [option or right of pre-emption] is ...
   (iv) the principal terms in which the option or right of pre-emption would be exercisable, including the consideration payable on its exercise, are ...

4. This notice constitutes an offer by CD to grant an [option or right of pre-emption] which may be accepted by the requisite majority of qualifying tenants of the flats contained in the premises.

5. This offer may be so accepted by [insert date], or the date two months after service of this notice or (if later) the date of service of this form of notice on the last of the qualifying tenants.

6. You and the other qualifying tenants have a further period of two months from the date of such acceptance to nominate a person or persons under section 6 of the Landlord and Tenant Act 1987.

7. Any notice accepting this offer or other communication concerning this notice should be sent to me [or to E] at [address].

Dated ...

(4) Notice under section 5D

To [AB Name (if known- otherwise 'the tenant') and address of tenant of flat]

1. CD [the landlord, or EF his agent on behalf of the CD landlord] of [address] proposes to dispose of his [freehold/leasehold] interest in [address of the building] in which the flat of which you are the tenant is situated.

2. The principal terms of the proposed disposal are as follows:
   (i) the property is ...
   (ii) the estate or interest in that property to which the contract relates is ...
   (iii) the consideration required by CD for the disposal of his interest is ...
   [(iv) insert any other principal terms of the disposal].

3. This notice constitutes an offer by CD to dispose of the property on the above terms which may be accepted by the requisite majority of qualifying tenants of the flats contained in the premises.

4. This offer may be so accepted by [insert date], or the date two months after service of this notice or (if later) the date of service of this form of notice on the last of the qualifying tenants.

5. You and the other qualifying tenants have a further period of two months from the date of such acceptance to nominate a person or persons under section 6 of the Landlord and Tenant Act 1987.

6. Any notice accepting this offer or other communication concerning this notice should be sent to me [or to EF] at [address].

Dated ....

(5) Notice complying with section 5E

Where the consideration required by the landlord does not consist, or does not wholly consist of money, the offer notice must, *in addition* to complying with one of the above notices, state as follows:

> An election may be made under section 8C of the Landlord and Tenant Act 1987. This means that, within the period for nominating a person or persons under section 6, the requisite majority of qualifying tenants may elect to allow the disposal by CD to proceed; in which case sections 11–17 of the Act shall have effect as if:
>
> (i) no notice under section 5 of the Act had been served;
>
> (ii) in section 11A(3) the period for serving notice requiring information shall be 28 days instead of four months;
>
> (iii) in sections 12A(2) and 12B(3) the period for exercise of the tenants' rights against the purchaser shall be two months instead of six months.
>
> So much of the consideration for the original disposal as did not consist of money shall be treated as such amount in money as was equivalent to its value on the hands of the landlord. The landlord or the nominated person may apply to have that amount determined by a leasehold valuation tribunal.

(6) Acceptance notice under section 6

To [the landlord]

We, the persons whose names are set out below, are the requisite majority of qualifying tenants of the constituent flats in [premises] and we accept the offer contained in your notice dated [insert].

[We hereby nominate [insert name and address[1] of nominee purchaser] as our nominee purchaser][2].

AB of Flat X ... , CD of Flat Y ... [Specify the names of all of the persons giving the notice and the addresses of the flats of which they are qualifying tenants[3]].

Dated ...

1 The LTA 1987 does not require the nominee purchaser's address to be included in the acceptance notice, but this is obviously sensible.
2 The acceptance notice need not include details of the nominee purchaser. This can be done by a later notice, provided it is served within the time limit set out in the offer notice for doing so.
3 LTA 1987, s 54(2). The notice does not have to be signed by the tenants, but see para **10.15**.

(7) Landlord's notice of withdrawal under section 8(3)(a)

To (the nominated person)

Take notice that AB, the landlord of the premises at [address], no longer intends to proceed with the disposal of the protected interest, that is the estate, interest or other subject-matter of his offer notice dated [insert].

Signed AB [or CD as agent for AB]

Dated [within one month beginning with the date of service of the notice of nomination].

(8) Nominated person's notice of withdrawal under section 8A(4)(a)

To (the landlord)

Take notice that AB, the nominated person, no longer intends to proceed with the acquisition of the protected interest, that is the estate, interest or other subject matter of your offer notice dated [insert].

Signed AB [or CD as AB's agent]

Dated [within two months of the period beginning with the date for which contract is sent, or such longer period as may be agreed].

(9) Nominated persons's notice of election under section 8B

To (the landlord)

Take notice that AB, the nominated person, hereby elects that the provisions of s 8B of the above Act shall apply, and to be sent a copy of the contract entered into at the auction referred to in your offer notice dated [insert].

You must send me a copy of the contract, if one is entered into at the auction, within the period of seven days beginning with the date of the auction.

Signed AB [or CD as AB's agent]

Dated [not less than 28 days before the date of the auction]

(10) Nominated person's notice of acceptance of contract under section 8B

To (the landlord)

Take notice that AB, the nominated person, having received a copy of the contract for sale of [premises] on [insert date] hereby accepts the terms of the contract, and is prepared to fulfil the conditions imposed by the purchaser on entering into the contract.

Signed AB [or CD as AB's agent]

Dated [within the period of 28 days beginning with the date on which a copy of the contract is sent].

(11) Notice of election under section 8C

To (the landlord)

Take notice that we, the requisite majority of qualifying tenants of the constituent flats in [premises], hereby elect that the provisions of section 8C of the above Act shall apply.

Accordingly, if you dispose of your protected interest on terms corresponding to those specified in your offer notice dated [insert], sections 11–17 will apply as if you had not served your offer notice, with adjustments as to the time limits for service of notices. The consideration for the original disposal as did not consist of money will be given a monetary equivalent.

[Set out the names of all the persons by whom the notice is served and the addresses of the flats of which they are qualifying tenants][1].

Dated [within the period specified in the offer notice for nominating person(s) for purposes of section 6 or such longer period as may be agreed between landlord and requisite majority].

1 LTA 1987, s 54(2).

(12) Landlord's notice under section 8E(3)

To (the nominated person)

Take notice that AB, the landlord of [premises] has:

(i) used his best endeavours to secure the consent of CD to the disposal of the protected interest to you, but CD has withheld his consent; and [if applicable]

(ii) applied for a declaration that CD has unreasonably withheld his consent to the disposal but the application was refused by [court] on [date].

Signed AB [or EF as AB's agent]

Dated [insert].

(13) Notice of withdrawal under section 9A(1)

To (the landlord)

Take notice that AB, the nominated person, no longer intends to proceed with the acquisition of your protected interest in [premises].

Signed [AB or CD as AB's agent]

Dated [insert].

(14) Notice of withdrawal under section 9A(2)

To (the landlord)

Take notice that AB, the nominated person, has become aware that the number of qualifying tenants of the constituent flats desiring to proceed with the acquisition of your protected interest in [premises] is less than the requisite majority and hereby gives notice of withdrawal.

Signed AB [or CD as AB's agent]

Dated [forthwith upon AB becoming aware].

(15) Notice of withdrawal under section 9B

To (the nominated person)

Take notice that AB, the landlord, no longer intends to proceed with the disposal of his protected interest in [premises].

Signed AB [or CD as AB's agent]

Dated [insert].

(16) Notice under section 10

To (the qualifying tenants of the constituent flats)[1]

Take notice that the premises at [address] have ceased to be premises to which Part I of the above Act applies [because ...][2] and, accordingly, the offer notice dated [insert] is to be treated as not having been served, and anything done in pursuance of that notice is to be treated as not having been done.

Upon the service of this notice, the provisions of Part I of the above Act cease to have effect in relation to the disposal referred to in the offer notice[3].

Signed AB, [the landlord, or CD as AB's agent]

Dated [insert][4].

1 The notice need be served on not less than 90% of the qualifying tenants, or (if there are less than ten) on all but one: LTA 1987, s 10(2).
2 The LTA 1987, s 10 does not require the reason to be stated in the notice, but it is advisable to explain why the landlord takes this view.
3 The LTA 1987, s10(1) provides that this is the effect, although the notice is not required to state it.
4 The notice cannot be served after a binding contract has been entered into between the landlord and the nominated person: LTA 1987, s 10(4).

(17) Notice under section 11A

To (the purchaser)

Section 11 of the above Act applies to the disposal of [premises] to you, no notice having been served under section 5 by [the landlord] <u>or</u> the disposal having been made in contravention of [insert which provision under sections 6–10].

We, the requisite majority of qualifying tenants of the constituent flats in [premises], require you:

(a) to give particulars of the terms on which the said premises were disposed of to you, including the deposit and consideration required, and the date of the disposal;

(b) [where the disposal consisted of entering into a contract] to provide a copy of the contract.

You must give these to AB of [address] within one month of the date of service of this notice.

[Set out the names of all the persons by whom the notice is served and the addresses of the flats of which they are qualifying tenants][1].

Dated [before the end of four months beginning with the date by which (a) notices under section 3A of the Landlord and Tenant Act 1985 relating to the original disposal, or (b) where that section does not apply, documents of any other description (i) indicating that the original disposal has taken place, and (ii) alerting the tenants to the existence of their rights under the 1987 Act and the time within which any such rights must be exercised, have been served on the requisite majority][2].

1 LTA 1987, s 54(2).
2 LTA 1987, s 11A(3).

(18) Notice under section 12A

To (the landlord)

Take notice that we, the requisite majority of qualifying tenants of the constituent flats in [premises], hereby elect that the contract by which you disposed of the premises shall have effect as if entered into not with [the purchaser], but with [AB, insert person(s)] nominated by us[1].

AB is prepared to fulfil the requirements as to the deposit required on entering into the contract and other conditions required to be fulfilled by the purchaser[2].

Any time limit in the contract shall start to run again on the service of this notice.

[Where the original disposal included other property] This notice only has effect in relation to [premises] and not in relation to [identify other premises], and the terms of the contract are to be modified [as follows [set out] or as determined by a leasehold valuation tribunal][3].

[Set out the names of all the persons by whom the notice is served and the addresses of the flats of which they are qualifying tenants][4].

Dated [before the end of six months after (i) date of purchaser's compliance with a notice under section 11A, alternatively (ii) the date of service on the requisite majority of qualifying tenants of documents of any description indicating the original disposal has taken place, and alerting the tenants to the existence of their rights under the 1987 Act and the time within which any such rights must be exercised].

1 This is how the nominated person is appointed: LTA 1987, s12D(1).
2 See the LTA 1987, s 12A(3). The notice does not require this statement to be included, but it is desirable to do so.
3 See the LTA 1987, s 12A(5).
4 LTA 1987, s 54(2).

(19) Notice under section 12B

To (the purchaser)

Take notice that we, the requisite majority of qualifying tenants of the constituent flats in [premises], hereby require you to dispose of the estate or interest that was the subject-matter of the disposal to you, on the terms on which it was made, including the consideration, to [AB, insert person(s)] nominated by us[1].

[Where the original disposal included other property] This notice only has effect in relation to [premises] and not in relation to [identify other premises], and the terms of the disposal are to be modified [as follows [set out] or as determined by a leasehold valuation tribunal][2].

If the property has become subject to any charge or other incumbrance, then unless the court orders otherwise,

(a) in the case of a charge to secure the payment of money or the performance of any other obligation by the purchaser or any other person, the disposal to AB shall operate to discharge the property from that charge; and

b) in the case of any other incumbrance, the property shall be disposed of subject to the incumbrance but with a reduction in the consideration payable to you corresponding to the amount by which the existence of the incumbrance reduces the value of the property[3].

[Set out the names of all the persons by whom the notice is served and the addresses of the flats of which they are qualifying tenants][4].

Dated [before the end of six months after (i) date of purchaser's compliance with a notice under section 11A, (ii) in any other case, the date by which notices under section 3A of the Landlord and Tenant Act 1985, alternatively documents of any description indicating the original disposal has taken place, and alerting the tenants to the existence of their rights under the 1987 Act and the time within which any such rights must be exercised, were served on the requisite majority of qualifying tenants of the constituent flats].

1 This is how the nominated person is appointed: LTA 1987, s 12D(1).
2 See the LTA 1987, s 12A(5).
3 See the LTA 1987, s 12B(5). The notice is not required to state this paragraph, but it is considered advisable to include it.
4 LTA 1987, s 54(2).

(20) Notice under section 12C

To (the purchaser)

Take notice that we, the requisite majority of qualifying tenants of the constituent flats in [premises], hereby require you to grant a new tenancy of the premises, which were the subject of the tenancy surrendered by AB [the landlord] 'the relevant tenancy' to [CD, insert person(s)] nominated by us[1]. The new tenancy is to be on the same terms as the relevant tenancy and must expire on the same date as the relevant tenancy would have expired.

[Insert if consideration paid for surrender] CD will pay to you the amount you paid as consideration for the surrender of the relevant tenancy[2].

[Where the premises the subject to the relevant tenancy included other premises] This notice only has effect in relation to [premises] and not in relation to [identify other premises], and the terms of the tenancy are to be modified [as follows [set out] or as determined by a leasehold valuation tribunal][3].

[Set out the names of all the persons by whom the notice is served and the addresses of the flats of which they are qualifying tenants][4].

Dated [before the end of six months after (i) date of purchaser's compliance with a notice under section 11A, alternatively (ii) the date of service on the requisite majority of qualifying tenants of documents of any description indicating the original disposal has taken place, and alerting the tenants to the existence of their rights under the 1987 Act and the time within which any such rights must be exercised].

1 This is how the nominated person is appointed: LTA 1987, s 12D(1).
2 See the LTA 1987, s 12C(4). The Act does not require this statement to be included in the notice, but it is considered advisable.
3 See the LTA 1987, s 12C(5).
4 LTA 1987, s 54(2).

(21) Notice of withdrawal under section 14(1)

To (the purchaser)

Take notice that AB, the nominated person, no longer intends to proceed with the disposal of your interest in [premises] pursuant to the notice served on you under sections [12B/12C].

Signed [AB or CD as AB's agent]

Dated [insert].

(22) Notice of withdrawal under section 14(2)

To (the purchaser)

Take notice that AB, the nominated person, has become aware that the number of qualifying tenants of the constituent flats desiring to proceed with the disposal of your interest in [premises] pursuant to section [12B/12C] is less than the requisite majority and hereby gives notice of withdrawal.

Signed AB [or CD as AB's agent]

Dated [forthwith upon AB becoming aware].

(23) Notice under section 16(2)

To AB [the person specified under section 11A to receive particulars of the original disposal]

Take notice that I, CD [the purchaser] no longer hold the estate or interest in [premises][1] referred to in the Notice dated [insert] served under section 11A of the above Act.

I have disposed of that estate or interest to EF of [address][2].

Signed CD [or GH as CD's agent]

Dated [insert].

1 If the purchaser has disposed only of part or parts of the estate or interest to one or more persons, this notice must give details: LTA 1987, s 16(5).
2 The purchaser must also serve on the subsequent purchaser a copy of the s 11A notice and of the particulars given by him in response to it: LTA 1987, s 16(2)(b).

(24) Notice under section 16(3)

To AB [the nominated person]

Take notice that I, CD [the purchaser] no longer hold the estate or interest in [premises][1] referred to in the notice dated [insert] served under s [12A/12B/12C] of the above Act.

I have disposed of that estate or interest to EF of [address][2].

Signed CD [or GH as CD's agent]

Dated [insert].

1 If the purchaser has disposed only of part or parts of the estate or interest to one or more persons, this notice must give details: LTA 1987, s 16(5).
2 The purchaser must also forward to the subsequent purchaser the s [12A/12B/12C] notice: LTA 1987, s 16(5).

(25) Notice under section 17(1)

To (the qualifying tenants of the constituent flats)[1]

Take notice that the premises at [address] have ceased to be premises to which Part I of the above Act applies [because ...][2] and, accordingly, the notice dated [insert] under s [11A/12A/12B/12C] is to be treated as not having been served, and anything done in pursuance of that notice, is to be treated as not having been done.

Upon the service of this notice, Part I of the above Act ceases to have effect in relation to me in connection with the original disposal[3].

Signed AB, [the purchaser[4], or CD as AB's agent]

Dated [insert].

1 The notice need be served on not less than 90% of the qualifying tenants, or (if there are less than ten) on all but one: LTA 1987, s 17(2).
2 Section 17 of the LTA 1987 does not require the reason to be stated in the notice, but it is advisable to explain why the landlord takes this view.
3 LTA 1987, s 17(5) provides that this is the effect, although the notice is not required to state it.
4 This includes a subsequent purchaser: LTA 1987, s 17(7).

(26) Notice under section 17(3)

To (the nominated person)

Take notice that a period of three months has expired since the service of the notice dated [insert] under s [12A/12B/12C] relating to [premises] without any binding contract having been entered into between us and without there having been made any application in connection with the notice to the court or to a leasehold valuation tribunal. Accordingly, the notice is to be treated as not having been served, and anything done in pursuance of that notice, is to be treated as not having been done.

Upon the service of this notice, Part I of the above Act ceases to have effect in relation to me in connection with the original disposal[1].

Signed AB, [the purchaser[2], or CD as AB's agent]

Dated [insert].

1 LTA 1987, s 17(5) provides that this is the effect, although the notice is not required to state it.
2 This includes a subsequent purchaser: LTA 1987, s 17(7).

(27) Notice under section 17(4)

To (the nominated person)

Take notice that a period of two months has expired since date of determination of the application to the [(insert) court/leasehold valuation tribunal] without any binding contract having been entered into between us and without there having been made any other application in connection with the notice to the court or to a leasehold valuation tribunal. Accordingly, the notice under s [12A/12B/12C] is to be treated as not having been served, and anything done in pursuance of that notice, is to be treated as not having been done.

Upon the service of this notice, Part I of the above Act ceases to have effect in relation to me in connection with the original disposal[1].

Signed AB, [the purchaser[2], or CD as AB's agent]

Dated [insert].

1 LTA 1987, s 17(5) provides that this is the effect, although the notice is not required to state it.
2 This includes a subsequent purchaser: LTA 1987, s 17(7).

(28) Notice under section 18

To (the tenant of a flat contained in [premises])

Take notice that your landlord AB is proposing to dispose of his estate or interest in [premises] to me, CD.

The general nature of the principal terms of the proposed disposal are as follows: [insert – the following must be included: the property to which the disposal would relate and the estate or interest in that property proposed to be disposed of by the landlord, and the consideration required for the disposal].

You are invited to serve on me a notice stating:

(i) Whether AB has served on you, or your predecessor in title as tenant, a notice under s 5 of the above Act with respect to the disposal referred to above.

(ii) If AB has not served any such notice, whether you are aware of any reason why you are not entitled to be served with such a notice by the landlord.

(iii) If you are not so aware, whether you would wish to avail yourself of the right of first refusal conferred by such a notice if it were served.

If I serve notices in this form on at least 80% of the tenants of the flats in [premises] and:

(a) not more than 50% of the tenants on whom those notices have been served serve on me notices in the form mentioned above by the end of two months from the date when the last of them is served with this notice; or

(b) more than 50% of those tenants serve notices on me in the form mentioned above, but the notices in each case indicate that the tenant either:

    (i) does not regard himself as being entitled to be served by the landlord with a notice under section 5 with respect to the disposal, or

    (ii) would not wish to avail himself of the right of first refusal conferred by such a notice if it were served,

the premises shall, in relation to the disposal, be treated as premises to which Part I of the above Act does not apply.

For this purpose, each of the flats in the premises shall be regarded as having one tenant, who shall count towards any of the percentages specified, whether he is a qualifying tenant of the flat or not.

Signed CD [or EF, as CD's agent]

Dated [insert].

(29) Default notice under section 19(2)

To (the landlord or purchaser alleged to be in default).

Take notice that you are in default of the following obligation imposed by the above Act: [specify].

You are hereby required to make good the default by [specify].

If you do not comply with this notice within 14 days, an application may be made to the court for an order requiring you to make good the default.

Signed AB (nominated person, qualifying tenant etc) [or DC, as AB's agent]

Dated [insert].

Appendix II

List of appendices

Landlord and Tenant Act 1985

3 Duty to inform tenant of assignment of landlord's interest

(1) If the interest of the landlord under a tenancy of premises which consist of or include a dwelling is assigned, the new landlord shall give notice in writing of the assignment, and of his name and address, to the tenant not later than the next day on which rent is payable under the tenancy or, if that is within two months of the assignment, the end of that period of two months.

(2) If trustees constitute the new landlord, a collective description of the trustees as the trustees of the trust in question may be given as the name of the landlord, and where such a collective description is given:

- (a) the address of the new landlord may be given as the address from which the affairs of the trust are conducted, and
- (b) a change in the persons who are for the time being the trustees of the trust shall not be treated as an assignment of the interest of the landlord.

(3) A person who is the new landlord under a tenancy falling within subsection (1) and who fails, without reasonable excuse, to give the notice required by that subsection, commits a summary offence and is liable on conviction to a fine not exceeding level 4 on the standard scale.

[(3A) The person who was the landlord under the tenancy immediately before the assignment ('the old landlord') shall be liable to the tenant in respect of any breach of any covenant, condition or agreement under the tenancy occurring before the end of the relevant period in like manner as if the interest assigned were still vested in him; and where the new landlord is also liable to the tenant in respect of any such breach occurring within that period, he and the old landlord shall be jointly and severally liable in respect of it.

(3B) In subsection (3A) 'the relevant period' means the period beginning with the date of the assignment and ending with the date when:

- (a) notice in writing of the assignment, and of the new landlord's name and address, is given to the tenant by the new landlord (whether in accordance with subsection (1) or not), or
- (b) notice in writing of the assignment, and of the new landlord's name and last-known address, is given to the tenant by the old landlord,

whichever happens first.]

(4) In this section:

- (a) 'tenancy' includes a statutory tenancy, and
- (b) references to the assignment of the landlord's interest include any conveyance other than a mortgage or charge.

Amendment

Sub-ss (3A), (3B): inserted by the Landlord and Tenant Act 1987, s 50.

[3A Duty to inform tenant of possible right to acquire landlord's interest]

[(1) Where a new landlord is required by section 3(1) to give notice to a tenant of an assignment to him, then if:

(a) the tenant is a qualifying tenant within the meaning of Part I of the Landlord and Tenant Act 1987 (tenants' rights of first refusal), and

(b) the assignment was a relevant disposal within the meaning of that Part affecting premises to which at the time of the disposal that Part applied,

the landlord shall give also notice in writing to the tenant to the following effect.

(2) The notice shall state:

(a) that the disposal to the landlord was one to which Part I of the Landlord and Tenant Act 1987 applied;

(b) that the tenant (together with other qualifying tenants) may have the right under that Part:

(i) to obtain information about the disposal, and

(ii) to acquire the landlord's interest in the whole or part of the premises in which the tenant's flat is situated; and

(c) the time within which any such right must be exercised, and the fact that the time would run from the date of receipt of notice under this section by the requisite majority of qualifying tenants (within the meaning of that Part).

(3) A person who is required to give notice under this section and who fails, without reasonable excuse, to do so within the time allowed for giving notice under section 3(1) commits a summary offence and is liable on conviction to a fine not exceeding level 4 on the standard scale.]

Amendment

Inserted by the Housing Act 1996, s 93(1).

Landlord and Tenant Act 1987, Part I

(ss 5–10 and 11–17 as they were before the Housing Act 1996 amendments are included in italics)

[Preliminary]

1 Qualifying tenants to have rights of first refusal on disposals by landlord

(1) A landlord shall not make a relevant disposal affecting any premises to which at the time of the disposal this Part applies unless:

- (a) he has in accordance with section 5 previously served a notice under that section with respect to the disposal on the qualifying tenants of the flats contained in those premises (being a notice by virtue of which rights of first refusal are conferred on those tenants); and
- (b) the disposal is made in accordance with the requirements of sections 6 to 10.

(2) Subject to subsections (3) and (4), this part applies to premises if:

- (a) they consist of the whole or part of a building; and
- (b) they contain two or more faults held by qualifying tenants; and
- (c) the number of flats held by such tenants exceeds 50 per cent of the total number of flats contained in the premises.

(3) This Part does not apply to premises falling within subsection (2) if:

- (a) any part or parts of the premises is or are occupied or intended to be occupied otherwise than for residential purposes; and
- (b) the internal floor area of that part or those parts (taken together) exceeds 50 per cent of the internal floor area of the premises (taken as a whole);

and for the purposes of this subsection the internal floor area of any common parts shall be disregarded.

(4) This Part also does not apply to any such premises at a time when the interest of the landlord in the premises is held by an exempt landlord or a residential landlord.

(5) The Secretary of State may by order substitute for the percentage for the time being specified in subsection (3)(*b*) such other percentage as is specified in the order.

2 Landlords for the purposes of Part I

(1) Subject to subsection (2) [and section 4(1A)], a person is for the purposes of this Part the landlord in relation to any premises consisting of the whole or part of a building if he is:

(a) the immediate landlord of the qualifying tenants of the flats contained in those premises, or

(b) where any of those tenants is a statutory tenant, the person who, apart from the statutory tenancy, would be entitled to possession of the flat in question.

(2) Where the person who is, in accordance with subsection (1), the landlord in relation to any such premises for the purposes of this Part ('the immediate landlord') is himself a tenant of those premises under a tenancy which is either:

(a) a tenancy for a term of less than seven years, or

(b) a tenancy for a longer term but terminable within the first seven years at the option of the person who is the landlord under that tenancy ('the superior landlord'),

the superior landlord shall also be regarded as the landlord in relation to those premises for the purposes of this Part and, if the superior landlord is himself a tenant of those premises under a tenancy falling within paragraph (a) or (b) above, the person who is the landlord under that tenancy shall also be so regarded (and so on).

Amendment

Sub-s (1): words in square brackets inserted by the Housing Act 1988, s 119, Sch 13, para 1.

3 Qualifying tenants

(1) Subject to the following provisions of this section, a person is for the purposes of this Part a qualifying tenant of a flat if he is the tenant of the flat under a tenancy other than:

(a) a protected shorthold tenancy as defined in section 52 of the Housing Act 1980;

(b) a tenancy to which Part II of the Landlord and Tenant Act 1954 (business tenancies) applies; < . . . >

(c) a tenancy terminable on the cessation of his employment [or

(d) an assured tenancy or assured agricultural occupancy within the meaning of Part I of the Housing Act 1988].

(2) A person is not to be regarded as being a qualifying tenant of any flat contained in any particular premises consisting of the whole or part of a building if [by virtue of one or more tenancies none of which falls within paragraphs (a) to (d) of subsection (1), he is the tenant not only of the flat in question but also of at least two other flats contained in those premises].

(3) For the purposes of subsection [(2)] any tenant of a flat contained in the premises in question who is a body corporate shall be treated as the tenant of any other flat so contained and let to an associated company.

(4) A tenant of a flat whose landlord is a qualifying tenant of that flat is not to be regarded as being a qualifying tenant of that flat.

Amendment

Sub-s (1): words omitted repealed, and words in square brackets inserted by the Housing Act 1988, ss 119, 140, Sch 13, para 2(1), Sch 18. Sub-ss (2), (3): amended by the Housing Act 1988, s 119, Sch 13, para 2(2).

4 Relevant disposals

(1) In this Part references to a relevant disposal affecting any premises to which this Part applies are references to the disposal by the landlord of any estate or interest (whether legal or equitable) in any such premises, including the disposal of any such estate or interest in any common parts of any such premises but excluding:

- (a) the grant of any tenancy under which the demised premises consist of a single flat (whether with or without any appurtenant premises); and
- (b) any of the disposals falling within subsection (2).

[(1A) Where an estate or interest of the landlord has been mortgaged, the reference in subsection (1) above to the disposal of an estate or interest by the landlord includes a reference to its disposal by the mortgagee in exercise of a power of sale or leasing, whether or not the disposal is made in the name of the landlord; and, in relation to such a proposed disposal by the mortgagee, any reference in the following provisions of this Part to the landlord shall be construed as a reference to the mortgagee.]

(2) The disposals referred to in subsection (1)(b) are:

- (a) a disposal of:
  - (i) any interest of a beneficiary in settled land within the meaning of the Settled Land Act 1925, [or]
  - (ii) < . . . >
  - (iii) any incorporeal hereditament;
- [(aa) a disposal < . . . > by way of security for a loan;]
- (b) a disposal to a trustee in bankruptcy or to the liquidator of a company;
- [(c) a disposal in pursuance of an order made under:
  - (i) *section 24* [section 23A, 24] of the Matrimonial Causes Act 1973 (property adjustment orders in connection with matrimonial proceedings),
  - (ii) section 24A of the Matrimonial Causes Act 1973 (orders for the sale of property in connection with matrimonial proceedings) where the order includes provision requiring the

property concerned to be offered for sale to a person or class of persons specified in the order,

(iii) section 2 of the Inheritance (Provision for Family and Dependants) Act 1975 (orders as to financial provision to be made from estate),

(iv) section 17(1) of the Matrimonial and Family Proceedings Act 1984 (property adjustment orders after overseas divorce, &c),

(v) section 17(2) of the Matrimonial and Family Proceedings Act 1984 (orders for the sale of property after overseas divorce, &c) where the order includes provision requiring the property concerned to be offered for sale to a person or class of persons specified in the order, or

(vi) paragraph 1 of Schedule 1 to the Children Act 1989 (orders for financial relief against parents);]

(d) a disposal in pursuance of a compulsory purchase order or in pursuance of an agreement entered into in circumstances where, but for the agreement, such an order would have been made or (as the case may be) carried into effect;

[(da) a disposal of any freehold or leasehold interest in pursuance of Chapter I of Part I of the Leasehold Reform, Housing and Urban Development Act 1993;]

(e) a disposal by way of gift to a member of the landlord's family or to a charity;

(f) a disposal by one charity to another of an estate or interest in land which prior to the disposal is functional land of the first-mentioned charity and which is intended to be functional land of the other charity once the disposal is made;

(g) a disposal consisting of the transfer of an estate or interest held on trust for any person where the disposal is made in connection with the appointment of a new trustee or in connection with the discharge of any trustee;

(h) a disposal consisting of a transfer by two or more persons who are members of the same family either:

(i) to fewer of their number, or

(ii) to a different combination of members of the family (but one that includes at least one of the transferors);

[(i) a disposal in pursuance of a contract, option or right of pre-emption binding on the landlord (except as provided by section 8D (application of sections 11 to 17 to disposal in pursuance of option or right of pre-emption));]

(j) a disposal consisting of the surrender of a tenancy in pursuance of any covenant, condition or agreement contained in it;

(k) a disposal to the Crown; and

[(l) a disposal by a body corporate to a company which has been an associated company of that body for at least two years.]

(3) In this Part 'disposal' means a disposal whether by the creation or the transfer of an estate or interest and:

(a) includes the surrender of a tenancy and the grant of an option or right of pre-emption, but

(b) excludes a disposal under the terms of will or under the law relating to intestacy;

and references in this Part to the transferee in connection with a disposal shall be construed accordingly.

(4) In this section 'appurtenant premises', in relation to any flat, means any yard, garden, outhouse or appurtenance (not being a common part of the building containing the flat) which belongs to, or is usually enjoyed with, the flat.

(5) A person is a member of another's family for the purposes of this section if:

(a) that person is the spouse of that other person, or the two of them live together as husband and wife, or

(b) that person is that other person's parent, grandparent, child, grandchild, brother, sister, uncle, aunt, nephew or niece.

(6) For the purposes of subsection (5)(b):

(a) a relationship by marriage shall be treated as a relationship by blood,

(b) a relationship of the half-blood shall be treated as a relationship of the whole blood,

(c) the stepchild of a person shall be treated as his child, and

(d) the illegitimate child shall be treated as the legitimate child of his mother and reputed father.

Amendment

Sub-s (1A): inserted by the Housing Act 1988, s 119, Sch 13, para 3(1).
Sub-s (2): in para (a) words in square brackets inserted, and words omitted repealed by the Housing Act 1988, ss 119, 140, Sch 13, para 3(2), Sch 18; para (aa) inserted by the Housing Act 1988, s 119, Sch 13, para 3(2), words omitted repealed by the Housing Act 1996, ss 92, 227, Sch 6, Part IV, para 1, Sch 19, Part III; para (c) substituted by the Housing Act 1996, s 216(3), Sch 18, para 18, words in italics prospectively repealed with savings and subsequent words in square brackets prospectively substituted with savings by the Family Law Act 1996, s 66(1), Sch 8, para 38, as from a day to be appointed, for savings see Sch 9, para 5 thereto; para (da) inserted by the Leasehold Reform, Housing and Urban Development Act 1993, s 187(1), Sch 21, para 26; paras (i), (l) substituted by the Housing Act 1996, ss 89(2), 90(1).

[4A Application of right of first refusal in relation to contracts]

[(1) The provisions of this Part apply to a contract to create or transfer an estate or interest in land, whether conditional or unconditional and whether or not enforceable by specific performance, as they apply in relation to a disposal consisting of the creation or transfer of such an estate or interest.

As they so apply:

(a) references to a disposal of any description shall be construed as references to a contract to make such a disposal;

(b) references to making a disposal of any description shall be construed as references to entering into a contract to make such a disposal; and

(c) references to the transferee under the disposal shall be construed as references to the other party to the contract and include a reference to any other person to whom an estate or interest is to be granted or transferred in pursuance of the contract.

(2) The provisions of this Part apply to an assignment of rights under such a contract as is mentioned in subsection (1) as they apply in relation to a disposal consisting of the transfer of an estate or interest in land.

As they so apply:

(a) references to a disposal of any description shall be construed as references to an assignment of rights under a contract to make such a disposal;

(b) references to making a disposal of any description shall be construed as references to making an assignment of rights under a contract to make such a disposal;

(c) references to the landlord shall be construed as references to the assignor; and

(d) references to the transferee under the disposal shall be construed as references to the assignee of such rights.

(3) The provisions of this Part apply to a contract to make such an assignment as is mentioned in subsection (2) as they apply (in accordance with subsection (1)) to a contract to create or transfer an estate or interest in land.

(4) Nothing in this section affects the operation of the provisions of this Part relating to options or rights of pre-emption.]

Amendment

Inserted by the Housing Act 1996, s 89(1).

[5 Landlord required to serve offer notice on tenants]

[(1) Where the landlord proposes to make a relevant disposal affecting premises to which this Part applies, he shall serve a notice under this section (an 'offer notice') on the qualifying tenants of the flats contained in the premises (the 'constituent flats').

(2) An offer notice must comply with the requirements of whichever is applicable of the following sections:

section 5A (requirements in case of contract to be completed by conveyance, &c),

section 5B (requirements in case of sale at auction),

section 5C (requirements in case of grant of option or right of pre-emption),

section 5D (requirements in case of conveyance not preceded by contract, &c);

and in the case of a disposal to which section 5E applies (disposal for non-monetary consideration) shall also comply with the requirements of that section.

(3) Where a landlord proposes to effect a transaction involving the disposal of an estate or interest in more than one building (whether or not involving the same estate or interest), he shall, for the purpose of complying with this section, sever the transaction so as to deal with each building separately.

(4) If, as a result of the offer notice being served on different tenants on different dates, the period specified in the notice as the period for accepting the offer would end on different dates, the notice shall have effect in relation to all the qualifying tenants on whom it is served as if it provided for that period to end with the latest of those dates.

(5) A landlord who has not served an offer notice on all of the qualifying tenants on whom it was required to be served shall nevertheless be treated as having complied with this section:

(a) if he has served an offer notice on not less than 90% of the qualifying tenants on whom such a notice was required to be served, or

(b) where the qualifying tenants on whom it was required to be served number less than ten, if he has served such a notice on all but one of them.]

Amendment

Substituted, together with ss 5A–5E, 6–8, 8A–8E, 9A, 9B, 10, for ss 5–10 as originally enacted, by the Housing Act 1996, s 92(1), Sch 6, Part I.

[5A Offer notice: requirements in case of contract to be completed by conveyance, &c]

[(1) The following requirements must be met in relation to an offer notice where the disposal consists of entering into a contract to create or transfer an estate or interest in land.

(2) The notice must contain particulars of the principal terms of the disposal proposed by the landlord, including in particular:

(a) the property, and the estate or interest in that property, to which the contract relates,

(b) the principal terms of the contract (including the deposit and consideration required).

(3) The notice must state that the notice constitutes an offer by the landlord to enter into a contract on those terms which may be accepted by the requisite majority of qualifying tenants of the constituent flats.

(4) The notice must specify a period within which that offer may be so accepted, being a period of not less than two months which is to begin with the date of service of the notice.

(5) The notice must specify a further period of not less than two months within which a person or persons may be nominated by the tenants under section 6.

(6) This section does not apply to the grant of an option or right of pre-emption (see section 5C).]

Amendment

Substituted, together with ss 5, 5B–5E, 6–8, 8A–8E, 9A, 9B, 10, for ss 5–10 as originally enacted, by the Housing Act 1996, s 92(1), Sch 6, Part I.

[5B Offer notice: requirements in case of sale by auction]

[(1) The following requirements must be met in relation to an offer notice where the landlord proposes to make the disposal by means of a sale at a public auction held in England and Wales.

(2) The notice must contain particulars of the principal terms of the disposal proposed by the landlord, including in particular the property to which it relates and the estate or interest in that property proposed to be disposed of.

(3) The notice must state that the disposal is proposed to be made by means of a sale at a public auction.

(4) The notice must state that the notice constitutes an offer by the landlord, which may be accepted by the requisite majority of qualifying tenants of the constituent flats, for the contract (if any) entered into by the landlord at the auction to have effect as if a person or persons nominated by them, and not the purchaser, had entered into it.

(5) The notice must specify a period within which that offer may be so accepted, being a period of not less than two months beginning with the date of service of the notice.

(6) The notice must specify a further period of not less than 28 days within which a person or persons may be nominated by the tenants under section 6.

(7) The notice must be served not less than four months or more than six months before the date of the auction; and:

(a) the period specified in the notice as the period within which the offer may be accepted must end not less than two months before the date of the auction, and

(b) the period specified in the notice as the period within which a person may be nominated under section 6 must end not less than 28 days before the date of the auction.

(8) Unless the time and place of the auction and the name of the auctioneers are stated in the notice, the landlord shall, not less than 28 days before the date of the auction, serve on the requisite majority of qualifying tenants of the constituent flats a further notice stating those particulars.]

Amendment

Substituted, together with ss 5, 5A, 5C–5E, 6–8, 8A–8E, 9A, 9B, 10, for ss 5–10 as originally enacted, by the Housing Act 1996, s 92(1), Sch 6, Part I.

[5C Offer title: requirements in case of grant or option or right of pre-emption]

[(1) The following requirements must be met in relation to an offer notice where the disposal consists of the grant of an option or right of pre-emption.

(2) The notice must contain particulars of the principal terms of the disposal proposed by the landlord, including in particular:

(a) the property, and the estate or interest in that property, to which the option or right of pre-emption relates,

(b) the consideration required by the landlord for granting the option or right of pre-emption, and

(c) the principal terms on which the option or right of pre-emption would be exercisable, including the consideration payable on its exercise.

(3) The notice must state that the notice constitutes an offer by the landlord to grant an option or right of pre-emption on those terms which may be accepted by the requisite majority of qualifying tenants of the constituent flats.

(4) The notice must specify a period within which that offer may be so accepted, being a period of not less than two months which is to begin with the date of service of the notice.

(5) The notice must specify a further period of not less than two months within which a person or persons may be nominated by the tenants under section 6.]

Amendment

Substituted, together with ss 5, 5A, 5B, 5D, 5E, 6–8, 8A–8E, 9A, 9B, 10, for ss 5–10 as originally enacted, by the Housing Act 1996, s 92(1), Sch 6, Part I.

[5D Offer notice: requirements in case of conveyance not preceded by contract, &c]

[(1) The following requirements must be met in relation to an offer notice where the disposal is not made in pursuance of a contract, option or right of pre-emption binding on the landlord.

(2) The notice must contain particulars of the principal terms of the disposal proposed by the landlord, including in particular:

(a) the property to which it relates and the estate or interest in that property proposed to be disposed of, and

(b) the consideration required by the landlord for making the disposal.

(3) The notice must state that the notice constitutes an offer by the landlord to dispose of the property on those terms which may be accepted by the requisite majority of qualifying tenants of the constituent flats.

(4) The notice must specify a period within which that offer may be so accepted, being a period of not less than two months which is to begin with the date of service of the notice.

(5) The notice must specify a further period of not less than two months within which a person or persons may be nominated by the tenants under section 6.]

Amendment

Substituted, together with ss 5, 5A–5C, 5E, 6–8, 8A–8E, 9A, 9B, 10, for ss 5–10 as originally enacted, by the Housing Act 1996, s 92(1), Sch 6, Part I.

[5E Offer notice: disposal for non-monetary consideration]

[(1) This section applies where, in any case to which section 5 applies, the consideration required by the landlord for making the disposal does not consist, or does not wholly consist, of money.

(2) The offer notice, in addition to complying with whichever is applicable of sections 5A to 5D, must state:

(a) that an election may be made under section 8C (explaining its effect), and

(b) that, accordingly, the notice also constitutes an offer by the landlord, which may be accepted by the requisite majority of qualifying tenants of the constituent flats, for a person or persons nominated by them to acquire the property in pursuance of sections 11 to 17.

(3) The notice must specify a period within which that offer may be so accepted, being a period of not less than two months which is to begin with the date of service of the notice.]

Amendment

Substituted, together with ss 5, 5A–5D, 6–8, 8A–8E, 9A, 9B, 10, for ss 5–10 as originally enacted, by the Housing Act 1996, s 92(1), Sch 6, Part I.

[6 Acceptance of landlord's offer: general provisions]

[(1) Where a landlord has served an offer notice, he shall not during:

(a) the period specified in the notice as the period during which the offer may be accepted, or

(b) such longer period as may be agreed between him and the requisite majority of the qualifying tenants of the constituent flats,

dispose of the protected interest except to a person or persons nominated by the tenants under this section.

(2) Where an acceptance notice is duly served on him, he shall not during the protected period (see subsection (4) below) dispose of the protected interest except to a person duly nominated for the purposes of this section by the requisite majority of qualifying tenants of the constituent flats (a 'nominated person').

(3) An 'acceptance notice' means a notice served on the landlord by the requisite majority of qualifying tenants of the constituent flats informing him that the persons by whom it is served accept the offer contained in his notice.

An acceptance notice is 'duly served' if it is served within:

(a) the period specified in the offer notice as the period within which the offer may be accepted, or

(b) such longer period as may be agreed between the landlord and the requisite majority of qualifying tenants of the constituent flats.

(4) The 'protected period' is the period beginning with the date of service of the acceptance notice and ending with:

(a) the end of the period specified in the offer notice as the period for nominating a person under this section, or

(b) such later date as may be agreed between the landlord and the requisite majority of qualifying tenants of constituent flats.

(5) A person is 'duly nominated' for the purposes of this section if he is nominated at the same time as the acceptance notice is served or at any time after that notice is served and before the end of:

(a) the period specified in the offer notice as the period for nomination, or

(b) such longer period as may be agreed between the landlord and the requisite majority of qualifying tenants of the constituent flats.

(6) A person nominated for the purposes of this section by the requisite majority of qualifying tenants of the constituent flats may be replaced by another person

so nominated if, and only if, he has (for any reason) ceased to be able to act as a nominated person.

(7) Where two or more persons have been nominated and any of them ceases to act without being replaced, the remaining person or persons so nominated may continue to act.]

Amendment

Substituted, together with ss 5, 5A–5E, 7, 8, 8A–8E, 9A, 9B, 10, for ss 5–10 as originally enacted, by the Housing Act 1996, s 92(1), Sch 6, Part I.

[7 Failure to accept landlord's offer or to make nomination]

[(1) Where a landlord has served an offer notice on the qualifying tenants of the constituent flats and:

(a) no acceptance notice is duly served on the landlord, or

(b) no person is nominated for the purposes of section 6 during the protected period,

the landlord may, during the period of 12 months beginning with the end of that period, dispose of the protected interest to such person as he thinks fit, but subject to the following restrictions.

(2) Where the offer notice was one to which section 5B applied (sale by auction), the restrictions are:

(a) that the disposal is made by means of a sale at a public auction, and

(b) that the other terms correspond to those specified in the offer notice.

(3) In any other case the restrictions are:

(a) that the deposit and consideration required are not less than those specified in the offer notice, and

(b) that the other terms correspond to those specified in the offer notice.

(4) The entitlement of a landlord, by virtue of this section or any other corresponding provision of this Part, to dispose of the protected interest during a specified period of 12 months extends only to a disposal of that interest, and accordingly the requirements of section 1(1) must be satisfied with respect to any other disposal by him during that period of 12 months (unless the disposal is not a relevant disposal affecting any premises to which at the time of the disposal this Part applies).]

Amendment

Substituted, together with ss 5, 5A–5E, 6, 8, 8A–8E, 9A, 9B, 10, for ss 5–10 as originally enacted, by the Housing Act 1996, s 92(1), Sch 6, Part I.

[8 Landlord's obligations in case of acceptance and nomination]

[(1) This section applies where a landlord serves an offer notice on the qualifying tenants of the constituent flat and:

(a) an acceptance notice is duly served on him, and

(b) a person is duly nominated for the purposes of section 6,

by the requisite majority of qualifying tenants of the constituent flats.

(2) Subject to the following provisions of this Part, the landlord shall not dispose of the protected interest except to the nominated person.

(3) The landlord shall, within the period of one month beginning with the date of service of notice of nomination, either:

(a) serve notice on the nominated person indicating an intention no longer to proceed with the disposal of the protected interest, or

(b) be obliged to proceed in accordance with the following provisions of this Part.

(4) A notice under subsection (3)(a) is a notice of withdrawal for the purposes of section 9B(2) to (4) (consequences of notice of withdrawal by landlord).

(5) Nothing in this section shall be taken as prejudicing the application of the provisions of this Part to any further offer notice served by the landlord on the qualifying tenants of the constituent flats.]

Amendment

Substituted, together with ss 5, 5A–5E, 6, 7, 8A–8E, 9A, 9B, 10, for ss 5–10 as originally enacted, by the Housing Act 1996, s 92(1), Sch 6, Part I.

[8A Landlord's obligation: general provisions]

[(1) This section applies where the landlord is obliged to proceed and the offer notice was not one to which section 5B applied (sale by auction).

(2) The landlord shall, within the period of one month beginning with the date of service of the notice of nomination, send to the nominated person a form of contract for the acquisition of the protected interest on the terms specified in the landlord's offer notice.

(3) If he fails to do so, the following provisions of this Part apply as if he had given notice under section 9B (notice of withdrawal by landlord) at the end of that period.

(4) If the landlord complies with subsection (2), the nominated person shall, within the period of two months beginning with the date on which it is sent or such longer period beginning with that date as may be agreed between the landlord and that person, either:

(a) serve notice on the landlord indicating an intention no longer to proceed with the acquisition of the protected interest, or

(b) offer an exchange of contracts, that is to say, sign the contract and send it to the landlord, together with the requisite deposit.

In this subsection 'the requisite deposit' means a deposit of an amount determined by or under the contract or an amount equal to 10 per cent of the consideration, whichever is the less.

(5) If the nominated person:

(a) serves notice in pursuance of paragraph (a) of subsection (4), or

(b) fails to offer an exchange of contracts within the period specified in that subsection,

the following provisions of this Part apply as if he had given notice under section 9A (withdrawal by nominated person) at the same time as that notice or, as the case may be, at the end of that period.

(6) If the nominated person offers an exchange of contracts within the period specified in subsection (4), but the landlord fails to complete the exchange within the period of seven days beginning with the day on which he received that person's contract, the following provisions of this Part apply as if the landlord had given notice under section 9B (withdrawal by landlord) at the end of that period.]

Amendment

Substituted, together with ss 5, 5A–5E, 6, 7, 8, 8B–8E, 9A, 9B, 10, for ss 5–10 as originally enacted, by the Housing Act 1996, s 92(1), Sch 6, Part I.

[8B Landlord's obligation: election in case of sale at auction]

[(1) This section applies where the landlord is obliged to proceed and the offer notice was one to which section 5B applied (sale by auction).

(2) The nominated person may, by notice served on the landlord not less than 28 days before the date of the auction, elect that the provisions of this section shall apply.

(3) If a contract for the disposal is entered into at the auction, the landlord shall, within the period of seven days beginning with the date of the auction, send a copy of the contract to the nominated person.

(4) If, within the period of 28 days beginning with the date on which such a copy is so sent, the nominated person:

(a) serves notice on the landlord accepting the terms of the contract, and

(b) fulfils any conditions falling to be fulfilled by the purchaser on entering into the contract, the contract shall have effect as if the nominated person, and not the purchaser, had entered into the contract.

(5) Unless otherwise agreed, any time limit in the contract as it has effect by virtue of subsection (4) shall start to run again on the service of notice under that subsection; and nothing in the contract as it has effect by virtue of a notice under this section shall require the nominated person to complete the purchase before the end of the period of 28 days beginning with the day on which he is deemed to have entered into the contract.

(6) If the nominated person:

(a) does not serve notice on the landlord under subsection (2) by the time mentioned in that subsection, or

(b) does not satisfy the requirements of subsection (4) within the period mentioned in that subsection,

the following provisions of this Part apply as if he had given notice under section 9A (withdrawal by nominated person) at the end of that period.]

Amendment

Substituted, together with ss 5, 5A–5E, 6, 7, 8A, 8C–8E, 9A, 9B, 10, for ss 5–10 as originally enacted, by the Housing Act 1996, s 92(1), Sch 6, Part I.

[8C Election in case of disposal for non-monetary consideration]

[(1) This section applies where an acceptance notice is duly served on the landlord indicating an intention to accept the offer referred to in section 5E (offer notice: disposal for non-monetary consideration).

(2) The requisite majority of qualifying tenants of the constituent flats may, by notice served on the landlord within:

(a) the period specified in the offer notice for nominating a person or persons for the purposes of section 6, or

(b) such longer period as may be agreed between the landlord and the requisite majority of qualifying tenants of the constituent flats,

elect that the following provisions shall apply.

(3) Where such an election is made and the landlord disposes of the protected interest on terms corresponding to those specified in his offer notice in accordance with section 5A, 5B, 5C or 5D, sections 11 to 17 shall have effect as if:

(a) no notice under section 5 had been served;

(b) in section 11A(3) (period for serving notice requiring information, &c), the reference to four months was a reference to 28 days; and

(c) in section 12A(2) and 12B(3) (period for exercise of tenants' rights against purchaser) each reference to six months was a reference to two months.

(4) For the purposes of sections 11 to 17 as they have effect by virtue of subsection (3) so much of the consideration for the original disposal as did not consist of money shall be treated as such amount in money as was equivalent to its value in the hands of the landlord.

The landlord or the nominated person may apply to have that amount determined by a leasehold valuation tribunal.]

Amendment

Substituted, together with ss 5, 5A–5E, 6, 7, 8, 8A, 8B, 8D, 8E, 9A, 9B, 10, for ss 5–10 as originally enacted, by the Housing Act 1996, s 92(1), Sch 6, Part I.

[8D Disposal in pursuance of option or right of pre-emption]

[(1) Where:

(a) the original disposal was the grant of an option or right of pre-emption, and

(b) in pursuance of the option or right, the landlord makes another disposal affecting the premises ('the later disposal') before the end of the period specified in subsection (2),

sections 11 to 17 shall have effect as if the later disposal, and not the original disposal, were the relevant disposal.

(2) The period referred to in subsection (1)(b) is the period of four months beginning with the date by which:

(a) notices under section 3A of the Landlord and Tenant Act 1985 (duty of new landlord to inform tenants of rights) relating to the original disposal, or

(b) where that section does not apply, documents of any other description:

(i) indicating that the original disposal has taken place, and

(ii) alerting the tenants to the existence of their rights under this Part and the time within which any such rights must be exercised,

have been served on the requisite majority of qualifying tenants of the constituent flats.]

Amendment

Substituted, together with ss 5, 5A–5E, 6, 7, 8A–8C, 8E, 9A, 9B, 10, for ss 5–10 as originally enacted, by the Housing Act 1996, s 92(1), Sch 6, Part I.

[8E Covenant &c affecting landlord's power to dispose]

[(1) Where the landlord is obliged to proceed but is precluded by a covenant, condition or other obligation from disposing of the protected interest to the nominated person unless the consent of some other person is obtained:

- (a) he shall use his best endeavours to secure that the consent of that person to that disposal is given, and
- (b) if it appears to him that that person is obliged not to withhold his consent unreasonably but has nevertheless so withheld it, he shall institute proceedings for a declaration to that effect.

(2) Subsection (1) ceases to apply if a notice of withdrawal is served under section 9A or 9B (withdrawal of either party from transaction) or if notice is served under section 10 (lapse of landlord's offer: premises ceasing to be premises to which this Part applies).

(3) Where the landlord has discharged any duty imposed on him by subsection (1) but any such consent as is there mentioned has been withheld, and no such declaration as is there mentioned has been made, the landlord may serve a notice on the nominated person stating that to be the case.

When such a notice has been served, the landlord may, during the period of 12 months beginning with the date of service of the notice, dispose of the protected interest to such person as he thinks fit, but subject to the following restrictions.

(4) Where the offer notice was one to which section 5B applied (sale by auction), the restrictions are:

- (a) that the disposal is made by means of a sale at a public auction, and
- (b) that the other terms correspond to those specified in the offer notice.

(5) In any other case the restrictions are:

- (a) that the deposit and consideration required are not less than those specified in the offer notice or, if higher, those agreed between the landlord and the nominated person (subject to contract), and
- (b) that the other terms correspond to those specified in the offer notice.

(6) Where notice is given under subsection (3), the landlord may recover from the nominated party and the qualifying tenants who served the acceptance notice any costs reasonably incurred by him in connection with the disposal between the end of the first four weeks of the nomination period and the time when that notice is served by him.

Any such liability of the nominated person and those tenants is a joint and several liability.]

Amendment

Substituted, together with ss 5, 5A–5E, 6, 7, 8, 8A–8D, 9A, 9B, 10, for ss 5–10 as originally enacted, by the Housing Act 1996, s 92(1), Sch 6, Part I.

[9A Notice of withdrawal by nominated person]

[(1) Where the landlord is obliged to proceed, the nominated person may serve notice on the landlord (a 'notice of withdrawal') indicating his intention no longer to proceed with the acquisition of the protected interest.

(2) If at any time the nominated person becomes aware that the number of the qualifying tenants of the constituent flats desiring to proceed with the acquisition of the protected interest is less than the requisite majority of qualifying tenants of those flats, he shall forthwith serve a notice of withdrawal.

(3) Where notice of withdrawal is given by the nominated person under this section, the landlord may, during the period of 12 months beginning with the date of service of the notice, dispose of the protected interest to such person as he thinks fit, but subject to the following restrictions.

(4) Where the offer notice was one to which section 5B applied (sale by auction), the restrictions are:

- (a) that the disposal is made by means of a sale at a public auction, and
- (b) that the other terms correspond to those specified in the offer notice.

(5) In any other case the restrictions are:

- (a) that the deposit and consideration required are not less than those specified in the offer notice or, if higher, those agreed between the landlord and the nominated person (subject to contract), and
- (b) that the other terms correspond to those specified in the offer notice.

(6) If notice of withdrawal is served under this section before the end of the first four weeks of the nomination period specified in the offer notice, the nominated person and the qualifying tenants who served the acceptance notice are not liable for any costs incurred by the landlord in connection with the disposal.

(7) If notice of withdrawal is served under this section after the end of those four weeks, the landlord may recover from the nominated person and the qualifying tenants who served the acceptance notice any costs reasonably incurred by him in connection with any disposal between the end of those four weeks and the time when the notice of withdrawal was served on him.

Any such liability of the nominated person and those tenants is a joint and several liability.

(8) This section does not apply after a binding contract for the disposal of the protected interest:

(a) has been entered into by the landlord and the nominated person, or

(b) has otherwise come into existence between the landlord and the nominated person by virtue of any provision of this Part.]

Amendment

Substituted, together with ss 5, 5A–5E, 6, 7, 8, 8A–8E, 9B, 10, for ss 5–10 as originally enacted, by the Housing Act 1996, s 92(1), Sch 6, Part I.

[9B Notice of withdrawal by landlord]

[(1) Where the landlord is obliged to proceed, he may serve notice on the nominated person (a 'notice of withdrawal') indicating his intention no longer to proceed with the disposal of the protected interest.

(2) Where a notice of withdrawal is given by the landlord, he is not entitled to dispose of the protected interest during the period of 12 months beginning with the date of service of the notice.

(3) If a notice of withdrawal is served before the end of the first four weeks of the nomination period specified in the offer notice, the landlord is not liable for any costs incurred in connection with the disposal by the nominated person and the qualifying tenants who served the acceptance notice.

(4) If a notice of withdrawal is served after the end of those four weeks, the nominated person and the qualifying tenants who served the acceptance notice may recover from the landlord any costs reasonably incurred by them in connection with the disposal between the end of those four weeks and the time when the notice of withdrawal was served.

(5) This section does not apply after a binding contract for the disposal of the protected interest:

(a) has been entered into by the landlord and the nominated person, or

(b) has otherwise come into existence between the landlord and the nominated person by virtue of any provision of this Part].

Amendment

Substituted, together with ss 5, 5A–5E, 6, 7, 8, 8A–8E, 9A, 10, for ss 5–10 as originally enacted, by the Housing Act 1996, s 92(1), Sch 6, Part I.

[10 Lapse of landlord's offer]

[(1) If after a landlord has served an offer notice the premises concerned cease to be premises to which this Part applies, the landlord may serve a notice on the qualifying tenants of the constituent flats stating:

(a) that the premises have ceased to be premises to which this Part applies, and

(b) that the offer notice, and anything done in pursuance of it, is to be treated as not having been served or done;

and on the service of such a notice the provisions of this Part cease to have effect in relation to that disposal.

(2) A landlord who has not served such a notice on all of the qualifying tenants of the constituent flats shall nevertheless be treated as having duly served a notice under subsection (1):

(a) if he has served such a notice on not less than 90% of those tenants, or

(b) where those qualifying tenants number less than ten, if he has served such a notice on all but one of them.

(3) Where the landlord is entitled to serve a notice under subsection (1) but does not do so, this Part shall continue to have effect in relation to the disposal in question as if the premises in question were still premises to which this Part applies.

(4) The above provisions of this section do not apply after a binding contract for the disposal of the protected interest:

(a) has been entered into by the landlord and the nominated person, or

(b) has otherwise come into existence between the landlord and the nominated person by virtue of any provision of this Part.

(5) Where a binding contract for the disposal of the protected interest has been entered into between the landlord and the nominated person but it has been lawfully rescinded by the landlord, the landlord may, during the period of 12 months beginning with the date of the rescission of the contract, dispose of that interest to such person (and on such terms) as he thinks fit.]

Amendment

Substituted, together with ss 5A–5E, 6, 7, 8, 8A–8E, 9A, 9B, for ss 5–10 as originally enacted, by the Housing Act 1996, s 92(1), Sch 6, Part I.

5

Requirement to serve notice conferring rights of first refusal

(1) Where, in the case of any premises to which this Part applies, the landlord proposes to make a relevant disposal affecting the premises, he shall serve a notice under this section on the qualifying tenants of the flats contained in the premises.

(2) A notice under this section must:

(a) contain particulars of the principal terms of the disposal proposed by the landlord, including in particular:

(i) the property to which it relates and the estate or interest in that property proposed to be disposed of, and

(ii) the consideration required by the landlord for making the disposal;

(b) state that the notice constitutes an offer by the landlord to dispose of the property on those terms which may be accepted by the requisite majority of qualifying tenants of the constituent flats;

(c) specify a period within which that offer may be so accepted, being a period of not less than two months which is to begin with the date of service of the notice; and

(d) specify a further period within which a person or persons may be nominated for the purposes of section 6, being a period of not less than two months which is to begin with the end of the period specified under paragraph (c).

(3) Where, as the result of a notice under this section being served on different tenants on different dates, the period specified in the notice under subsection (2)(c) would, apart from this subsection, end on different dates:

(a) the notice shall have effect in relation to all the qualifying tenants on whom it is served as if it provided for that period to end with the latest of those dates, and for the period specified in the notice under subsection (2)(d) to begin with the end of that period; and

(b) references in this Part to the period specified in the notice under subsection (2)(c) or (as the case may be) subsection (2)(d) shall be construed accordingly.

(4) Where a landlord has not served a notice under this section on all of the qualifying tenants on whom it was required to be served by virtue of subsection (1), he shall nevertheless be treated as having complied with that subsection if:

(a) he has served such a notice on not less than 90 per cent of the qualifying tenants on whom it was so required to be served, or

(b) where the qualifying tenants on whom it was so required to be served number less than ten, he has served such a notice on all but one of them.

(5) Where a landlord proposes to effect a transaction that would involve both:

(a) a disposal of an estate or interest in the whole or part of a building constituting a relevant disposal affecting any premises to which this Part applies, and

(b) a disposal of an estate or interest in the whole or part of another building (whether or not constituting a relevant disposal affecting any premises to which this Part applies) or more than one such disposal,

the landlord shall, for the purpose of complying with this section in relation to any relevant disposal falling within paragraph (a) or (b) above, sever the transaction in such a way as to secure that, in the notice served by him under this section with respect to that disposal, the terms specified in pursuance of subsection (2)(a) are the terms on which he is willing to make that disposal.

(6) References in this Part to the requisite majority of qualifying tenants of the constituent flats are references to qualifying tenants of those flats with more than 50 per cent of the available votes; and for the purposes of this subsection:

- *(a) the total number of available votes shall be determined as follows, namely:*
  - *(i) in a case where a notice has been served under this section, that number shall correspond to the total number of constituent flats let to qualifying tenants on the date when the period specified in that notice under subsection (2)(c) expires,*
  - *(ii) in a case where a notice is served under section 11 without a notice having been previously served under this section, that number shall correspond to the total number of constituent flats let to qualifying tenants on the date of service of the notice under section 11, and*
  - *(iii) in a case where a notice is served under section 12 or 15 without a notice having been previously served under this section or under section 11, that number shall correspond to the total number of constituent flats let to qualifying tenants on the date of service of the notice under section 12 or 15; and*
- *(b) there shall be one available vote in respect of each of the flats so let on the date referred to in the relevant provision of paragraph (a) which shall be attributed to the qualifying tenant to whom it is let.*

(7) Nothing in this Part shall be construed as requiring the persons constituting the requisite majority of qualifying tenants in any one context to be the same as the persons constituting any such majority in any other context.

(8) For the purpose of:

- *(a) subsection (2) above and sections 6 to 10, and*
- *(b) subsection (6) above so far as it has effect for the purposes of those provisions,*

a flat is a constituent flat if it is contained in the premises affected by the relevant disposal with respect to which the notice was served under this section; and for the purposes of sections 11 to 17, and subsection (6) above so far as it has effect for the purposes of those sections, a flat is a constituent flat if it is contained in the premises affected by the relevant disposal referred to in section 11(1)(a).

6

Acceptance of landlord's offer

(1) Where:

- *(a) the landlord has, in accordance with the provisions of section 5, served an offer notice on the qualifying tenants of the constituent flats, and*
- *(b) within the period specified in that notice under section 5(2)(c), a notice is served on him by the requisite majority of qualifying tenants of the constituent flats informing him that the persons by whom it is served accept the offer contained in his notice,*

the landlord shall not during the relevant period dispose of the protected interest except to a person or persons nominated for the purposes of this section by the requisite majority of qualifying tenants of the constituent flats.

(2) In subsection (1) 'the relevant period' means:

(a) in every case, the period beginning with the date of service of the acceptance notice and ending with the end of the period specified in the offer notice under section 5(2)(d), and

(b) if any person is nominated for the purposes of this section within that period, an additional period of three months beginning with the end of the period so specified.

(3) If no person has been nominated for the purposes of this section during the period so specified, the landlord may, during the period of 12 months beginning with the end of that period, dispose of the protected interest to such person as he thinks fit, but subject to the following restrictions, namely:

(a) that the consideration required by him for the disposal must not be less than that specified in the offer notice, and

(b) that the other terms on which the disposal is made must, so far as relating to any matters covered by the terms specified in the offer notice, correspond to those terms.

(4) It is hereby declared that the entitlement of a landlord, by virtue of subsection (3) or any other corresponding provision of this Part, to dispose of a particular estate or interest in any property during a specified period of 12 months extends only to a disposal of that estate or interest in the property, and accordingly the requirements of section 1(1) must be satisfied with respect to any other disposal by him affecting that property and made during that period of 12 months (unless the disposal is not a relevant disposal affecting any premises to which at the time of the disposal this Part applies).

(5) A person nominated for the purposes of this section by the requisite majority of qualifying tenants of the constituent flats may only be replaced by another person so nominated if he has (for any reason) ceased to be able to act as a person so nominated.

(6) Where two or more persons have been so nominated and any of them ceases to act as such a person without being replaced in accordance with subsection (5), any remaining person or persons so nominated shall be entitled to continue to act in his or their capacity as such.

(7) Where subsection (1) above applies to the landlord, and he is precluded by virtue of any covenant, condition or other obligation from disposing of the protected interest to the nominated person unless the consent of some other person is obtained, then, subject to subsection (8):

(a) he shall use his best endeavours to secure that the consent of that person to that disposal is given, and

(b) if it appears to him that that person is obliged not to withhold his consent unreasonably but has nevertheless so withheld it, he shall institute proceedings for a declaration to that effect.

(8) Subsection (7) shall not apply once a notice is served by or on the landlord in accordance with any provision of section 9 or 10.

(9) In this Part:

'acceptance notice' means a notice served on the landlord in pursuance of subsection (1)(b);

'offer notice' means a notice served under section 5; and

'the protected interest' means (subject to section 9(9)) any such estate or interest in any property as is specified in an offer notice in pursuance of section 5(2)(a).

7

Rejection of landlord's offer: counter-offer by tenants

(1) Where:

(a) a landlord has, in accordance with section 5, served an offer notice on the qualifying tenants of the constituent flats, and

(b) an acceptance notice is not served on the landlord by the requisite majority of qualifying tenants of the constituent flats within the period specified in the offer notice under section 5(2)(c), and

(c) paragraph (b) of subsection (2) below does not apply,

the landlord may, during the period of 12 months beginning with the end of that period, dispose of the protected interest to such person as he thinks fit, but subject to the restrictions mentioned in section 6(3)(a) and (b).

(2) Where:

(a) a landlord has served an offer notice as mentioned in subsection 1(a), and

(b) within the period specified in the offer notice under section 5(2)(c), a notice is served on the landlord by the requisite majority of qualifying tenants of the constituent flats stating that the persons by whom it is served are making him a counter-offer for the acquisition by them of such estate or interest in the property specified in the offer notice under section 5(2)(a) as is specified in their notice,

the landlord shall serve on such person as is specified in that notice in pursuance of subsection (3)(b) a notice which either accepts the counter-offer or rejects it.

(3) Any notice making a counter-offer in accordance with subsection 2(b) must specify:

(a) the terms (including those relating to the consideration payable) on which the counter-offer is made; and

(b) the name and address of a person on whom any notice by the landlord under subsection (2) is to be served.

(4) If the landlord serves a notice under subsection (2) above accepting the counter-offer, section 6(1) and the other provisions of section 6 shall apply to him as if an acceptance notice had been served on him as mentioned in section 6(1)(b), except that:

(a) any reference to the protected interest shall be read as a reference to any such estate or interest as is specified in the notice making the counter-offer in accordance with subsection (2)(b) above;

(b) *any reference in section 6(3) to the offer notice shall be read as a reference to the notice making the counter-offer; and*

(c) *where the landlord's notice is served under subsection (2) above after the end of the period specified under section 5(2)(c), section 6(2) and (3) shall have effect as if the period specified under section 5(2)(d) began with the date of service of the landlord's notice.*

(5) If the landlord serves a notice under subsection (2) above rejecting the counter-offer, then, unless it is a notice falling within section 8(1), subsection (1) above shall apply to him as if no such notice as is mentioned in subsection (2)(b) above had been served on him (except that where he serves his notice under subsection (2) above after the end of the period specified under section 5(2)(c), subsection (1) above shall have effect as if the period of 12 months there mentioned began with the date of service of that notice).

8

Fresh offer by landlord: further negotiations between parties

(1) This section applies where the landlord serves a notice under subsection (2) of section 7 rejecting a counter-offer but the notice:

(a) *states that it constitutes a fresh offer by the landlord to dispose of an estate or interest in the property specified in the offer notice under section 5(2)(a)*

which may be accepted by the requisite majority of qualifying tenants of the constituent flats;

(b) *contains particulars of the estate or interest in that property which he proposes to dispose of, the consideration required by him for the disposal and the other principal terms of the disposal; and*

(c) *specifies a period within which the offer may be accepted as mentioned in paragraph (a) above.*

(2) If, within the period specified in the landlord's notice under subsection (1)(c) above, a notice is served on the landlord by the requisite majority of qualifying tenants of the constituent flats informing him that the persons by whom it is served accept the offer contained in the landlord's notice, section 6(1) and the other provisions of section 6 shall apply to the landlord as if an acceptance notice had been served on him as mentioned in section 6(1)(b), except that:

(a) *any reference to the protected interest shall be read as a reference to any such estate or interest as is specified in the landlord's notice in pursuance of subsection (1)(b) above; and*

(b) *any reference in section 6(3) to the offer notice shall be read as a reference to the landlord's notice under subsection (1) above; and*

(c) *where the notice served on the landlord in pursuance of this subsection is served after the end of the period specified under section 5(2)(c), section 6(2) and (3) shall have effect as if the period specified under section 5(2)(d) began with the date of service of that notice.*

(3) If, within the period specified in the landlord's notice under subsection (1)(c) above, no notice is served on the landlord as mentioned in subsection (2) above and subsection (4) below does

not apply, the landlord may, during the period of 12 months beginning with the end of that period dispose of any such estate or interest as is specified in the landlord's notice under subsection (1)(b) above to such person as he thinks fit, but subject to the following restrictions, namely:

- *(a) that the consideration required by him for the disposal must not be less than that specified in his notice under subsection (1), and*
- *(b) that the other terms on which the disposal is made must, so far as relating to any matters covered by the terms specified in that notice, correspond to those terms.*

(4) If, within the period so specified in the landlord's notice, a notice is served on him by the requisite majority of qualifying tenants of the constituent flats stating that the persons by whom it is served are making him a further counter-offer for the acquisition by them of such estate or interest in the property specified in the offer notice under section 5(2)(a) as is specified in their notice, the provisions of subsection (2) to (5) of section 7 and the provisions of this section (including this subsection) shall apply, with any necessary modifications, in relation to any such notice as they apply in relation to a notice served as mentioned in subsection (2)(b) of section 7.

9

Withdrawal of either party from transaction

(1) Where:

- *(a) section 6(1) applies to a landlord by virtue of any provision of sections 6 to 8, and*
- *(b) any person has been nominated for the purposes of section 6 by the requisite majority of qualifying tenants of the constituent flats within the period specified by the landlord in his offer notice under section 5(2)(d) (taking into account any postponement of the commencement of that period effected by any of the preceding provisions of this Part), and*
- *(c) the nominated person serves a notice on the landlord indicating an intention no longer to proceed with the acquisition of the protected interest,*

the landlord may, during the period of 12 months beginning with the date of service of the nominated person's notice, dispose of the protected interest to such person as he thinks fit, but subject to the restrictions mentioned in subsection (2).

(2) The restrictions referred to in subsection (1) are:

- *(a) that the consideration required by him for the disposal must not be less than the amount which has been agreed to by the parties (subject to contract) for the disposal of the protected interest, and*
- *(b) that the other terms on which the disposal is made must correspond to those so agreed to by the parties in relation to the disposal.*

(3) If at any time the nominated person becomes aware that the number of the qualifying tenants of the constituent flats desiring to proceed with the acquisition of the protected interest is less than the requisite majority of qualifying tenants of those flats, he shall forthwith serve on the landlord such a notice as is mentioned in subsection (1)(c).

(4) Where:

(a) paragraphs (a) and (b) of subsection (1) apply, and

(b) the landlord serves a notice on the nominated person indicating an intention no longer to proceed with the disposal of the protected interest,

the landlord shall not be entitled to dispose of that interest in accordance with that subsection but the notice shall have the consequences set out in subsection (5) or (6) (as the case may be).

(5) If any notice served in pursuance of subsection (1), (3) or (4) above is served not later than the end of the first four weeks of the period referred to in subsection (1)(b) above, the party serving it shall not be liable for any costs incurred by the other party in connection with the disposal.

(6) If any such notice is served after the end of those four weeks, the party on whom it is served may recover from the other party any costs reasonably incurred by the first-mentioned party in connection with the disposal between the end of those four weeks and the time when that notice is served on him.

(7) For the purposes of this section the parties are:

(a) the landlord, and

(b) the qualifying tenants who served the acceptance notice or other notice accepting an offer by the landlord, or (as the case may be) the notice making the counter-offer which was accepted by the landlord, together with the nominated person,

and any liability of those tenants and the nominated person which arises under this section shall be a joint and several liability.

(8) Nothing in this section applies where a binding contract for the disposal of the protected interest has been entered into by the landlord and the nominated person.

(9) In this section and section 10:

'the nominated person' means the person or persons for the time being nominated for the purposes of section 6 by the requisite majority of qualifying tenants of the constituent flats; and

'the protected interest' means:

(a) except where section 6(1) applies to the landlord by virtue of section 7(4) or 8(2), the protected interest as defined by section 6(9); and

(b) where section 6(1) applies to the landlord by virtue of section 7(4) or 8(2), any such estate or interest as is mentioned in section 7(4)(a) or (as the case may be) in section 8(2)(a).

10

Lapse of landlord's offer

(1) If, at any time after a landlord has served an offer notice with respect to any relevant disposal affecting any premises to which this Part applies, those premises cease to be premises to which this Part applies, the landlord may serve a notice on the qualifying tenants of the constituent flats stating:

(a) that the premises have ceased to be premises to which this Part applies, and

(b) that the offer notice, and anything done in pursuance of it, is to be treated as not having been served or done;

and, on the service of any such notice, the provisions of this Part shall cease to have effect in relation to that disposal.

(2) Subsection (4) of section 5 shall apply to a notice under subsection (1) above as it applies to a notice under that section, but as if the references to the qualifying tenants on whom such a notice is required to be served by virtue of subsection (1) of that section were references to the qualifying tenants mentioned in subsection (1) above.

(3) In a case where a landlord is entitled to serve a notice under subsection (1) above but does not do so, this Part shall continue to have effect in relation to the disposal in question as if the premises in question were still premises to which this Part applies.

(4) Where:

(a) in the case of a landlord to whom section 6(7) applies:

(i) the landlord has discharged any duty imposed on him by that provision, and

(ii) any such consent as is there mentioned has been withheld, and

(iii) no such declaration as is there mentioned has been made, or

(b) the period specified in section 6(2)(b) has expired without any binding contract having been entered into between the landlord and the nominated person,

and the landlord serves a notice on the nominated person stating that paragraph (a) or (b) above applies, the landlord may, during the period of 12 months beginning with the end of the period specified in section 6(2)(b), dispose of the protected interest to such person as he thinks fit, but subject to the restrictions mentioned in section 9(2). References in this subsection to section 6(2)(b) include references to that provision as it has effect by virtue of section 7(4)(c) or 8(2)(c).

(5) Where any such notice is served in a case to which paragraph (b) of subsection (4) applies, the landlord may recover from the other party any costs reasonably incurred by him in connection with the disposal to the nominated person between the end of the first four weeks of the period referred to in section 9(1)(b) and the time when that notice is served by him; and section 9(7) shall apply for the purposes of this section as it applies for the purposes of section 9.

(6) Where any binding contract with respect to the disposal of the protected interest has been entered into between the landlord and the nominated person but it has been lawfully rescinded by the landlord, the landlord may, during the period of 12 months beginning with the date of the rescission of the contract, dispose of that interest to such person (and on such terms) as he thinks fit.

(7) Section 9(9) applies for the purposes of this section.

[10A Offence of failure to comply with requirements of Part I]

[(1) A landlord commits an offence if, without reasonable excuse, he makes a relevant disposal affecting premises to which this Part applies:

(a) without having first complied with the requirements of section 5 as regards the service of notices on the qualifying tenants of flats contained in the premises, or

(b) in contravention of any prohibition or restriction imposed by sections 6 to 10.

(2) A person guilty of an offence under this section is liable on summary conviction to a fine not exceeding level 5 on the standard scale.

(3) Where an offence under this section committed by a body corporate is proved:

(a) to have been committed with the consent or connivance of a director, manager, secretary or other similar officer of the body corporate, or a person purporting to act in such a capacity, or

(b) to be due to any neglect on the part of such an officer or person,

he, as well as the body corporate, is guilty of the offence and liable to be proceeded against and punished accordingly.
Where the affairs of a body corporate are managed by its members, the above provision applies in relation to the acts and defaults of a member in connection with his functions of management as if he were a director of the body corporate.

(4) Proceedings for an offence under this section may be brought by a local housing authority (within the meaning of section 1 of the Housing Act 1985).

(5) Nothing in this section affects the validity of the disposal.]

Amendment

Inserted by the Housing Act 1996, s 91(1).

[Enforcement by tenants of rights against purchaser]

[11 Circumstances in which tenants' rights enforceable against purchaser]

[(1) The following provisions of this Part apply where a landlord has made a relevant disposal affecting premises to which at the time of the disposal this Part applied ('the original disposal'), and either:

(a) no notice was served by the landlord under section 5 with respect to that disposal, or

(b) the disposal was made in contravention of any provision of sections 6 to 10,

and the premises are still premises to which this Part applies.

(2) In those circumstances the requisite majority of the qualifying tenants of the flats contained in the premises affected by the relevant disposal (the 'constituent flats') have the rights conferred by the following provisions:

section 11A (right to information as to terms of disposal, &c),

section 12A (right of qualifying tenants to take benefit of contract),

section 12B (right of qualifying tenants to compel sale, &c by purchaser), and

section 12C (right of qualifying tenants to compel grant of new tenancy by superior landlord).

(3) In those sections the transferee under the original disposal (or, in the case of the surrender of a tenancy, the superior landlord) is referred to as 'the purchaser'.

This shall not be read as restricting the operation of those provisions to disposals for consideration.]

Amendment

Substituted, together with ss 11A, 12A–12D, 13, 14, for ss 11–15 as originally enacted, the Housing Act 1996, s 92(1), Sch 6, Part II.

[11A Right to information as to terms of disposal, &c]

[(1) The requisite majority of qualifying tenants of the constituent flats may serve a notice on the purchaser requiring him:

(a) to give particulars of the terms on which the original disposal was made (including the deposit and consideration required) and the date on which it was made, and

(b) where the disposal consisted of entering into a contract, to provide a copy of the contract.

(2) The notice must specify the name and address of the person to whom (on behalf of the tenants) the particulars are to be given, or the copy of the contract provided.

(3) Any notice under this section must be served before the end of the period of four months beginning with the date by which:

(a) notices under section 3A of the Landlord and Tenant Act 1985 (duty of new landlord to inform tenants of rights) relating to the original disposal, or

(b) where that section does not apply, documents of any other description:

(i) indicating that the original disposal has taken place, and

(ii) alerting the tenants to the existence of their rights under this Part and the time within which any such rights must be exercised,

have been served on the requisite majority of qualifying tenants of the constituent flats.

(4) A person served with a notice under this section shall comply with it within the period of one month beginning with the date on which it is served on him.]

Amendment

Substituted, together with ss 11, 12A–12D, 13, 14, for ss 11–15 as originally enacted, by the Housing Act 1996, s 92(1), Sch 6, Part II.

[12A Right of qualifying tenants to take benefit of contract]

[(1) Where the original disposal consisted of entering into a contract, the requisite majority of qualifying tenants of the constituent flats may by notice to the landlord elect that the contract shall have effect as if entered into not with the purchaser but with a person or persons nominated for the purposes of this section by the requisite majority of qualifying tenants of the constituent flats.

(2) Any such notice must be served before the end of the period of six months beginning:

- (a) if a notice was served on the purchaser under section 11A (right to information as to terms of disposal, &c), with the date on which the purchaser complied with that notice;
- (b) in any other case, with the date by which documents of any description:
  - (i) indicating that the original disposal took place, and
  - (ii) alerting the tenants to the existence of their rights under this Part and the time within which any such rights must be exercised,

have been served on the requisite majority of qualifying tenants of the constituent flats.

(3) The notice shall not have effect as mentioned in subsection (1) unless the nominated person:

- (a) fulfils any requirements as to the deposit required on entering into the contract, and
- (b) fulfils any other conditions required to be fulfilled by the purchaser on entering into the contract.

(4) Unless otherwise agreed, any time limit in the contract as it has effect by virtue of a notice under this section shall start to run again on the service of that notice; and nothing in the contract as it has effect by virtue of a notice under this section shall require the nominated person to complete the purchase before the end of the period of 28 days beginning with the day on which he is deemed to have entered into the contract.

(5) Where the original disposal related to other property in addition to the premises to which this Part applied at the time of the disposal:

(a) a notice under this section has effect only in relation to the premises to which this Part applied at the time of the original disposal, and

(b) the terms of the contract shall have effect with any necessary modifications.

In such a case the notice under this section may specify the subject-matter of the disposal, and the terms on which the disposal is to be made (whether doing so expressly or by reference to the original disposal), or may provide for that estate or interest, or any such terms, to be determined by a leasehold valuation tribunal.]

Amendment

Substituted, together with ss 11, 12B–12D, 13, 14, for ss 11–15 as originally enacted, by the Housing Act 1996, s 92(1), Sch 6, Part II.

[12B Right of qualifying tenants to compel sale, &c by purchaser]

[(1) This section applies where:

(a) the original disposal consisted of entering into a contract and no notice has been served under section 12A (right of qualifying tenants to take benefit of contract), or

(b) the original disposal did not consist of entering into a contract.

(2) The requisite majority of qualifying tenants of the constituent flats may serve a notice (a 'purchase notice') on the purchaser requiring him to dispose of the estate or interest that was the subject-matter of the original disposal, on the terms on which it was made (including those relating to the consideration payable), to a person or persons nominated for the purposes of this section by any such majority of qualifying tenants of those flats.

(3) Any such notice must be served before the end of the period of six months beginning:

(a) if a notice was served on the purchaser under section 11A (right to information as to terms of disposal, &c), with the date on which the purchaser complied with that notice;

(b) in any other case, with the date by which:

(i) notices under section 3A of the Landlord and Tenant Act 1985 (duty of new landlord to inform tenants of rights) relating to the original disposal, or

(ii) where that section does not apply, documents of any other description indicating that the original disposal has taken place, and alerting the tenants to the existence of their rights under this Part and the time within which any such rights must be exercised,

have been served on the requisite majority of qualifying tenants of the constituent flats.

(4) A purchase notice shall where the original disposal related to other property in addition to premises to which this Part applied at the time of the disposal:

(a) require the purchaser only to make a disposal relating to those premises, and

(b) require him to do so on the terms referred to in subsection (2) with any necessary modifications.

In such a case the purchase notice may specify the subject-matter of the disposal, and the terms on which the disposal is to be made (whether doing so expressly or by reference to the original disposal), or may provide for those matters to be determined by a leasehold valuation tribunal.

(5) Where the property which the purchaser is required to dispose of in pursuance of the purchase notice has since the original disposal become subject to any charge or other incumbrance, then, unless the court by order directs otherwise:

(a) in the case of a charge to secure the payment of money or the performance of any other obligation by the purchaser or any other person, the instrument by virtue of which the property is disposed of by the purchaser to the person or persons nominated for the purposes of this section shall (subject to the provisions of Part I of Schedule 1) operate to discharge the property from that charge; and

(b) in the case of any other incumbrance, the property shall be so disposed of subject to the incumbrance but with a reduction in the consideration payable to the purchaser corresponding to the amount by which the existence of the incumbrance reduces the value of the property.

(6) Subsection (5)(a) and Part I of Schedule 1 apply, with any necessary modifications, to mortgages and liens as they apply to charges; but nothing in those provisions applies to a rentcharge.

(7) Where the property which the purchaser is required to dispose of in pursuance of the purchase notice has since the original disposal increased in monetary value owing to any change in circumstances (other than a change in the value of money), the amount of the consideration payable to the purchaser for the disposal by him of the property in pursuance of the purchase notice shall be the amount that might reasonably have been obtained on a corresponding disposal made on the open market at the time of the original disposal if the change in circumstances had already taken place.]

Amendment

Substituted, together with ss 11, 12A, 12C, 12D, 13, 14, for ss 11–15 as originally enacted, by the Housing Act 1996, s 92(1), Sch 6, Part II.

[12C Rights of qualifying tenants to compel grant of new tenancy by superior landlord]

[(1) This section applies where the original disposal consisted of the surrender by the landlord of a tenancy held by him ('the relevant tenancy').

(2) The requisite majority of qualifying tenants of the constituent flats may serve a notice on the purchaser requiring him to grant a new tenancy of the premises which were subject to the relevant tenancy, on the same terms as those of the relevant tenancy and so as to expire on the same date as that tenancy would have expired, to a person or persons nominated for the purposes of this section by any such majority of qualifying tenants of those flats.

(3) Any such notice must be served before the end of the period of six months beginning:

(a) if a notice was served on the purchaser under section 11A (right to information as to terms of disposal, &c), with the date on which the purchaser complied with that notice;

(b) in any other case, with the date by which documents of any description:

(i) indicating that the original disposal has taken place, and

(ii) alerting the tenants to the existence of their rights under this Part and the time within which any such rights must be exercised,

have been served on the requisite majority of qualifying tenants of the constituent flats.

(4) If the purchaser paid any amount to the landlord as consideration for the surrender by him of that tenancy, the nominated person shall pay that amount to the purchaser.

(5) Where the premises subject to the relevant tenancy included premises other than premises to which this Part applied at the time of the disposal, a notice under this section shall:

(a) require the purchaser only to grant a new tenancy relating to the premises to which this Part then applied, and

(b) require him to do so on the terms referred to in subsection (2) subject to any necessary modifications.

(6) The purchase notice may specify the subject-matter of the disposal, and the terms on which the disposal is to be made (whether doing so expressly or by reference to the original disposal), or may provide for those matters to be determined by a leasehold valuation tribunal.]

Amendment

Substituted, together with ss 11, 12A, 12B, 12D, 13, 14, for ss 11–15 as originally enacted, by the Housing Act 1996, s 92(1), Sch 6, Part II.

[12D Nominated persons: supplementary provisions]

[(1) The person or persons initially nominated for the purposes of section 12A, 12B or 12C shall be nominated in the notice under that section.

(2) A person nominated for those purposes by the requisite majority of qualifying tenants of the constituent flats may be replaced by another person so nominated if, and only if, he has (for any reason) ceased to be able to act as a nominated person.

(3) Where two or more persons have been nominated and any of them ceases to act without being replaced, the remaining person or persons so nominated may continue to act.

(4) Where, in the exercise of its power to award costs, the court or the Lands Tribunal makes, in connection with any proceedings arising under or by virtue of this Part, an award of costs against the person or persons so nominated, the liability for those costs is a joint and several liability of that person or those persons together with the qualifying tenants by whom the relevant notice was served.]

Amendment

Substituted, together with ss 11, 12A–12C, 13, 14, for ss 11–15 as originally enacted, by the Housing Act 1996, s 92(1), Sch 6, Part II.

[13 Determination by rent assessment committees of questions relating to purchase notices]

[(1) A leasehold valuation tribunal has jurisdiction to hear and determine:

(a) any question arising in relation to any matters specified in a notice under section 12A, 12B or 12C, and

(b) any question arising for determination as mentioned in section 8C(4), 12A(5) or 12B(4) (matters left for determination by tribunal).

(2) On an application under this section the interests of the persons by whom the notice was served under section 12A, 12B or 12C shall be represented by the nominated person; and accordingly the parties to any such application shall not include those persons.]

Amendment

Substituted, together with ss 11, 12A–12D, 14, for ss 11–15 as originally enacted, by the Housing Act 1996, s 92(1), Sch 6, Part II.

[14 Withdrawal of nominated person from transaction]

[(1) Where notice has been duly served on the landlord under:

section 12B (right of qualifying tenants to compel sale, &c by purchaser), or

section 12C (right of qualifying tenants to compel grant of new tenancy by superior landlord), the nominated person may at any time before a binding contract is entered into in pursuance of the notice, serve notice under this section on the purchaser (a 'notice of withdrawal') indicating an intention no longer to proceed with the disposal.

(2) If at any such time the nominated person becomes aware that the number of qualifying tenants of the constituent flats desiring to proceed with the disposal is less than the requisite majority of those tenants, he shall forthwith serve a notice of withdrawal.

(3) If a notice of withdrawal is served under this section the purchaser may recover from the nominated person any costs reasonably incurred by him in connection with the disposal down to the time when the notice is served on him.

(4) If a notice of withdrawal is served at a time when proceedings arising under or by virtue of this Part are pending before the court or the Lands Tribunal, the liability of the nominated person for any costs incurred by the purchaser as mentioned in subsection (3) shall be such as may be determined by the court or (as the case may be) by the Tribunal.

(5) The costs that may be recovered by the purchaser under this section do not include any costs incurred by him in connection with an application to a leasehold valuation tribunal.]

Amendment

Substituted, together with ss 11, 12A–12D, 13, for ss 11–15 as originally enacted, by the Housing Act 1996, s 92(1), Sch 6, Part II.

[Enforcement by tenants of rights against subsequent purchasers]

[16 Right of qualifying tenants to compel sale etc by subsequent purchaser]

[(1) This section applies where, at the time when a notice is served on the purchaser under section 11A, 12A, 12B or 12C, he no longer holds the estate or interest that was the subject-matter of the original disposal.

(2) In the case of a notice under section 11A (right to information as to terms of disposal, &c) the purchaser shall, within the period for complying with that notice:

- (a) serve notice on the person specified in the notice as the person to whom particulars are to be provided of the name and address of the person to whom he has disposed of that estate or interest ('the subsequent purchaser'), and
- (b) serve on the subsequent purchaser a copy of the notice under section 11A and of the particulars given by him in response to it.

(3) In the case of a notice under section 12A, 12B or 12C the purchaser shall forthwith:

(a) forward the notice to the subsequent purchaser, and

(b) serve on the nominated person notice of the name and address of the subsequent purchaser.

(4) Once the purchaser serves a notice in accordance with subsection (2)(a) or (3)(b), sections 12A to 14 shall, instead of applying to the purchaser, apply to the subsequent purchaser as if he were the transferee under the original disposal.

(5) Subsections (1) to (4) have effect, with any necessary modifications, in a case where, instead of disposing of the whole of the estate or interest referred to in subsection (1) to another person, the purchaser has disposed of it in part or in parts to one or more other persons.

In such a case, sections 12A to 14:

(a) apply to the purchaser in relation to any part of that estate or interest retained by him, and

(b) in relation to any part of that estate or interest disposed of to any other person, apply to that other person instead as if he were (as respects that part) the transferee under the original disposal.]

Amendment

Substituted by the Housing Act 1996, s 92(1), Sch 6, Part II.

[Termination of rights against new landlords etc]

[17 Termination of rights against new landlord or subsequent purchaser]

[(1) If, at any time after a notice has been served under section 11A, 12A, 12B or 12C, the premises affected by the original disposal cease to be premises to which this Part applies, the purchaser may serve a notice on the qualifying tenants of the constituent flats stating:

(a) that the premises have ceased to be premises to which this Part applies, and

(b) that any such notice served on him, and anything done in pursuance of it, is to be treated as not having been served or done.

(2) A landlord who has not served such a notice on all of the qualifying tenants of the constituent flats shall nevertheless be treated as having duly served a notice under subsection (1):

(a) if he has served such a notice on not less than 90% of those tenants, or

(b) where those qualifying tenants number less than ten, if he has served such a notice on all but one of them.

(3) Where a period of three months beginning with the date of service of a notice under section 12A, 12B or 12C on the purchaser has expired:

(a) without any binding contract having been entered into between the purchaser and the nominated person, and

(b) without there having been made any application in connection with the notice to the court or to a leasehold valuation tribunal,

the purchaser may serve on the nominated person a notice stating that the notice, and anything done in pursuance of it, is to be treated as not having been served or done.

(4) Where any such application as is mentioned in subsection (3)(b) was made within the period of three months referred to in that subsection, but:

(a) a period of two months beginning with the date of the determination of that application has expired,

(b) no binding contract has been entered into between the purchaser and the nominated person, and

(c) no other such application as is mentioned in subsection (3)(b) is pending,

the purchaser may serve on the nominated person a notice stating that any notice served on him under section 12A, 12B or 12C, and anything done in pursuance of any such notice, is to be treated as not having been served or done.

(5) Where the purchaser serves a notice in accordance with subsection (1), (3) or (4), this Part shall cease to have effect in relation to him in connection with the original disposal.

(6) Where a purchaser is entitled to serve a notice under subsection (1) but does not do so, this Part shall continue to have effect in relation to him in connection with the original disposal as if the premises in question were still premises to which this Part applies.

(7) References in this section to the purchaser include a subsequent purchaser to whom sections 12A to 14 apply by virtue of section 16(4) or (5).]

Amendment

Substituted by the Housing Act 1996, s 92(1), Sch 6, Part II.

Noticed served by prospective purchasers

11

Duty of new landlord to furnish particulars of disposal made in contravention of Part I

(1) Where:

(a) *a landlord has made a relevant disposal affecting any premises to which at the time of the disposal this Part applied ('the original disposal'), and*

(b) *either no notice was served by the landlord under section 5 with respect to that disposal or it was made in contravention of any provisions of sections 6 to 10, and*

(c) *those premises are still premises to which this Part applies,*

the requisite majority of qualifying tenants of the constituent flats may, before the end of the period specified in subsection (2) below, serve a notice on the transferee under the original disposal requiring him to furnish a person (whose name and address are specified for the purpose in the notice) with particulars of the terms on which the original disposal was made (including those relating to the consideration payable) and the date on which it was made; and in the following provisions of this Part the transferee under that disposal is referred to as 'the new landlord'.

(2) *The period referred to in subsection (1) is the period of two months beginning with the date by which:*

(a) *notices under section 3 of the Landlord and Tenant Act 1985 (in this Act referred to as 'the 1985 Act') relating to the original disposal, or*

(b) *documents of any other description indicating that the original disposal has taken place,*

have been served on the requisite majority of qualifying tenants of the constituent flats.

(3) *Any person served with a notice in accordance with subsection (1) shall comply with the notice within the period of one month beginning with the date on which it is served on him.*

12

Right of qualifying tenants to compel sale etc by new landlord

(1) *Where:*

(a) *paragraphs (a) and (b) of section 11(1) apply to a relevant disposal affecting any premises to which at the time of the disposal this Part applied (other than a disposal consisting of such a surrender as is mentioned in section 15(1)(b)), and*

(b) *those premises are still premises to which this Part applies,*

the requisite majority of qualifying tenants of the constituent flats may, before the end of the period specified in subsection (2), serve a notice ('a purchase notice') on the new landlord requiring him (except as provided by the following provisions of this Part) to dispose of the estate or interest that was the subject-matter of the original disposal, on the terms on which it was made (including those relating to the consideration payable), to a person or persons nominated for the purposes of this section by any such majority of qualifying tenants of those flats.

(2) *The period referred to in subsection (1) is:*

(a) *in a case where a notice has been served on the new landlord under section 11(1), the period of three months beginning with the date on which a notice is served by him under section 11(3); and*

(b) *in any other case, the period of three months beginning with the date mentioned in section 11(2).*

(3) A purchase notice:

(a) shall, where the estate or interest that was the subject-matter of the original disposal related to any property in addition to the premises to which this Part applied at the time of the disposal:

(i) require the new landlord to dispose of that estate or interest only so far as relating to those premises, and

(ii) require him to do so on the terms referred to in subsection (1) subject to such modifications as are necessary or expedient in the circumstances;

(b) may, instead of specifying the estate or interest to be disposed of or any particular terms on which the disposal is to be made by the new landlord (whether doing so expressly or by reference to the original disposal), provide for that estate or interest, or (as the case may be) for any such terms, to be determined by a rent assessment committee in accordance with section 13.

(4) Where the property which the new landlord is required to dispose of in pursuance of the purchase notice has at any time since the original disposal become subject to any charge or other incumbrance, then, unless the court by order directs otherwise:

(a) in the case of a charge to secure the payment of money or the performance of any other obligation by the new landlord or any other person, the instrument by virtue of which the property is disposed of by the new landlord to the person or persons nominated for the purposes of this section shall (subject to the provisions of Part I of Schedule 1) operate to discharge the property from that charge; and

(b) in the case of any other incumbrance, the property shall be so disposed of subject to the incumbrance but with a reduction in the consideration payable to the new landlord corresponding to the amount by which the existence of the incumbrance reduces the value of the property.

(5) Subsection (4)(a) and Part I of Schedule 1 shall apply, with any necessary modifications, to mortgages and liens as they apply to charges; but nothing in those provisions shall apply to a rentcharge.

(6) Where the property referred to in subsection (4) has at any time since the original disposal increased in monetary value owing to any change in circumstances (other than a change in the value of money), the amount of the consideration payable to the new landlord for the disposal by him of the property in pursuance of the purchase notice shall be the amount that might reasonably have been obtained on a corresponding disposal made on the open market at the time of the original disposal if the change in circumstances had already taken place.

(7) The person or persons initially nominated for the purposes of this section shall be so nominated in the purchase notice; and any such person may only be replaced by another person so nominated by the requisite majority of qualifying tenants of the constituent flats if he has (for any reason) ceased to be able to act as a person so nominated.

(8) Where two or more persons have been so nominated and any of them ceases to act as such a person without being replaced in accordance with subsection (7), any remaining person or persons so nominated shall be entitled to continue to act in his or their capacity as such.

(9) Where, in the exercise of its power to award costs, the court or the Lands Tribunal makes, in connection with any proceedings arising under or by virtue of this Part, an award of costs against the person or person so nominated, the liability for those costs shall be the joint and several

liability of that person or those persons together with the qualifying tenants by whom the relevant purchase notice was served.

13

Determination by rent assessment committees of questions relating to purchase notices

(1) A rent assessment committee shall have jurisdiction to hear and determine:

(a) any question arising in relation to any matters specified in a purchase notice (whether relating to the nature of the estate or interest, or the identity of the property, to be disposed of or relating to any other terms on which the disposal by the new landlord is to be made); and

(b) any question arising for determination in consequence of a provision in a purchase notice such as is mentioned in section 12(3)(b).

(2) An application to a rent assessment committee under this section must [comply with such requirements (if any) as to the form of, or the particulars to be contained in, any such application], as the Secretary of State may by regulations prescribe.

(3) On any application under this section the interests of the persons by whom a purchase notice has been served shall be represented by the nominated person, and accordingly the parties to any such application shall not include those persons.

(4) Any costs incurred by a party to an application under this section in connection with the application shall be borne by that party.

(5) A rent assessment committee shall, when constituted for the purpose of hearing and determining any question falling within subsection (1) above, be known as a leasehold valuation tribunal, and paragraphs 1 to 3 and 7 of Schedule 22 to the Housing Act 1980 (provisions relating to leasehold valuation tribunals) shall accordingly apply to any such committee when so constituted.

(6) In this section and sections 14, 16 and 17 'the nominated person' means (subject to section 15(5)) the person or persons for the time being nominated for the purposes of section 12 by the requisite majority of qualifying tenants of the constituent flats.

14

Withdrawal of nominated person from transaction

(1) Where, at any time before a binding contract is entered into in pursuance of a purchase notice, the nominated person serves a notice on the new landlord indicating an intention no longer to proceed with the disposal required by the purchase notice, the new landlord may recover from that person any costs reasonably incurred by him in connection with that disposal down to the time when the notice is served on him under this subsection.

(2) If, at any such time as is mentioned in subsection (1) above, the nominated person becomes aware that the number of qualifying tenants of the constituent flats desiring to proceed with the disposal required by the purchase notice is less than the requisite majority of those tenants, he shall forthwith serve on the new landlord a notice indicating such an intention as is mentioned in subsection (1), and that subsection shall apply accordingly.

(3) If a notice is served under this section at a time when any proceedings arising under or by virtue of this Part are pending before the court or the Lands Tribunal, the liability of the nominated person for any costs incurred by the new landlord as mentioned in subsection (1) above shall be such as may be determined by the court or (as the case may be) by the Tribunal.

(4) By virtue of section 13(4) the costs that may be recovered by the new landlord under the preceding provisions of this section do not include any costs incurred by him in connection with an application to a rent assessment committee.

(5) Any liability for costs to which a nominated person becomes subject by virtue of this section shall be such a joint and several liability as is mentioned in section 12(9).

(6) Section 13(6) applies for the purposes of this section.

15

Right of qualifying tenants to compel grant of new tenancy by superior landlord

(1) Where:

- *(a) paragraphs (a) and (b) of section 11(1) apply to a relevant disposal affecting any premises to which at the time of the disposal this Part applied, and*
- *(b) the disposal consisted of the surrender by the landlord of a tenancy held by him ('relevant tenancy'), and*
- *(c) those premises are still premises to which this Part applies,*

the requisite majority of qualifying tenants of the constituent flats may, before the end of the period specified in section 12(2), serve a notice on the new landlord requiring him (except as provided by the following provisions of this Part) to grant a new tenancy of the premises subject to the relevant tenancy, on the terms referred to in subsection (2) below and expiring on the date on which that tenancy would have expired, to a person or persons nominated for the purposes of this section by any such majority of qualifying tenants of those flats.

(2) Those terms are:

- *(a) the terms of the relevant tenancy; and*
- *(b) if the new landlord paid any amount to the landlord as consideration for the surrender by him of that tenancy, that any such amount is paid to the new landlord by the person or persons so nominated.*

(3) A notice under this section:

- *(a) shall, where the premises subject to the relevant tenancy included premises other than those to which this Part applied at the time of the original disposal:*
  - *(i) require the new landlord to grant a new tenancy only of the premises to which this Part so applied, and*
  - *(ii) require him to do so on the terms referred to in subsection (2) subject to such modifications as are necessary or expedient in the circumstances;*
- *(b) may, instead of specifying the premises to be demised under the new tenancy or any particular terms on which that tenancy is to be granted by the new landlord (whether doing so expressly or by reference to the relevant tenancy), provide for*

those premises, or (as the case may be) for any such terms, to be determined by a rent assessment committee in accordance with section 13 (as applied by subsection (4) below).

(4) The following provisions, namely:

section 12(7) to (9),

sections 13 and 14, and

sections 16 and 17,

shall apply in relation to a notice under this section as they apply in relation to a purchase notice (whether referred to as such or as a notice served under section 12(1)) but subject to the modifications specified in subsection (5) below.

(5) Those modifications are as follows:

(a) any reference to the purposes of section 12 shall be read as a reference to the purposes of this section;

(b) the reference in section 13(1)(b) to section 12(3)(b) shall be read as a reference to subsection (3)(b) above;

(c) the references in section 16 to the estate or interest that was the subject-matter of the original disposal shall be read as a reference to the estate or interest which, prior to the surrender of the relevant tenancy, constituted the reversion immediately expectant on it; and

(d) the references in sections 16 and 17 to sections 12 to 14 shall be read as references to sections 12(7) to (9), 13 and 14 (as applied by subsection (4) above) and this section.

16

Right of qualifying tenants to compel sale etc by subsequent purchaser

(1) Where, at the time when a notice is served under section 11(1) or 12(1) on the new landlord, he no longer holds the estate or interest that was the subject-matter of the original disposal, then:

(a) in the case of a notice served under section 11(1), the new landlord shall, within the period specified in section 11(3):

(i) furnish such person as is specified in the notice with the information that he is required to furnish by virtue of it, and

(ii) serve on that person a notice informing him of the name and address of the person to whom the new landlord disposed of that estate or interest ('the subsequent purchaser'), and

(iii) serve on the subsequent purchaser a copy of the notice under section 11(1) and of the information furnished by him under sub-paragraph (i) above;

(b) in the case of a notice served under section 12(1), the new landlord shall forthwith:

(i) forward the notice to the subsequent purchaser, and

(ii) serve on the nominated person such a notice as is mentioned in paragraph (a)(ii) above.

(2) If the new landlord serves a notice in accordance with subsection (1)(a)(ii) or (b)(ii) above, sections 12 to 14 shall, instead of applying to the new landlord, apply to the subsequent purchaser as if he were the transferee under the original disposal.

(3) Subsections (1) and (2) above shall have effect, with any necessary modifications, in a case where, instead of disposing of the whole of the estate or interest referred to in subsection (1) to another person, the new landlord has disposed of it in part or in parts to one or more other persons and accordingly sections 12 to 14 shall:

(a) in relation to any part of that estate or interest retained by the new landlord, apply to the new landlord, and

(b) in relation to any part of that estate or interest disposed of to any other person, apply to that other person instead as if he were (as respects that part) the transferee under the original disposal.

(4) Subsection (1) shall not apply in a case where the premises affected by the original disposal have ceased to be premises to which this Part applies.

(5) Section 13(6) applies for the purposes of this section.

Termination of rights against new landlords etc

17

Termination of rights against new landlord or subsequent purchaser

(1) If, at any time after a notice has been served under section 11(1) or 12(1), the premises affected by the original disposal cease to be premises to which this Part applies, the new landlord may serve a notice on the qualifying tenants of the constituent flats stating:

(a) that the premises have ceased to be premises to which this Part applies, and

(b) that any notice served on him under section 11(1) or 12(1), and anything done in pursuance of it, is to be treated as not having been served or done.

(2) Subsection (4) of section 5 shall apply to a notice under subsection (1) above as it applies to a notice under that section, but as if the references to the qualifying tenants on whom such a notice is required to be served by virtue of subsection (1) of that section were references to the qualifying tenants mentioned in subsection (1) above.

(3) Where a period of three months beginning with the date of service of a purchase notice on the new landlord has expired:

(a) without any binding contract having been entered into between the new landlord and the nominated person, and

(b) without there having been made any application in connection with the purchase notice to the court or to a rent assessment committee under section 13,

the new landlord may serve on the nominated person a notice containing such a statement as is mentioned in subsection (1)(b) above.

(4) Where:

- *(a) any such application as is mentioned in paragraph (b) of subsection (3) was made within the period of three months referred to in that subsection, but*
- *(b) a period of two months beginning with the date of the determination of that application has expired, and*
- *(c) no binding contract has been entered into between the new landlord and the nominated person, and*
- *(d) no other such application as is mentioned in subsection (3)(b) is pending,*

the new landlord may serve on the nominated person a notice containing such a statement as is mentioned in subsection (1)(b).

(5) Where the new landlord serves a notice in accordance with subsection (1), (3) or (4), this Part shall cease to have effect in relation to him in connection with the original disposal.

(6) In a case where a new landlord is entitled to serve a notice under subsection (1) above but does not do so, this Part shall continue to have effect in relation to him in connection with the original disposal as if the premises in question were still premises to which this Part applies.

(7) References in this section to the new landlord shall be read as including references to any other person to whom sections 12 to 14 apply by virtue of section 16(2) or (3).

(8) Section 13(6) applies for the purposes of this section.

18 Notices served by prospective purchasers to ensure that rights of first refusal do not arise

(1) Where:

- (a) any disposal of an estate or interest in any premises consisting of the whole or part of a building is proposed to be made by a landlord, and
- (b) it appears to the person who would be the transferee under that disposal ('the purchaser') that any such disposal would, or might, be a relevant disposal affecting premises to which this Part applies,

the purchaser may serve notices under this subsection on the tenants of the flats contained in the premises referred to in paragraph (a) ('the flats affected').

(2) Any notice under subsection (1) shall:

- (a) inform the person on whom it is served of the general nature of the principal terms of the proposed disposal, including in particular:
  - (i) the property to which it would relate and the estate or interest in that property proposed to be disposed of by the landlord, and
  - (ii) the consideration required by him for making the disposal;

(b) invite that person to serve a notice on the purchaser stating:

(i) whether the landlord has served on him, or on any predecessor in title of his, a notice under section 5 with respect to the disposal, and

(ii) if the landlord has not so served any such notice, whether he is aware of any reason why he is not entitled to be served with any such notice by the landlord, and

(iii) if he is not so aware, whether he would wish to avail himself of the right of first refusal conferred by any such notice if it were served; and

(c) inform that person of the effect of the following provisions of this section.

(3) Where the purchaser has served notices under subsection (1) on at least 80 per cent. of the tenants of the flats affected and:

(a) not more than 50 per cent of the tenants on whom those notices have been served by the purchaser have served notices on him in pursuance of subsection (2)(b) by the end of the period of [two months] beginning with the date on which the last of them was served by him with a notice under this section, or

(b) more than 50 per cent. of the tenants on whom those notices have been served by the purchaser have served notices on him in pursuance of subsection (2)(b) but the notices in each case indicate that the tenant serving it either:

(i) does not regard himself as being entitled to be served by the landlord with a notice under section 5 with respect to the disposal, or

(ii) would not wish to avail himself of the right of first refusal conferred by such a notice if it were served,

the premises affected by the disposal shall, in relation to the disposal, be treated for the purposes of this Part as premises to which this Part does not apply.

(4) For the purposes of subsection (3) each of the flats affected shall be regarded as having one tenant, who shall count towards any of the percentages specified in that subsection whether he is a qualifying tenant of the flat or not.

Amendment

Para (3): words in square brackets in sub-para (a) substituted by SI 1996/2371, reg 2.

Supplementary

[18A The requisite majority of qualifying tenants]

[(1) In this Part 'the requisite majority of qualifying tenants of the constituent flats' means qualifying tenants of constituent flats with more than 50 per cent of the available votes.

(2) The total number of available votes shall be determined as follows:

(a) where an offer notice has been served under section 5, that number is equal to the total number of constituent flats let to qualifying tenants on the date when the period specified in that notice as the period for accepting the offer expires;

(b) where a notice is served under section 11A without a notice having been previously served under section 5, that number is equal to the total number of constituent flats let to qualifying tenants on the date of service of the notice under section 11A;

(c) where a notice is served under section 12A, 12B or 12C without a notice having been previously served under section 5 or section 11A, that number is equal to the total number of constituent flats let to qualifying tenants on the date of service of the notice under section 12A, 12B or 12C, as the case may be.

(3) There is one available vote in respect of each of the flats so let on the date referred to in the relevant paragraph of subsection (2), which shall be attributed to the qualifying tenant to whom it is let.

(4) The persons constituting the requisite majority of qualifying tenants for one purpose may be different from the persons constituting such a majority for another purpose.]

Amendment

Inserted by the Housing Act 1996, s 92(1), Sch 6, Part IV, para 2.

19 Enforcement of obligations under Part I

(1) The court may, on the application of any person interested, make an order requiring any person who has made default in complying with any duty imposed on him by any provision of this Part to make good the default within such time as is specified in the order.

(2) An application shall not be made under subsection (1) unless:

(a) a notice has been previously served on the person in question requiring him to make good the default, and

(b) more than 14 days have elapsed since the date of service of that notice without his having done so.

(3) The restriction imposed by section 1(1) may be enforced by an injunction granted by the court.

20 Construction of Part I and power of Secretary of State to prescribe modifications

(1) In this Part:

['acceptance notice' has the meaning given by section 6(3);]

'associated company', in relation to a body corporate, means another body corporate which is (within the meaning of section 736 of the Companies Act 1985) that body's holding company, a subsidiary of that body or another subsidiary of that body's holding company;

['constituent flat' shall be construed in accordance with section 5(1) or 11(2), as the case may require;]

'disposal' [shall be construed in accordance with section 4(3) and section 4A (application of provisions to contracts)] and references to the acquisition of an estate or interest shall be construed accordingly;

'landlord', in relation to any premises, shall be construed in accordance with section 2;

< . . . >

['the nominated person' means the person or persons for the time being nominated by the requisite majority of the qualifying tenants of the constituent flats;]

'offer notice' means a notice served by a landlord under section 5;

'the original disposal' means the relevant disposal referred to in section 11(1);

['the protected interest' means the estate, interest or other subject-matter of an 'offer notice';]

['the protected period' has the meaning given by section 6(4);]

['purchase notice' has the meaning given by section 12B(2);]

['purchaser' has the meaning given by section 11(3);]

'qualifying tenant', in relation to a flat, shall be construed in accordance with section 3;

'relevant disposal' shall be construed in accordance with section 4;

'the requisite majority', in relation to qualifying tenants, shall be construed in accordance with [section 18A];

'transferee', in relation to a disposal, shall be construed in accordance with section 4(3).

(2) In this Part:

(a) any reference to an offer < . . . > is a reference to an offer < . . . > made subject to contract, and

(b) any reference to the acceptance of an offer < . . . > is a reference to its acceptance subject to contract.

(3) Any reference in this Part to a tenant of a particular description shall be construed, in relation to any time when the interest under his tenancy has ceased to be vested in him, as a reference to the person who is for the time being the successor in title to that interest.

(4) The Secretary of State may by regulations make such modifications of any of the provisions of sections 5 to 18 as he considers appropriate, and any such regulations may contain such incidental, supplemental or transitional provisions as he considers appropriate in connection with the regulations.

(5) In subsection (4) 'modifications' includes additions, omissions and alterations.

Amendment

Sub-s (1): definitions 'acceptance notice', 'constituent flat', 'the protected interest', and 'purchase notice' substituted, definitions 'the nominated person', 'the protected period', and 'purchaser' inserted, in definitions 'disposal' and 'the requisite majority' words in square brackets substituted, and definition 'the new landlord' repealed, by the Housing Act 1996, ss 89(3), 92(1), 227, Sch 6, Part IV, para 3, Sch 19, Part III.
Sub-s (2): words omitted repealed by the Housing Act 1996, ss 92(1), 227, Sch 6, Part IV, para 4, Sch 19, Part III.

The Landlord and Tenant Act 1987, Part VII

52 Jurisdiction of county courts

(1) A county court shall have jurisdiction to hear and determine any question arising under any provision to which this section applies (other than a question falling within the jurisdiction of a [leasehold valuation tribunal] by virtue of section 13(1) or 31(1)).

(2) This section applies to:

(a) any provision of [Parts I, III and IV];

(b) any provision of section 42; and

(c) any provision of sections 46 to 48.

(3) Where any proceedings under any provision to which this section applies are being taken in a county court, the county court shall have jurisdiction to hear and determine any other proceedings joined with those proceedings, notwithstanding that the other proceedings would, apart from this subsection, be outside the court's jurisdiction.

(4) If a person takes any proceedings under any such provision in the High Court he shall not be entitled to recover any more costs of those proceedings than those to which he would have been entitled if the proceedings had been taken in a county court; and in any such case the taxing master shall have the same power of directing on what county court scale costs are to be allowed, and of allowing any item of costs, as the judge would have had if the proceedings had been taken in a county court.

(5) Subsection (4) shall not apply where the purpose of taking the proceedings in the High Court was to enable them to be joined with any proceedings already pending before that court (not being proceedings taken under any provision to which this section applies).

Amendment

Sub-s (1): words in square brackets substituted by the Housing Act 1996, s 92(1), Sch 6, Part IV, para 6.
Sub-s (2): words in square brackets substituted by the Housing Act 1996, s 86(6).
Sub-ss (4), (5): prospectively repealed by the Courts and Legal Services Act 1990, s 125(7), Sch 20, as from a day to be appointed.

[52A Jurisdiction of leasehold valuation tribunal under Part I or II]

[(1) Any jurisdiction conferred by Part I or III of this Act on a leasehold valuation tribunal is exercisable by a rent assessment committee constituted in accordance with Schedule 10 to the Rent Act 1977 which when so constituted for the purposes of exercising any such jurisdiction shall be known as a leasehold valuation tribunal.

(2) The power to make regulations under section 74(1)(b) of the Rent Act 1977 (procedure of rent assessment committees) extends to prescribing the procedure to be followed in connection with any proceedings before a leasehold valuation tribunal under this Act.

(3) Any application under this Act to a leasehold valuation tribunal must be in such form, and contain such particulars, as the Secretary of State may by regulations prescribe.

(4) Any costs incurred by a party to any such application in connection with the application shall be borne by that party.

(5) Paragraphs 1, 2, 3 and 7 of Schedule 22 to the Housing Act 1980 (supplementary provisions relating to leasehold valuation tribunals: constitution, appeals and provision of information) apply to a leasehold valuation tribunal constituted for the purposes of this section.]

Amendment

Inserted by the Housing Act 1996, s 92(1), Sch 6, Part IV, para 7.

53 Regulations and orders

(1) Any power of the Secretary of State to make an order or regulations under this Act shall be exercisable by statutory instrument and may be exercised so as to make different provision for different cases, including different provision for different areas.

(2) A statutory instrument containing:

- (a) an order made under section 1(5), 25(6), 42(5) or 55, or
- (b) any regulations made under [section 52A(3)] or under section 20(4),

shall be subject to annulment in pursuance of a resolution of either House of Parliament.

Amendment

Sub-s (2): words in square brackets substituted by the Housing Act 1996, s 92(1), Sch 6, Part IV, para 8.

54 Notices

(1) Any notice required or authorised to be served under this Act:

- (a) shall be in writing; and
- (b) may be sent by post.

(2) Any notice purporting to be a notice served under any provision of Part I or III by the requisite majority of any qualifying tenants (as defined for the

purposes of that provision) shall specify the names of all of the persons by whom it is served and the addresses of the flats of which they are qualifying tenants.

(3) The Secretary of State may by regulations prescribe:

(a) the form of any notices required or authorised to be served under or in pursuance of any provision of Parts I to III, and

(b) the particulars which any such notices must contain (whether in addition to, or in substitution for, any particulars required by virtue of the provision in question).

(4) Subsection (3)(*b*) shall not be construed as authorising the Secretary of State to make regulations under subsection (3) varying [any of the periods specified in section 5A(4) or (5), 5B(5) or (6), 5C(4) or (5), 5D(4) or (5) or 5E(3)] (which accordingly can only be varied by regulations under section 20(4)).

Amendment

Sub-s (4): words in square brackets substituted by the Housing Act 1996, s 92(1), Sch 6, Part IV, para 9.

55 Application to Isle of Scilly

This Act shall apply to the Isles of Scilly subject to such exceptions, adaptations and modifications as the Secretary of State may by order direct.

56 Crown land

(1) This Act shall apply to a tenancy from the Crown if there has ceased to be a Crown interest in the land subject to it.

(2) A variation of any such tenancy effected by or in pursuance of an order under section 38 shall not, however, be treated as binding on the Crown, as a predecessor in title under the tenancy, by virtue of section 39(1).

(3) Where there exists a Crown interest in any land subject to a tenancy from the Crown and the person holding that tenancy is himself the landlord under any other tenancy whose subject-matter comprises the whole or part of that land, this Act shall apply to that other tenancy, and to any derivative sub-tenancy, notwithstanding the existence of that interest.

(4) For the purposes of this section 'tenancy from the Crown' means a tenancy of land in which there is, or has during the subsistence of the tenancy been, a Crown interest superior to the tenancy, and 'Crown interest' means:

(a) an interest comprised in the Crown Estate;

(b) an interest belonging to Her Majesty in right of the Duchy of Lancaster;

(c) an interest belonging to the Duchy of Cornwall;

(d) any other interest belonging to a government department or held on behalf of Her Majesty for the purposes of a government department.

57 Financial provision

There shall be paid out of money provided by Parliament any increase attributable to this Act in the sums payable out of money so provided under any other Act.

58 Exempt landlords and resident landlords

(1) In this Act 'exempt landlord' means a landlord who is one of the following bodies, namely:

(a) a district, county[, county borough] or London borough council, the Common Council of the City of London, [the London Fire and Emergency Planning Authority,] the Council of the Isles of Scilly, [a police authority established under [section 3 of the Police Act 1996]][, the Service Authority for the National Criminal Intelligence Service, the Service Authority for the National Crime Squad] < . . . > , or a joint authority established by Part IV of the Local Government Act 1985;

(b) the Commission for the New Towns or a development corporation established by an order made (or having effect as if made) under the New Towns Act 1981;

(c) an urban development corporation within the meaning of Part XVI of the Local Government, Planning and Land Act 1980;

[(ca) a housing action trust established under Part III of the Housing Act 1988];

(d) < . . . >

[(dd) the Broads Authority;]

[(de) a National Park authority;]

(e) the Housing Corporation;

[(ea) < . . . >];

(f) a housing trust (as defined in section 6 of the Housing Act 1985) which is a charity;

[(g) a registered social landlord, or a fully mutual housing association which is not a registered social landlord; or]

(h) an authority established under section 10 of the Local Government Act 1985 (joint arrangements for waste disposal functions).

[(1A) In subsection (1)(g):

'fully mutual housing association' has the same meaning as in the Housing Associations Act 1985 (see section 1(1) and (2) of that Act); and 'registered social landlord' has the same meaning as in the Housing Act 1985 (see section 5(4) and (5) of that Act).]

(2) For the purposes of this Act the landlord of any premises consisting of the whole or part of a building is a resident landlord of those premises at any time if:

(a) the premises are not, and do not form part of, a purpose-built block of flats; and

(b) at that time the landlord occupies a flat contained in the premises as his only or principal residence; and

(c) he has so occupied such a flat throughout a period of not less than 12 months ending with that time.

(3) In subsection (2) 'purpose-built block of flats' means a building which contained as constructed, and contains, two or more flats.

Amendment

Sub-s (1): in para (a) words, 'county borough' in square brackets inserted by the Local Government (Wales) Act 1994, s 22(2), Sch 8, para 8.
Sub-s (1): in para (a) words 'the London Fire and Emergency Planning Authority', in square brackets inserted by the Greater London Authority Act 1999, s 328, Sch 29, Pt I, para 48.
Date in force: 3 July 2000: see SI 2000/1094, art 4(h).
Sub-s (1): in para (a) words beginning with the words 'a police authority established under' in square brackets inserted by the Police and Magistrates' Courts Act 1994, s 43, Sch 4, para 61.
Sub-s (1): in para (a) words 'section 3 of the Police Act 1996' in square brackets substituted by the Police Act 1996, s 103, Sch 7, para 1(2)(z).
Sub-s (1): in para (a) words from, 'the Service Authority' to 'National Crime Squad' in square brackets inserted by the Police Act 1997, s 134(1), Sch 9, para 52.
Sub-s (1): in para (a) words omitted repealed by the Education Reform Act 1988, s 237, Sch 13, Pt I.
Sub-s (1): para (ca) inserted by the Housing Act 1988, s 119, Sch 13, para 7.
Sub-s (1): para (d) repealed by the Government of Wales Act 1998, s 152, Sch 18, Pt IV.
Date in force: 1 October 1998: see SI 1998/2244, art 4.
Sub-s (1): para (dd) inserted by the Norfolk and Suffolk Broads Act 1988, s 21, Sch 6, para 28.
Sub-s (1): para (de) inserted by the Environment Act 1995, s 78, Sch 10, para 26.
Sub-s (1): para (ea) inserted by the Housing Act 1988, s 140, Sch 17, Pt II.
Sub-s (1): para (ea) repealed by the Government of Wales Act 1998, s 152, Sch 18, Pt VI.
Date in force: 1 November 1998: see SI 1998/2244, art 5.
Sub-s (1): para (g) substituted by SI 1996/2325, art 5, Sch 2, para 17(2).
Sub-s (1A): inserted by SI 1996/2325, art 5, Sch 2, para 17(3).

59 Meaning of 'lease', 'long lease' and related expressions

(1) In this Act 'lease' and 'tenancy' have the same meaning; and both expressions include:

- (a) a sub-lease or sub-tenancy, and
- (b) an agreement for a lease or tenancy (or for a sub-lease or sub-tenancy).

(2) The expressions 'landlord' and 'tenant', and references to letting, to the grant of a lease or to covenants or the terms of a lease shall be construed accordingly.

(3) In this Act 'long lease' means:

- (a) a lease granted for a term certain exceeding 21 years, whether or not it is (or may become) terminable before the end of that term by notice given by the tenant or by re-entry or forfeiture;
- (b) a lease for a term fixed by law under a grant with a covenant or obligation for perpetual renewal, other than a lease by sub-demise from one which is not a long lease; or
- (c) a lease granted in pursuance of Part V of the Housing Act 1985 (the right to buy)[, including a lease granted in pursuance of that Part as it has effect by virtue of section 17 of the Housing Act 1996 (the right to acquire)].

Amendment

Sub-s (3): words in square brackets in para (c) inserted by SI 1997/627, art 4, Schedule, para 5.

60 General interpretation

(1) In this Act:

'the 1985 Act' means the Landlord and Tenant Act 1985;

'charity' means a charity within the meaning of [the Charities Act 1993], and 'charitable purposes', in relation to a charity, means charitable purposes whether of that charity or of that charity and other charities;

'common parts', in relation to any building or part of a building, includes the structure and exterior of that building or part and any common facilities within it;

'the court' means the High Court or a county court;

'dwelling' means a building or part of a building occupied or intended to be occupied as a separate dwelling, together with any yard, garden, outhouses and appurtenances belonging to it or usually enjoyed with it;

'exempt landlord' has the meaning given by section 58(1);

'flat' means a separate set of premises, whether or not on the same floor, which:

(a) forms part of a building, and

(b) is divided horizontally from some other part of that building, and

(c) is constructed or adapted for use for the purposes of a dwelling;

'functional land', in relation to a charity, means land occupied by the charity, or by trustees for it, and wholly or mainly used for charitable purposes;

'landlord' (except for the purposes of Part I) means the immediate landlord or, in relation to a statutory tenant, the person who, apart from the statutory tenancy, would be entitled to possession of the premises subject to the tenancy;

'lease' and related expressions shall be construed in accordance with section 59(1) and (2);

'long lease' has the meaning given by section 59(3);

'mortgage' includes any charge or lien, and references to a mortgagee shall be construed accordingly;

'notices in proceedings' means notices or other documents served in, or in connection with, any legal proceedings;

< . . . >

'resident landlord' shall be construed in accordance with section 58(2);

'statutory tenancy' and 'statutory tenant' mean a statutory tenancy or statutory tenant within the meaning of the Rent Act 1977 or the Rent (Agriculture) Act 1976;

'tenancy' includes a statutory tenancy.

(2) < . . . >

Amendment

Sub-s (1): in definition 'charity' words in square brackets substituted by the Charities Act 1993, s 98(1), Sch 6, para 30; definition 'rent assessment committee' repealed by the Housing Act 1996, ss 92(1), 227, Sch 6, Part IV, para 10, Sch 19, Part III. Sub-s (2): repealed by the Housing Act 1988, s 140, Sch 18.

61 Consequential amendments and repeals

(1) The enactments mentioned in Schedule 4 shall have effect subject to the amendments there specified (being amendments consequential on the preceding provisions of this Act).

(2) The enactments mentioned in Schedule 5 are hereby repealed to the extent specified in the third column of that Schedule.

62 Short title, commencement and extent

(1) This Act may be cited as the Landlord and Tenant Act 1987.

(2) This Act shall come into force on such day as the Secretary of State may by order appoint.

(3) An order under subsection (2):

- (a) may appoint different days for different provisions or for different purposes; and
- (b) may make such transitional, incidental, supplemental or consequential provision or saving as the Secretary of State considers necessary or expedient in connection with the coming into force of any provision of this Act or the operation of any enactment which is repealed or amended by a provision of this Act during any period when the repeal or amendment is not wholly in force.

(4) This Act extends to England and Wales only.

The Landlord and Tenant Act 1987, Schedule 1, Part I

Construction

1

In this Part of this Schedule:

'the consideration payable' means the consideration payable to *the new landlord* [the purchaser] for the disposal by him of the property referred to in *section 12(4)* [section 12B(7)];

['the purchaser'] has the same meaning as in section 12, and accordingly includes any person to whom that section applies by virtue of [section 16(4) or (5)]; and

'the nominated person' means the person or persons nominated as mentioned in [section 12B(2)].

Duty of nominated person to redeem mortgages

2

(1) Where in accordance with [section 12B(5)(a)] an instrument will operate to discharge any property from a charge to secure the payment of money, it shall be the duty of the nominated person to apply the consideration payable, in the first instance, in or towards the redemption of any such charge (and, if there are more than one, then according to their priorities).

(2) Where sub-paragraph (1) applies to any charge or charges, then if (and only if) the consideration payable is applied by the nominated person in accordance with that sub-paragraph or paid into court by him in accordance with paragraph 4, the instrument in question shall operate as mentioned in sub-paragraph (1) notwithstanding that the consideration payable is insufficient to enable the charge or charges to be redeemed in its or their entirety.

(3) Subject to sub-paragraph (4), sub-paragraph (1) shall not apply to a charge which is a debenture holders' charge, that is to say, a charge (whether a floating charge or not) in favour of the holders of a series of debentures issued by a company or other body of persons, or in favour of trustees for such debenture holders; and any such charge shall be disregarded in determining priorities for the purposes of sub-paragraph (1).

(4) Sub-paragraph (3) above shall not have effect in relation to a charge in favour of trustees for debenture holders which at the date of the instrument by virtue of which the property is disposed of by [the purchaser] is (as regards that property) a specific and not a floating charge.

Determination of amounts due in respect of mortgages

3

(1) For the purpose of determining the amount payable in respect of any charge under paragraph 2(1), a person entitled to the benefit of a charge to which

that provision applies shall not be permitted to exercise any right to consolidate that charge with a separate charge on other property.

(2) For the purpose of discharging any property from a charge to which paragraph 2(1) applies, a person may be required to accept three months or any longer notice of the intention to pay the whole or part of the principal secured by the charge, together with interest to the date of payment, notwithstanding that the terms of the security make other provision or no provision as to the time and manner of payment; but he shall be entitled, if he so requires, to receive such additional payment as is reasonable in the circumstances in respect of the costs of re-investment or other incidental costs and expenses and in respect of any reduction in the rate of interest obtainable on re-investment.

Payments into court

4

(1) Where under [section 12B(5)(a)] any property is to be discharged from a charge and, in accordance with paragraph 2(1), a person is or may be entitled in respect of the charge to receive the whole or part of the consideration payable, then if:

(a) for any reason difficulty arises in ascertaining how much is payable in respect of the charge, or

(b) for any reason mentioned in sub-paragraph (2) below difficulty arises in making a payment in respect of the charge,

the nominated person may pay into court on account of the consideration payable the amount, if known, of the payment to be made in respect of the charge or, if that amount is not known, the whole of that consideration or such lesser amount as the nominated person thinks right in order to provide for that payment.

(2) Payment may be made into court in accordance with sub-paragraph (1)(a) where the difficulty arises for any of the following reasons, namely:

(a) because a person who is or may be entitled to receive payment cannot be found or ascertained;

(b) because any such person refuses or fails to make out a title, or to accept payment and give a proper discharge, or to take any steps reasonably required of him to enable the sum payable to be ascertained and paid;

(c) because a tender of the sum payable cannot, by reason of complications in the title to it or the want of two or more trustees or for other reasons, be effected, or not without incurring or involving unreasonable cost or delay.

(3) Without prejudice to sub-paragraph (1)(a), the whole or part of the consideration payable shall be paid into court by the nominated person if, before execution of the instrument referred to in paragraph 2(1), notice is given to him:

(a) that [the purchaser] or a person entitled to the benefit of a charge on the property in question requires him to do so for the purpose of protecting the rights of persons so entitled, or for reasons related to the bankruptcy or winding up of [the purchaser], or

(b) that steps have been taken to enforce any charge on [the purchaser's] interest in that property by the bringing of proceedings in any court, or by the appointment of a receiver or otherwise;

and where payment into court is to be made by reason only of a notice under this sub-paragraph, and the notice is given with reference to proceedings in a court specified in the notice other than a county court, payment shall be made into the court so specified.

Savings

5

(1) Where any property is discharged by [section 12B(5)(a)] from a charge (without the obligations secured by the charge being satisfied by the receipt of the whole or part of the consideration payable), the discharge of that property from the charge shall not prejudice any right or remedy for the enforcement of those obligations against other property comprised in the same or any other security, nor prejudice any personal liability as principal or otherwise of [the purchaser] or any other person.

(2) Nothing in this Schedule shall be construed as preventing a person from joining in the instrument referred to in paragraph 2(1) for the purpose of discharging the property in question from any charge without payment or for a lesser payment than that to which he would otherwise be entitled; and, if he does so, the persons to whom the consideration payable ought to be paid shall be determined accordingly.

Amendment

Paras 1, 2, 4, 5: words in square brackets substituted by the Housing Act 1996, s 92(1), Sch 6, Part IV, para 11.

Rent Assessment Committee (England and Wales) (Leasehold Valuation Tribunal) Regulations 1993

(Preamble)

The Secretary of State for the Environment, as respects England, and the Secretary of State for Wales, as respects Wales, in exercise of the powers conferred upon them by section 21(4A) of the Leasehold Reform Act 1967, section 74(1) of the Rent Act 1977, sections 13(2) and 31(5) of the Landlord and Tenant Act 1987, and sections 75(4), 88(5) and 91(6) of the Leasehold Reform, Housing and Urban Development Act 1993 and of all other powers enabling them in that behalf, and after consultation with the Council on Tribunals, hereby make the following Regulations

1

These Regulations may be cited as the Rent Assessment Committee (England and Wales) (Leasehold Valuation Tribunal) Regulations 1993 and shall come into force on 1st November 1993.

2

[In these Regulations:

'applicant' means:

(i) the person making an application to a tribunal, or

(ii) the plaintiff in proceedings before a court where the court has ordered the transfer to the tribunal of so much of the proceedings as relate to the determination of a question falling within the jurisdiction of the tribunal;]

['application' means an application to a tribunal under:

section 21(1) of the Leasehold Reform Act 1967 (jurisdiction of leasehold valuation tribunals);

section 19 of the Landlord and Tenant Act 1985 (determination of reasonableness of service charges;

section 20C of that Act (limitation of service charges: costs of proceedings);

paragraph 8 of the Schedule to that Act (right to challenge landlord's choice of insurers);

section 13 of the Landlord and Tenant Act 1987 (determination of questions by leasehold valuation tribunal);

Part II of that Act (appointment of manager by leasehold valuation tribunal);

section 31 of that Act (determination by leasehold valuation tribunal of terms where acquisition order);

Part I of the 1993 Act (collective enfranchisement and grant of new lease) and includes, except where the contrary is indicated, a scheme application; or

a transferred application;

'Part II application' means an application for an order under section 22(3), section 24(1) or section 24(9) of the Landlord and Tenant Act 1987 (appointment of manager);]

'party' includes (as regards a scheme application) two or more landlords or a representative body under section 71 (applications by two or more landlords or by representative body) of the 1993 Act, and the relevant authority for the purposes of section 73 (applications by certain public bodies) of that Act;

'person making representations' means such a person as is mentioned in section 70(6) of the 1993 Act;

['representative application' has the meaning given in regulation 4C(1);

'respondent' means the person against whom the applicant seeks an order or determination and in a case which is transferred to the tribunal from a court it means the defendant or respondent in the court application;]

['scheme application' means an application under:

(a) section 19 of the Leasehold Reform Act 1967 (retention of management powers for general benefit of neighbourhood) as it has effect by virtue of section 75 of the 1993 Act (variation of existing schemes), or

(b) Chapter IV of Part I of the 1993 Act, including that Chapter as it has effect by virtue of section 118(1) of the Rousing Act 1996 (estate management schemes in connection with enfranchisement by virtue of section 106),

'transferred application' means so much of proceedings before a court as relate to a question falling within the jurisdiction of the tribunal which have been transferred to the tribunal for determination by order of the court;

'1985 Act application' means an application under section 19, section 20C of, or paragraph 8 of the Schedule to, the Landlord and Tenant Act 1985;]

'the 1993 Act' means the Leasehold Reform, Housing and Urban Development Act 1993; and

'tribunal' means a leasehold valuation tribunal.

Amendment

Words 'In these Regulations—' and definition 'applicant' substituted, for words 'In these Regulations—' as originally enacted, definitions 'application' and 'Part

II application' substituted, for definition 'application' as originally enacted, definitions 'representative application' and 'respondent' inserted, and definitions 'scheme application', 'transferred application' and '1985 Act application' substituted, for definition 'scheme application' as originally enacted, by SI 1997/1854, reg 3.

3

(1) The particulars to be included in an application, except a scheme application, [a 1985 Act application and a Part II application,] are those specified in Schedule 1 to these Regulations.

(2) The particulars to be included in a scheme application are those specified in Schedule 2 to these Regulations.

Amendment

Para (1): words in square brackets inserted by SI 1997/1854, reg 4.
[ss 4A–4F are here]

[4G]

[(1) The tribunal may, whether of their own motion or on an application by a party, order a pre-trial review to be held in respect of an application.

(2) At the pre-trial review the tribunal shall:

- (a) give any direction that appears to the tribunal necessary or desirable for securing the just, expeditious and economical disposal of proceedings,
- (b) endeavour to secure that the parties make all such admissions and agreements as ought reasonably to be made by them in relation to the proceedings, and
- (c) may record in the order made on the pre-trial review any such admission or agreement or any refusal to make such admission or agreement.

(3) Where a party seeks a specific direction he shall, so far as is practicable, apply for such a direction at the pre-trial review and shall give the tribunal not less than 7 days' notice (or such shorter period as the tribunal may allow) of his intention to do so.

(4) Where the tribunal has received notice of any specific direction which a party intends to seek at the pre-trial review the tribunal shall give every other party notice of the requested direction.

(5) The functions of the tribunal in relation to, or at, a pre-trial review may be exercised by any single member of the panel provided for in Schedule 10 to the Rent Act 1977 who was appointed to that panel by the Lord Chancellor.]

Amendment

Inserted by SI 1997/1854, reg 5.

[4H]

[In any case where a fee which is payable for an application, a transferred application or a hearing is not paid, the tribunal shall not proceed further until the fee is paid and where a fee is unpaid for a period of six months from the date of the request for payment issued by the tribunal the application shall be treated as withdrawn.]

Amendment

Inserted by SI 1997/1854, reg 5.

5

(1) [Subject to regulations 4C(3), 4D(3) and 4E(3),] a hearing shall be on the date and at the time and place appointed by the tribunal.

(2) The tribunal shall give notice of the appointed date, time and place to the parties not less than 21 days (or such shorter period as the parties may agree) before the appointed date, and the tribunal shall send a copy of the notice:

- (a) to any other person who has indicated to the tribunal an intention to appear at the hearing; and
- (b) in the case of a scheme application, to any person making representations.

(3) The notice shall contain a statement that an appeal to the Lands Tribunal may only be made by a person who appeared before the tribunal in proceedings to which he was a party.

(4) The tribunal may, where they consider it appropriate, arrange that an application shall be heard together with one or more other applications.

(5) A hearing shall be in public unless, for special reasons, the tribunal decide that a hearing or part of a hearing should be held in private.

Amendment

Para (1): words in square brackets inserted by SI 1997/1854, reg 6.

6

At a hearing:

- (a) the tribunal shall determine the procedure (subject to these Regulations), and the order in which the persons appearing before them are to be heard;

(b) a person appearing before the tribunal may do so either in person or by a representative authorised by him, whether or not that representative is of counsel or a solicitor; and

(c) a person appearing before the tribunal may give evidence on his own behalf, call witnesses, and cross-examine any witnesses called by any other person appearing.

7

If a party or person mentioned in regulation 5(2) does not appear at a hearing, the tribunal may proceed with the hearing if they are satisfied that notice has been given to that party or person in accordance with these Regulations.

8

(1) The tribunal may postpone or adjourn a hearing at their discretion either of their own motion, or at the request of the parties or of one or more of the persons appearing before them, but they shall not do so at the request of one party or person except where they consider it reasonable to do so having regard to the grounds for the request, the time at which the request is made and the convenience of the other persons appearing before them.

(2) The tribunal shall give reasonable notice of any postponed or adjourned hearing to the persons appearing before them.

9

(1) Before the date of a hearing, the tribunal shall take all reasonable steps to ensure that each of the parties and persons making representations is given:

(a) a copy of, or sufficient extracts from or particulars of, any document relevant to the proceedings which has been received from a party or person making representations (other than a document already in the possession of that party or one of which he has previously been supplied with a copy); and

(b) a copy of any document which embodies the results of any enquiries made by or for the tribunal for the purposes of the proceedings.

(2) At a hearing, if a person appearing before the tribunal does not have in his possession a relevant document or a copy of, or sufficient extracts from or particulars of, a relevant document, then unless:

(a) that person consents to the continuation of the hearing; or

(b) the tribunal consider that that person has a sufficient opportunity to deal with the document without an adjournment of the hearing,

the tribunal shall adjourn the hearing for a period which they consider will give that person a sufficient opportunity to deal with the document.

10

(1) The tribunal may (subject to any necessary consent being obtained) inspect the house, premises or area which are the subject of the proceedings.

(2) An inspection may be made before, during or after the close of a hearing, as the tribunal may decide, and the tribunal shall give the persons appearing before them an opportunity to attend.

(3) Notice of an inspection shall be given as if it were notice of a hearing, but the requirements for notice may be dispensed with or relaxed with the consent of the persons appearing before the tribunal or if the tribunal are satisfied that such persons have received sufficient notice.

(4) Where an inspection is made after the close of a hearing, the tribunal shall, if they consider it expedient to do so on account of any matter arising from the inspection, reopen the hearing; and if the hearing is to be reopened regulation 5(2) shall apply as it applied to the original hearing, except that its requirements may be dispensed with or relaxed with the consent of the parties and persons mentioned in regulation 5(2) or if the tribunal are satisfied that such parties and persons have received sufficient notice.

(5) This regulation shall apply, so far as is reasonable and practicable, to any comparable house, premises or area to which the attention of the tribunal is directed.

11

(1) The decision of the tribunal shall be recorded in a document signed by the chairman of the tribunal (or, in the event of his absence or incapacity, by another member of the tribunal) which shall contain the reasons for the decision.

(2) The chairman (or, in the event of his absence or incapacity, another member of the tribunal) shall have power, by certificate under his hand, to correct any clerical mistakes in the document or any errors arising in it from an accidental slip or omission.

(3) A copy of the document and of any such correction shall be sent by the tribunal to each party and person making representations.

[11A]

[Where the tribunal is considering requiring any party to the proceedings to reimburse any other party to the proceedings the whole or part of any fees paid by him to the tribunal in respect of the proceedings, the tribunal shall not make any such requirement unless the tribunal has:

- (a) given notice to the parties that the tribunal is considering making such a requirement,
- (b) given notice to the parties of the appointed date, time and place at which the tribunal will consider the representations of the parties

in respect of the making of such a requirement which shall be not less than 21 (or such shorter period as the parties may agree) days before the appointed date, and

(c) has considered the representations of the parties.]

Amendment

Inserted by SI 1997/1854, reg 7.

[11B]

[Where a party makes an application to a tribunal for leave to appeal to the Lands Tribunal:

(a) the application for leave shall be made to the tribunal within the period of 21 days starting on the date on which the determination which is the subject of the application was sent to that party by the tribunal (or such further period as the tribunal may allow), and

(b) an application for leave to appeal shall be served by the tribunal on every other party to the hearing.]

Amendment

Inserted by SI 1997/1854, reg 7.

12

Nothing in these Regulations shall prevent a member of the Council on Tribunals in that capacity from attending any hearing or inspection or from being present during the tribunal's deliberations as to their decision; but a member of the Council on Tribunals may not take part in such deliberations.

13

(1) Where a tribunal requires information to be given under paragraph 7 of Schedule 22 to the Housing Act 1980, the notice shall contain a statement to the effect that any person who fails without reasonable cause to comply with the notice is liable on summary conviction to a fine not exceeding level 3 on the standard scale.

(2) Paragraph (1) above shall not apply in the case of a notice addressed to an appropriate authority in relation to a Crown interest.

14

Where any notice or other document is required under these Regulations to be given or sent by the tribunal, it shall be sufficient compliance with these Regulations if the notice or other document is sent by pre-paid post or by facsimile transmission addressed to the person for whom it is intended at his usual or last known address or (if a person has appointed an agent to act on his behalf) to his agent at the address of the agent supplied to the tribunal.

[14A]

[If any person to whom any notice or other document is required to be given or sent under these regulations:

(a) cannot be found after all diligent enquiries have been made,

(b) has died and has no personal representative,

(c) is out of the United Kingdom and there is no known address for service in England and Wales, or

(d) for any other reason service upon him cannot readily be effected in accordance with these regulations,

the tribunal may dispense with service upon that person, or may give directions for substituted service in such other form (whether by advertisement in a newspaper or otherwise) as the tribunal may think fit.]

Schedule 1

PARTICULARS TO BE INCLUDED IN APPLICATIONS

1

The address of the property which is the subject of the application.

2

A statement of the purpose of the application, identifying the relevant statutory provision.

3

The name and address of the applicant.

4

The name, address and profession of the applicant's representative, if any.

5

Whether the applicant is the reversioner or other freeholder or landlord, nominated person, nominee purchaser, or tenant; or, if none of the former, the capacity in which the applicant makes the application.

6

The name and address of the respondent and whether the respondent is the reversioner or other freeholder or landlord, nominated person, nominee purchaser or tenant; or, if none of the former, the capacity of the respondent.

7

If the respondent is not the freeholder, the name and address of the freeholder.

8

The name and address of any intermediate landlord, which the applicant knows or could reasonably obtain.

9

The name and address of any person having a mortgage or other charge over an interest in the property held by the freeholder or other landlord, which the applicant knows or could reasonably obtain.

10

Copies of:

(a) any lease;

(b) any notice served by any party;

(c) any application to court or court order; and

(d) any other document

which are relevant to the application and which the applicant has or could reasonably obtain.

11

Any terms which have already been determined or agreed between the parties, including a copy of any draft conveyance or lease.

12

Any terms which are in dispute.

13

If an amount or price is in dispute, the amount or price which the applicant considers to be appropriate.

14

If the application is for determination of the amount of compensation payable under section 17 or 18 of the Leasehold Reform Act 1967, details of the circumstances under which the claim for compensation arises.

15

If the application includes an application for determination of the amount of a sub-tenant's share of compensation under section 21(2) of the Leasehold Reform Act 1967, the name and address of the sub-tenant, and a copy of any agreement for a sub-tenancy.

[15A

If the application is made under subsection (4) of section 8C (election in case of disposal for non-monetary consideration) of the Landlord and Tenant Act 1987, particulars of the non-monetary consideration.]

16

If the application is made under section 13 of the Landlord and Tenant Act 1987, the date on which the landlord acquired the property, and the terms of acquisition, including the sums paid.

17

If the application is made under the Landlord and Tenant Act 1987 or under the 1993 Act, a map or plan showing the property and any appurtenant property which is relevant to the application.

18

If the application is for apportionment of an amount under section 91(2)(e) of the 1993 Act, the circumstances by which the need for apportionment arises, and the apportionment which the applicant considers to be appropriate.

19

If the application relates to the grant of leases back to a former freeholder under Schedule 9 to the 1993 Act, the name and address of any secure tenant, [introductory tenant,] tenant under housing association tenancy, or sub-tenant to whose interests the tribunal is required to have particular regard.

20

The date of the application.

Amendment

Para 15A: inserted by SI 1996/2305, reg 2(b).
Para 19: words in square brackets inserted by SI 1997/74, art 2, Schedule, para 11.

Lands Tribunal Rules 1996

(Preamble)

The Lord Chancellor, in exercise of the powers conferred on him by section 3 of the Lands Tribunal Act 1949 and by section 84(3A) of the Law of Property Act 1925, after consultation with the Council on Tribunals in accordance with section 8(1) of the Tribunals and Inquiries Act 1992, hereby makes the following Rules:

Part 1
Preliminary

1 Citation and commencement

These Rules may be cited as the Lands Tribunal Rules 1996 and shall come into force on 1st May 1996.

2 Interpretation

(1) In these Rules:

'the Act' means the Lands Tribunal Act 1949;

'the 1961 Act' means the Land Compensation Act 1961;

['appeal' means an appeal against a determination of any question by an authority in respect of whose decision an appeal lies to the Lands Tribunal;]

'authority' means the person or body in respect of whose decision an appeal is brought;

'the office' means the office for the time being of the Lands Tribunal;

'party' in relation to an appeal, means the appellant, the authority and any person who has served notice of intention to respond in accordance with rule 7;

'the President' means the President of the Lands Tribunal, or the member appointed under section 2(3) of the Act to act for the time being as deputy for the President;

'proceedings' means proceedings before the Lands Tribunal;

'rating appeal' means an appeal from the decision of a valuation tribunal in relation to non-domestic rating;

'the registrar' means the registrar of the Lands Tribunal or, as respects any powers or functions of the registrar, an officer of the Lands Tribunal authorised by the Lord Chancellor to exercise those powers or functions;

'the Tribunal' means the member or members of the Lands Tribunal selected under section 3(2) of the Act to deal with a case;

'valuation officer' means a valuation officer appointed under section 61 of the Local Government Finance Act 1988 or any officer authorised by him in writing to act on his behalf;

(2) In these Rules, a form referred to by number alone means the form so numbered in Schedule 1 to these Rules.

Amendment

Definition 'appeal' substituted by SI 1997/1965, r 3.

Part II
Composition and Hearings of the Tribunal

3 Selection and powers of members of Tribunal

(1) The President may at any time substitute a member of the Lands Tribunal for a member that he has previously selected to sit as the Tribunal or as a member of the Tribunal to hear a case.

(2) Where members of the Lands Tribunal have been selected for a class or group of cases under the provisions of section 3(2) of the Act, the President may from time to time vary the members selected.

(3) Where the President has appointed a member of the Lands Tribunal to be the chairman of any members selected under paragraphs (1) or (2) the chairman shall have the same power as the President to substitute or vary the members selected.

(4) A member of the Tribunal selected to hear a case shall have power to do anything, in relation to that case, which the President has power to do under these Rules.

4 Notice of hearings and sittings of the Tribunal

(1) The registrar shall, as soon as practicable after the commencement of proceedings before the Tribunal, send to each party a notice informing him of the date, time and place of the hearing.

(2) Upon receipt of a notice of intention to respond from a person who is not already a party to the proceedings, the registrar shall send to that person a notice informing him of the date, time and place of the hearing.

5 Hearings to be in public: exceptions

(1) All hearings by the Tribunal shall be in public except where:

(a) it is acting as an arbitrator under a reference by consent under section 1(5) of the Act; or

(b) it is satisfied that, by reason of disclosure of confidential matters or matters concerning national security, it is just and reasonable for the hearing or any part of the hearing to be in private.

(2) The following persons shall be entitled to attend a hearing whether or not it is in private:

(a) the President or any member of the Tribunal notwithstanding that they do not constitute the Tribunal for the purpose of the hearing; and

(b) a member of the Council on Tribunals.

(3) The Tribunal, with the consent of the parties, may permit any other person to attend a hearing which is held in private.

[Part IIA
Applications for Leave to Appeal]

[5A Application of Part IIA]

[Part IIA applies to applications to the Lands Tribunal for leave to appeal against a decision of the Leasehold Valuation Tribunal under section 31A of the Landlord and Tenant Act 1985 or section 24A of the Landlord and Tenant Act 1987.]

Amendment

Inserted by SI 1997/1965, r 4.

[5B Interpretation]

[(1) A respondent to an application for leave to appeal is any party in the proceedings before the Leasehold Valuation Tribunal, other than the applicant, who was present or represented at the hearing before that Tribunal.

(2) A respondent to an application for leave to appeal shall not be a respondent to any subsequent appeal unless he gives notice of intention to respond to the appeal in accordance with rule 7.]

Amendment

Inserted by SI 1997/1965, r 4.

[5C Application for leave to appeal]

[(1) A person ('the applicant') may only apply to the Lands Tribunal for leave to appeal if he has made an application to the Leasehold Valuation Tribunal for such leave and that application has been refused.

(2) An application for leave must be made to the Lands Tribunal within 28 days of the date on which the decision of the Leasehold Valuation Tribunal to refuse leave to appeal was sent to the applicant.

(3) The application for leave shall contain:

- (a) the name and address of the applicant;
- (b) the name and address of every respondent;
- (c) the grounds of appeal against the decision in respect of which leave to appeal is sought;
- (d) where the applicant is represented, the name, address and profession of the representative; and
- (e) the signature of the applicant or his representative and the date the application was signed.

(4) The application for leave shall be accompanied by:

- (a) a copy of the decision against which leave to appeal is being sought;
- (b) a copy of the decision of the Leasehold Valuation Tribunal refusing leave to appeal;
- (c) the fee payable to the Lands Tribunal in respect of the proposed appeal.

(5) The applicant shall deliver or send the application for leave to appeal to the Lands Tribunal together with sufficient copies for service upon each respondent.

(6) Upon receiving an application for leave to appeal the registrar shall:

- (a) serve a copy of the application on each respondent;
- (b) inform the applicant of the date on which this was done; and
- (c) enter details of the application in the register of appeals.

(7) The registrar shall, when serving a copy of the application, notify each respondent of the time limit, specified by the Tribunal, within which any written representations relating to the application must be made to the Tribunal.]

Amendment

Inserted by SI 1997/1965, r 4.

[5D Determination of application]

[(1) The Tribunal shall determine an application for leave without a hearing unless it considers that there are special circumstances which make a hearing necessary or desirable.

(2) The registrar shall serve on the applicant and each respondent a notice recording the decision of the Tribunal on the application for leave.]

Amendment

Inserted by SI 1997/1965, r 4.

[5E Refusal of leave to appeal]

[If the Tribunal refuses leave to appeal the registrar shall refund to the applicant the fee paid in respect of the appeal.]

Amendment

Inserted by SI 1997/1965, r 4.

[5F Leave to appeal]

[(1) If the Tribunal grants leave to appeal it may do so on such conditions as it thinks fit including conditions relating to the costs of the appeal.

(2) The registrar shall note in the register of appeals that the appeal is proceeding unless the applicant notifies him, within 14 days of the date of service of the notice recording the decision to grant leave, that he does not wish to proceed with the appeal.

(3) The registrar shall serve notice on each respondent that the appeal is proceeding with details of the number of the appeal entered on the register which shall constitute the title of the appeal.]

Amendment

Inserted by SI 1997/1965, r 4.

[5G Application of Part III (Appeals)]

[Where an appeal proceeds following the grant of leave to appeal under this Part:

- (a) rule 6 shall not apply to the appeal; and
- (b) rule 7 shall apply as if the reference to the notice of appeal was a reference to the notice that the appeal is proceeding referred to in rule 5F(3).]

Amendment

Inserted by SI 1997/1965, r 4.

[5H Application of Part III (General Procedure)]

[In Part VIII, reference to an appeal shall include reference to an application for leave to appeal under this Part.]

Amendment

Inserted by SI 1997/1965, r 4.

Part III
Appeals

6 Notice of appeal

[(1) An appeal to the Lands Tribunal shall be made by sending to the registrar a written notice indicating an intention to appeal so that it is received by the registrar:

- (a) within 28 days of the date on which the decision appealed against ('the disputed decision') was sent to the applicant, or within such other time as is prescribed by the enactment conferring the right to appeal; or
- (b) where the appeal is made following the grant of leave to appeal by the authority, within 28 days of the date on which the decision granting leave to appeal was sent to the applicant.]

(2) Where the notice referred to in paragraph (1) does not conform with the requirements set out in paragraph (3), the appellant shall, within such time as the registrar may direct, send to the registrar a notice which does so conform.

(3) The notice of appeal shall state that it is a notice of appeal and shall contain:

- (a) the name and address of the appellant;
- (b) the date and any reference number of the disputed decision and the name and address of the Authority;
- (c) the grounds of appeal;
- (d) where the appellant is represented, the name, address and profession of the representative; and
- (e) the signature of the appellant or his representative and the date the notice was signed.

[(4) The appellant shall attach to the notice of appeal:

- (a) a copy of the disputed decision; and
- (b) where the appeal is made following grant of leave to appeal by the authority, a copy of the decision granting leave to appeal; and
- (c) where the appeal relates to a rating appeal, a copy of the proposal or determination that was the subject of the proceedings which led to the disputed decision.]

(5) The appellant shall deliver or send the notice of appeal to the Lands Tribunal together with sufficient copies for service upon each of the parties to the proceedings which led to the disputed decision and upon the authority, and where appropriate, the valuation officer.

(6) Upon receiving a notice of appeal the registrar shall:

- (a) enter particulars of the appeal in the [register of appeals];
- (b) serve a copy of the notice on the parties to the proceedings which led to the disputed decision other than the appellant, on the authority and, where applicable, on the valuation officer and inform the appellant of the date on which this was done; and
- (c) inform the appellant and all persons on whom a copy of the notice of appeal is served of the number of the appeal entered on the Register which shall constitute the title of the appeal.

Amendment

Paras (1), (4): substituted by SI 1997/1965, rr 5, 6.
Para (6): words in square brackets in sub-para (a) substituted by SI 1997/1965, r 7.

7 Notice of intention to respond

(1) If a person on whom a copy of the notice of appeal is served intends to respond, he shall give written notice of his intention, signed and dated, stating:

- (a) whether he intends to respond separately or jointly with some other person;
- (b) the grounds on which he opposes the appeal; and
- (c) an address for service of notices and other documents on him.

(2) The notice of intention to respond shall be served on the registrar and the appellant within 28 days of the date of service of the copy of the notice of appeal.

(3) Where the registrar receives more than one notice of intention to respond, he shall serve a copy of each such notice on all parties other than the appellant.

8 Statement of case

(1) A person giving notice of intention to respond is, in this rule, called a 'respondent'.

(2) Within 28 days of service of a notice of intention to respond, the appellant shall serve on the respondent from whom it is received, a statement of his case, including full particulars of the facts relied upon and any points of law on which he intends to rely at the hearing.

(3) Within 28 days of service of the appellant's statement, a respondent shall serve on the appellant a reply stating his case including full particulars of the facts relied upon and any points of law on which he intends to rely at the hearing.

(4) Where a party receives from the registrar a copy of a notice of intention to respond from another party in accordance with rule 7(3), he shall, within 28 days of service of such notice on him, send to that other party a copy of the reply referred to in paragraph (3).

(5) Where a party serves a statement or reply in accordance with paragraphs (2) or (3), he shall at the same time send a copy to the registrar with confirmation that the statement or reply has been served in accordance with this rule.

(6) A statement or reply served in accordance with this rule shall be accompanied by:

(a) every valuation which the party proposes to put in evidence (which shall include all particulars and computations in support of the valuation), or a statement of the value or values which the parties have agreed, and

(b) either:

(i) full particulars of any comparable properties and transactions to which the party intends to refer at the hearing in support of his case and a statement of the purpose for which the comparison is made; or

(ii) a statement that no comparable properties or transactions will be referred to.

(7) If at the hearing of an appeal a party seeks to rely upon any valuation or other document which appears to the Tribunal not to have been served in accordance with this rule, it may adjourn the hearing on such terms as to costs or otherwise as it thinks fit.

[Parts IV, V, VI and VII follow]

Part VIII
General Procedure

27 Determination of proceedings without a hearing

(1) The Tribunal may, with the consent of the parties to the proceedings, order that the proceedings be determined without an oral hearing.

(2) Where the Tribunal makes an order under paragraph (1), any party to the proceedings may submit written representations to the Tribunal.

(3) On or after making an order under paragraph (1), the Tribunal shall give such directions relating to the lodging of documents and representations as it considers appropriate.

(4) Rule 42 shall apply to proceedings to which this rule applies as if references to the calling of witnesses and the hearing of evidence in that rule were references to representations.

(5) The Tribunal may at any time, on the application of a party to the proceedings or of its own motion, order that the proceedings should be heard and in that event may give directions for the disposal of the proceedings in accordance with these Rules.

28 Simplified procedure

(1) A member or the registrar may, with the consent of the applicant or appellant or, in relation to proceedings under Part IV, the consent of the person who is claiming compensation, direct that proceedings shall be determined in accordance with this rule.

(2) The registrar shall send a copy of any direction made under paragraph (1) on all the parties to the proceedings and any party who objects to the direction may, within 7 days of service of the copy on him, send written notice of his objection to the registrar.

(3) Rule 38(6) to (9) and (11) shall apply as appropriate where an objection is received by the registrar under paragraph (2).

(4) Paragraphs (5) to (12) shall apply to proceedings in respect of which the registrar has made a direction under paragraph (1).

(5) Where the proceedings relate to an appeal under Part III, rule 8 shall not apply.

(6) The registrar shall:

- (a) give directions concerning the filing and contents of a statement of claim by the applicant or appellant and a reply by the other parties to the proceedings; and
- (b) give the parties not less than 21 days' notice of the day fixed for the hearing of the proceedings.

(7) The following directions shall take effect:

- (a) each party shall, not less than 14 days before the date fixed for the hearing, send to every other party copies of all documents in his possession on which he intends to rely at the hearing; and
- (b) each party shall not less than 7 days before the date fixed for the hearing send to the registrar and to every other party a copy of any expert report on which he intends to rely at the hearing and a list of the witnesses whom he intends to call at the hearing.

(8) The registrar may from time to time, whether on application or of his own motion, amend or add to any direction issued if he thinks it necessary to do so in the circumstances of the case.

(9) The hearing shall be informal and shall take place before a single member of the Lands Tribunal who shall act as if he were an arbitrator and who shall adopt any procedure that he considers to be fair.

(10) Strict rules of evidence shall not apply to the hearing and evidence shall not be taken on oath unless the Tribunal orders otherwise.

(11) No award shall be made in relation to the costs of the proceedings except in cases to which section 4 of the 1961 Act apply, save that the Tribunal may make an award of costs

(a) in cases where an offer of settlement has been made by a party and the Tribunal considers it appropriate to have regard to the fact that such an offer has been made; or

(b) in cases in which the Tribunal regards the circumstances as exceptional,

and if, exceptionally, an award of costs is made the amount shall not exceed that which would be allowed if the proceedings had been heard in a county court.

(12) The Tribunal may at any time, on the application of a party to the proceedings or of its own motion, order that this rule shall no longer apply to the proceedings and in that event may give directions for the disposal of the proceedings in accordance with these Rules.

29 Site inspections

(1) Subject to paragraph (2), the Tribunal may enter and inspect:

(a) the land or property which is the subject of proceedings, and

(b) as far as is practicable, any comparable land or property to which the attention of the Tribunal is drawn.

(2) When the Tribunal intends to enter any premises in accordance with paragraph (1) it shall give notice to the parties who shall be entitled to be represented at the inspection; where the Tribunal deems it appropriate, such representation shall be limited to one person to represent those parties having the same interest in the proceedings.

[29A Assessors]

[(1) If it appears to the President that any case coming before the Tribunal calls for special knowledge he may direct that the Tribunal shall hear the case with the aid of one or more assessors appointed by him.

(2) The remuneration to be paid to an assessor appointed under this rule shall be determined by the President with the approval of the Treasury.]

Amendment

Inserted, in relation to proceedings commenced before 1 February 1998 as well as to proceedings commenced on or after that date, by SI 1998/22, rr 3, 5.
Date in force: 1 February 1998: see SI 1998/22, r 1.

30 Consolidation of proceedings

(1) Where two or more notices of appeal, references or applications have been made which:

(a) are in respect of the same land or buildings; or

(b) relate to different interests in the same land or buildings; or

(c) raise the same issues;

the President or the Tribunal may, on his or its own motion or on the application of a party to the proceedings, order that the appeals, references or applications be consolidated or heard together.

(2) An order may be made with respect to some only of the matters to which the appeals, references or applications relate.

31 Power to select test case of appeals or references

(1) Where the President is of the opinion that two or more appeals or references involve the same issues he may, with the written consent of all the parties to the appeals or references, select one or more appeal or reference to be heard in the first instance as a test case or test cases and the parties to each appeal or reference shall be bound by the decision of the Tribunal on that appeal or reference.

(2) Paragraph (1) is without prejudice to the right of the parties to each appeal or reference to require the Tribunal to state a case for the decision of the Court of Appeal.

[32 Application of Arbitration Act 1996]

[The following provisions of the Arbitration Act 1996 shall apply to all proceedings as they apply to an arbitration:

(a) section 47 (awards on different issues, etc), as if the words 'unless otherwise agreed by the parties' were omitted from subsection (1) and so that the reference to 'award' shall include a reference to any decision of the Lands Tribunal;

(b) section 49 (interest) subject to any enactment that prescribes a rate of interest;

(c) section 57(3) to (7) (correction of award or additional award);]

[(d) section 66 (enforcement of the award).]

Amendment

Substituted by SI 1997/1965, r 9.
Para (d): inserted, in relation to proceedings commenced before 1 February 1998 as well as to proceedings commenced on or after that date, by SI 1998/22, rr 4, 5.
Date in force: 1 February 1998: see SI 1998/22, r 1.

33 Evidence

(1) Evidence before the Tribunal may be given orally and may be on oath or affirmation or, if the parties to the proceedings consent or the Tribunal or President so orders, by affidavit.

(2) Notwithstanding paragraph (1), the Tribunal may at any stage of the proceedings require the personal attendance of any deponent for examination or cross-examination.

(3) Paragraphs (2) to (7) of rule 38 shall apply to an application to the President for leave to give evidence by affidavit but as if for 'registrar' in those paragraphs there were substituted 'President'.

(4) Nothing in the Civil Evidence Act 1972, or in rules of court made under it, shall prevent expert evidence from being given before the Tribunal by any party even if no application has been made to the Tribunal for a direction as to the disclosure of that evidence to any other party to the proceedings.

34 Power to order discovery etc

(1) The Tribunal, or subject to any directions given by the Tribunal, the registrar may, on the application of any party to the proceedings or of its or his own motion, order any party:

- (a) to deliver to the registrar any document or information which the Tribunal may require and which it is in the power of the party to deliver;
- (b) to afford to every other party to the proceedings an opportunity to inspect those documents (or copies of them) and to take copies;
- (c) to deliver to the registrar an affidavit or make a list stating whether any document or class of document specified or described in the order or application is, or has at any time been in his possession, custody or power and stating when he parted with it;
- (d) to deliver to the registrar a statement in the form of a pleading setting out further and better particulars of the grounds on which he intends to rely and any relevant facts or contentions;
- (e) to answer interrogatories on affidavit relating to any matter at issue between the applicant and the other party;
- (f) to deliver to the registrar a statement of agreed facts, facts in dispute and the issue or issues to be tried by the Tribunal; or
- (g) to deliver to the registrar witness statements or proofs of evidence.

(2) Where an order is made under paragraph (1) the Tribunal or registrar may give directions as to the time within which any document is to be sent to the registrar (being at least 14 days from the date of the direction) and the parties to whom copies of the document are to be sent.

(3) Rule 38 shall apply to this rule as appropriate both in relation to applications and where the registrar acts of his own motion.

35 Extension of time

(1) The time appointed by or under these Rules for doing any act or taking any steps in connection with any proceedings may be extended on application to the registrar under rule 38.

(2) The registrar may extend the time limit on such terms as he thinks fit and may order an extension even if the application is not made until after the time limit has expired.

36 Appellant limited to grounds of appeal

(1) On the hearing of an appeal under Part III or of an application under Part V, the appellant or applicant may rely only on the grounds stated in his notice of appeal, statement of case or application unless the Tribunal permits additional grounds to be put forward.

(2) If the Tribunal permits additional grounds to be put forward in accordance with paragraph (1) it may do so on such terms as to costs, adjournment or otherwise as it thinks fit.

37 Right of audience

(1) Subject to paragraph (2), in any proceedings a party may appear in person or be represented by counsel or solicitor or by any other person with the leave of the Tribunal, or, in the case of an interlocutory application, the leave of the President or the registrar.

(2) Where a valuation officer is a party to proceedings, he may not appear in person except with the leave of the Tribunal or, in the case of an interlocutory application, the leave of the President or the registrar.

38 Interlocutory applications

(1) Except where these Rules make other provision or the President otherwise orders, an application for directions of an interlocutory nature in connection with any proceedings shall be made to the registrar.

(2) The application shall be made in writing and shall state the title of the proceedings, and the grounds upon which the application is made.

(3) If the application is made with the consent of all parties, it shall be accompanied by consents signed by or on behalf of the parties.

(4) If the application is not made with the consent of every party the applicant shall serve a copy of the proposed application on every other party before it is made and the application shall state that this has been done.

(5) A party who objects to an application may, within 7 days of service of a copy on him, send written notice of his objection to the registrar.

(6) Before making an order on an application the registrar shall consider all the objections that he has received and may allow any party who wishes to appear before him the opportunity to do so.

(7) In dealing with an application the registrar shall have regard to the convenience of all the parties and the desirability of limiting so far as practicable the costs of the proceedings and shall inform the parties in writing of his decision.

(8) The registrar may refer the application to the President for a decision and he shall do so if requested by the applicant or a party objecting to the application.

(9) A party may appeal to the President from a decision of the registrar under this rule by giving written notice to the registrar within 7 days of service of the notice of decision or such further time as the registrar may allow.

(10) An appeal under paragraph (9) shall not act as a stay of proceedings unless the President so orders.

(11) Where an application under this rule is made:

- (a) with respect to a case that has been included by the President in a class or group of cases under section 3(2) of the Act, or
- (b) with respect to a case for which a member or members of the Lands Tribunal has or have been selected,

the powers and duties of the President under this rule may be exercised and discharged in relation to the application by any member or members of the Lands Tribunal authorised by the President for that purpose.

39 Pre-trial review

(1) The Tribunal and, subject to any direction given by the Tribunal, the registrar may, on the application of a party to the proceedings or of its or his own motion order a pre-trial review to be held and the registrar shall send to each party to the proceedings a notice informing him of the place and date of the pre-trial review.

(2) Unless the parties agree otherwise, the date of the pre-trial review shall be not less than 14 days from the making of the order that the pre-trial review should be held.

(3) The Tribunal or the registrar:

- (a) shall at the pre-trial review give any direction that appears necessary or desirable for securing the just, expeditious and economical disposal of the proceedings; and
- (b) shall at the pre-trial review endeavour to secure that the parties make all such admissions and agreements as ought reasonably to be made by them in relation to the proceedings;
- (c) may record in the order made on the review any admission or agreement made under sub-paragraph (b) or any refusal to make any admission or agreement.

(4) Where a party seeks a specific direction he shall, so far as is practicable, apply for such direction at the pre-trial review and shall give the registrar and every other party notice of his intention to do so.

(5) If an application which might have been made at the pre-trial review is made subsequently the applicant shall pay the costs of and occasioned by the application unless the Tribunal considers that there was sufficient reason for the application not having been made at the review.

(6) Paragraphs (6) to (11) of rule 38 shall apply to a pre-trial review as if it were an interlocutory application.

(7) If any party does not appear at the pre-trial review the Tribunal or the registrar may, after giving the parties the opportunity to be heard, make such order as may be appropriate for the purpose of expediting or disposing of the proceedings.

40 Certificates of value

A party may apply in writing to the registrar for a certificate of value under section 35 of the 1961 Act and shall provide the registrar, at his request, with the information necessary to enable the certificate to be given.

41 Administration of oaths

The registrar and the Tribunal shall have power to administer oaths and take affirmations for the purpose of affidavits to be used in proceedings or for the purpose of the giving of oral evidence at hearings.

42 Expert witnesses

(1) This rule applies to any proceedings except an application for a certificate under Part VI.

(2) Subject to paragraph (3), only one expert witness on either side shall be heard unless the Tribunal orders otherwise.

(3) Where the proceedings relate to mineral valuations or business disturbance, not more than two expert witnesses on either side shall be heard unless the Tribunal orders otherwise.

(4) An application for leave to call more than the number of expert witnesses permitted by this rule may be made to the registrar in accordance with rule 38, or to the Tribunal at the hearing.

(5) A party shall, within 28 days of receiving a request from the registrar, send to him and to the other parties to the proceedings a copy of each of the following documents relating to the evidence to be given by each expert witness:

- (a) the expert witness's report, including every plan and valuation of the land or property to which the proceedings relate (which shall include full particulars and computations in support of the valuation) which it is proposed to put in evidence; and

(b) either:

(i) full particulars of any comparable properties and transactions to which the party intends to refer at the hearing in support of his case and a statement of the purpose for which the comparison is made; or

(ii) a statement that no comparable properties or transactions will be referred to.

(6) If:

(a) an application for leave under paragraph (4) is made at the hearing and granted by the Tribunal; or

(b) at the hearing any party seeks to rely on documents not sent to the registrar or to the other parties in accordance with paragraph (5);

the Tribunal may adjourn the hearing on such terms as to costs or otherwise as it thinks fit.

43 Preliminary issues

(1) The President or the Tribunal may, on the application of any party to proceedings, order any preliminary issue in the proceedings to be disposed of at a preliminary hearing.

(2) If in the opinion of the Tribunal the decision on the preliminary issue disposes of the proceedings, it may order that the preliminary hearing shall be treated as the hearing of the case or may make such other order as it thinks fit.

(3) Paragraphs (2) to (7) of rule 38 shall apply to an application under paragraph (1) above as if for 'registrar' in those paragraphs there were substituted 'President'.

44 Sealed offers

(1) Where any party unconditionally offers or is ready to accept, any sum as compensation or by way of price, or to agree a rent or a rateable value, a copy of the offer or indication of the readiness to accept enclosed in a sealed cover may be sent to the registrar or delivered to the Tribunal at the hearing by the party who made the offer or indicated the readiness to accept and shall be opened by the Tribunal after it has determined the proceedings.

(2) An offer or an indication of readiness to accept which is sent to the registrar or delivered to the Tribunal in accordance with paragraph (1), shall not be disclosed to the Tribunal until it has decided the amount of such sum, rent or rateable value.

45 Withdrawal or dismissal of appeal etc, before hearing

(1) An appeal, reference or application may be withdrawn by sending to the registrar a written notice of withdrawal signed by all parties to the proceedings or by their representatives.

(2) A party may, at any time before the hearing of the proceedings, apply to the President for an order to dismiss the proceedings and the President may make such order as he thinks fit.

(3) Paragraphs (2) and (4) to (7) of rule 38 shall apply to an application under paragraph (2) as if for 'registrar' there were substituted 'President'.

46 Failure to pursue proceedings or comply with Rules

(1) If it appears to the Tribunal that any party to proceedings has failed to send a copy of any document to any other party or to the registrar as required by these Rules, it may:

(a) direct that a copy be sent;

(b) adjourn the further hearing of the proceedings; and

(c) require the party at fault to pay any additional costs occasioned as a result of the failure.

(2) Where a party has failed to pursue any proceedings with due diligence or has failed to comply with any of the provisions of these Rules, the registrar [or the Tribunal], on the application of any party or of his [or its] own motion, after giving the parties an opportunity to be heard may make:

(a) an order that the proceedings be heard by the Tribunal; or

(b) an order that the proceedings be dismissed or that any party be debarred from taking any further part in the proceedings; or

(c) such other order as may be appropriate for expediting or disposing of the proceedings including an order for costs.

(3) Paragraphs (9) and (10) of rule 38 shall apply to any order made by the registrar under paragraph (2).

Amendment

Para (2): words in square brackets inserted by SI 1997/1965, r 10.

47 Failure to comply with the Rules not to render proceedings invalid

Any failure by any person to comply with these Rules shall not render the proceedings or anything done in pursuance of them invalid unless the President or the Tribunal so directs.

48 Procedure at hearing

Subject to these Rules and to any direction by the President, the procedure at the hearing of any proceedings shall be such as the Tribunal may direct.

49 Default of appearance at hearing

(1) If on an appeal under Part III or an application under Part V the appellant or applicant fails to attend or be represented at the hearing the Tribunal may dismiss the appeal or application.

(2) If any party to proceedings referred to in paragraph (1) other than the appellant or applicant, or any party to a reference under Part IV fails to attend or be represented at the hearing, the Tribunal may hear and determine the appeal, application or reference in his absence and may make such order as to costs as it thinks fit.

(3) Where proceedings have been dismissed or determined under this rule, the Tribunal may, on the application of the party who has failed to attend within 7 days of the dismissal or determination, if it is satisfied that he had sufficient reason for his absence, set aside the dismissal or determination on such terms as to costs as it thinks fit.

50 Decision of Tribunal

(1) Subject to paragraph (2), the decision of the Tribunal on an appeal, reference or application shall be given in writing, and shall state the reasons for the decision.

(2) The Tribunal may give its decision orally in cases where it is satisfied that this would not result in any injustice or inconvenience to the parties.

(3) The Tribunal may, and on the application of any party to the proceedings shall, issue an order incorporating its decision.

(4) Where an amount awarded or value determined by the Tribunal is dependent upon the decision of the Tribunal on a question of law which is in dispute in the proceedings, the Tribunal shall ascertain, and shall state in its decision, any alternative amount or value which it would have awarded or determined if it had come to a different decision on the point of law.

(5) [The Registrar shall serve] a copy of the decision or, where the decision is given orally an order stating its effect, [on every party] who has appeared before the Tribunal in the proceedings, and:

- (a) in the case of an appeal against the decision of a valuation tribunal to the clerk of that tribunal and, if the appeal is a rating appeal, to the valuation officer;
- (b) in the case of any other appeal under Part III, to the authority.

(6) If the Court of Appeal directs that any decision of the Tribunal, on which a case has been stated for the decision of the Court of Appeal, should be amended the registrar shall send copies of the amended decision to every person who was notified of the original decision.

Amendment

Para (5): words in square brackets substituted by SI 1997/1965, r 11.

51 Consent orders

Where the parties to proceedings have agreed the terms of an order to be made by the Tribunal, particulars of those terms signed by all the parties or by their representatives shall be sent to the registrar and an order may be made by the Tribunal in accordance with those terms in the absence of the parties.

52 Costs

(1) Subject to the provisions of section 4 of the 1961 Act and of rule 28(11), the costs of and incidental to any proceedings shall be in the discretion of the Tribunal.

(2) The registrar may make an order as to costs in respect of any application or proceedings heard by him.

(3) A person dissatisfied with the order of the registrar under paragraph (2) may, within 10 days of the order, appeal to the President who may make such order as to the payment of costs, including the costs of the appeal, as he thinks fit.

(4) If the Tribunal directs that the costs of a party to the proceedings be paid by another party it may settle the amount of costs by fixing a lump sum or direct that the costs be taxed by the registrar on such basis as the Tribunal thinks fit, being a basis that would be applied on a taxation of the costs of High Court or county court proceedings.

(5) A party dissatisfied with a taxation of costs under paragraph (4) may, within 7 days of the taxation, serve on any other interested party and on the registrar written objection specifying the items objected to and applying for the taxation to be reviewed in respect of those items.

(6) Upon such application the registrar shall review the taxation of the items objected to and shall state in writing the reasons for his decision.

(7) A person dissatisfied with the decision of the registrar under paragraph (6) may, within 10 days of the decision, apply to the President to review the taxation and the President may make such order as he thinks fit including an order as to payment of the costs of the review.

(8) Paragraphs (8) and (10) of rule 38 shall apply to any application under this rule.

53 Solicitor to be on the record

(1) Where a solicitor commences or responds to proceedings on behalf of a party to those proceedings he shall be noted on the record of the Tribunal as acting for that party.

(2) A party who has previously carried on proceedings in person may appoint a solicitor at any time to act on his behalf and if he does so shall notify the Tribunal who shall note on the record that the solicitor is acting for that party.

(3) A party who has previously been represented by a solicitor may change his solicitor at any time, or may decide to continue the proceedings in person but unless such change or decision is notified to the Tribunal the former solicitor shall be considered the representative of the party until the conclusion of the proceedings.

(4) The notifications referred to in paragraphs (2) and (3) may be given by the party or his solicitor and the person giving the notification shall send a copy to every other party to the proceedings.

(5) A solicitor who is on the record of the Tribunal as acting for a party shall be responsible for the payment of all fees of the Tribunal which are the responsibility of that party whilst he remains on the record.

54 Service of notices

(1) Every party to proceedings shall notify the registrar of an address for service of documents on him.

(2) Where a party to proceedings is represented by a person other than a solicitor he shall:

- (a) send to the registrar written authority for that representative to act on his behalf; and
- (b) notify the registrar if the representative ceases to act on his behalf and, if replaced, shall give the registrar details of the new representative together with the written authority for the new representative to act on his behalf.

(3) Any document to be served on any person under these Rules shall be deemed to have been served if sent by pre-paid post to that person at his address for service.

(4) Any document to be sent to the registrar under these Rules shall be sent to him at the office.

(5) Any application or communication to be made to the President or to any member of the Lands Tribunal in respect of any case shall be addressed to the registrar at the office.

55 Change of address

A party to any proceedings may at any time by notice in writing to the registrar and to every other party to the proceedings change his address for service under these Rules.

56 Substituted service

If any person to whom any notice or other document is required to be sent under these Rules:

(a) cannot be found after all diligent enquiries have been made;

(b) has died and has no personal representative; or

(c) is out of the United Kingdom;

or for any other reason service upon him cannot readily be effected in accordance with these Rules, the President or the Tribunal may dispense with service upon that person or make an order for substituted service in such other form (whether by advertisement in a newspaper or otherwise) as the President or Tribunal may think fit.

Part IX
Transitional Provisions

57 Transitional provisions, repeals, etc

(1) The Rules shall apply to proceedings commenced before the date on which they come into force as well as to proceedings commenced on or after that date.

(2) The Rules set out in Schedule 2 are hereby revoked.

[Sch 1 follows here]

SCHEDULE 2
REVOCATIONS

(1)	(2)
Rules revoked	**References**
The Lands Tribunal Rules 1975	SI 1975/299
The Lands Tribunal (Amendment) Rules 1977	SI 1977/1820
The Lands Tribunal (Amendment) Rules 1981	SI 1981/105
The Lands Tribunal (Amendment No 2) Rules 1981	SI 1981/600
The Lands Tribunal (Amendment) Rules 1984	SI 1984/793
The Lands Tribunal (Amendment) Rules 1986	SI 1986/1322
The Lands Tribunal (Amendment) Rules 1990	SI 1990/1382

Civil Procedure Rules 1998, Part 8

Rule 8.1 Types of claim in which Part 8 procedure may be followed

(1) The Part 8 procedure is the procedure set out in this Part.

(2) A claimant may use the Part 8 procedure where:

- (a) he seeks the court's decision on a question which is unlikely to involve a substantial dispute of fact; or
- (b) paragraph (6) applies.

(3) The court may at any stage order the claim to continue as if the claimant had not used the Part 8 procedure and, if it does so, the court may give any directions it considers appropriate.

(4) Paragraph (2) does not apply if a practice direction provides that the Part 8 procedure may not be used in relation to the type of claim in question.

(5) Where the claimant uses the Part 8 procedure he may not obtain default judgment under Part 12.

(6) A rule or practice direction may, in relation to a specified type of proceedings:

- (a) require or permit the use of the Part 8 procedure; and
- (b) disapply or modify any of the rules set out in this Part as they apply to those proceedings.

(Rule 8.9 provides for other modifications to the general rules where the Part 8 procedure is being used).

Rule 8.2 Contents of the claim form

Where the claimant uses the Part 8 procedure the claim form must state:

- (a) that this Part applies;
- (b)
  - (i) the question which the claimant wants the court to decide; or
  - (ii) the remedy which the claimant is seeking and the legal basis for the claim to that remedy;
- (c) if the claim is being made under an enactment, what that enactment is;
- (d) if the claimant is claiming in a representative capacity, what that capacity is; and
- (e) if the defendant is sued in a representative capacity, what that capacity is.

(Part 22 provides for the claim form to be verified by a statement of truth).

(Rule 7.5 provides for service of the claim form).

[(The costs practice direction sets out the information about a funding arrangement to be provided with the claim form where the claimant intends to seek to recover an additional liability).

('Funding arrangement' and 'additional liability' are defined in rule 43.2).]

Amendment

Third and fourth cross-references inserted by SI 2000/1317, r 5.
Date in force: 3 July 2000 (with transitional provisions relating to proceedings started in respect of a claim the subject of a funding arrangement entered into before that date): see SI 2000/1317, rr 1, 39.

[Rule 8.2A Issue of claim form without naming defendants]

[(1) A practice direction may set out the circumstances in which the court may give permission for a claim form to be issued under this Part without naming a defendant.

(2) An application for permission must be made by application notice before the claim form is issued.

[(1) A practice direction may set out the circumstances in which a claim form may be issued under this Part without naming a defendant.

(2) The practice direction may set out those cases in which an application for permission must be made by application notice before the claim form is issued.]

(3) The application notice for permission:

- (a) need not be served on any other person; and
- (b) must be accompanied by a copy of the claim form that the applicant proposes to issue.

(4) Where the court gives permission it will give directions about the future management of the claim.]

Amendment

Inserted by SI 2000/221, r 5.
Date in force: 2 May 2000: see SI 2000/221, r 1(b).
Paras (1), (2): substituted by SI 2001/256, r 5.
Date in force: 26 March 2001: see SI 2001/256, r 1(a).

Rule 8.3 Acknowledgment of service

(1) The defendant must:

- (a) file an acknowledgment of service in the relevant practice form not more than 14 days after service of the claim form; and

(b) serve the acknowledgment of service on the claimant and any other party.

(2) The acknowledgment of service must state:

(a) whether the defendant contests the claim; and

(b) if the defendant seeks a different remedy from that set out in the claim form, what that remedy is.

(3) The following rules of Part 10 (acknowledgment of service) apply:

(a) rule 10.3(2) (exceptions to the period for filing an acknowledgment of service); and

(b) rule 10.5 (contents of acknowledgment of service).

(4) Part 11 (disputing the court's jurisdiction) applies subject to the modification that in rule 11(4)(a) and (5)(b) (time limit for application disputing court's jurisdiction) references to the period for filing a defence are treated as if they were references to a period of 14 days from the filing of an acknowledgment of service.

[(The costs practice direction sets out the information about a funding arrangement to be provided with the acknowledgment of service where the defendant intends to seek to recover an additional liability).

('Funding arrangement' and 'additional liability' are defined in rule 43.2).]

Amendment

First and second cross-references inserted by SI 2000/1317, r 6.
Date in force: 3 July 2000 (with transitional provisions relating to proceedings started in respect of a claim the subject of a funding arrangment entered into before that date): see SI 2000/1317, rr 1, 39.

Rule 8.4 Consequence of not filing an acknowledgment of service

(1) This rule applies where:

(a) the defendant has failed to file an acknowledgment of service; and

(b) the time period for doing so has expired.

(2) The defendant may attend the hearing of the claim but may not take part in the hearing unless the court gives permission.

Rule 8.5 Filing and serving written evidence

(1) The claimant must file any written evidence on which he intends to rely when he files his claim form.

(2) The claimant's evidence must be served on the defendant with the claim form.

(3) A defendant who wishes to rely on written evidence must file it when he files his acknowledgment of service.

(4) If he does so, he must also, at the same time, serve a copy of his evidence on the other parties.

(5) The claimant may, within 14 days of service of the defendant's evidence on him, file further written evidence in reply.

(6) If he does so, he must also, within the same time limit, serve a copy of his evidence on the other parties.

(7) The claimant may rely on the matters set out in his claim form as evidence under this rule if the claim form is verified by a statement of truth.

Rule 8.6 Evidence—general

(1) No written evidence may be relied on at the hearing of the claim unless:

- (a) it has been served in accordance with rule 8.5; or
- (b) the court gives permission.

(2) The court may require or permit a party to give oral evidence at the hearing.

(3) The court may give directions requiring the attendance for cross-examination of a witness who has given written evidence.

(Rule 32.1 contains a general power for the court to control evidence).

Rule 8.7 Part 20 claims

Where the Part 8 procedure is used, Part 20 (counterclaims and other additional claims) applies except that a party may not make a Part 20 claim (as defined by rule 20.2) without the court's permission.

Rule 8.8 Procedure where defendant objects to use of the Part 8 procedure

(1) Where the defendant contends that the Part 8 procedure should not be used because:

- (a) there is a substantial dispute of fact; and
- (b) the use of the Part 8 procedure is not required or permitted by a rule or practice direction, he must state his reasons when he files his acknowledgment of service.

(Rule 8.5 requires a defendant who wishes to rely on written evidence to file it when he files his acknowledgment of service).

(2) When the court receives the acknowledgment of service and any written evidence it will give directions as to the future management of the case.

(Rule 8.1(3) allows the court to make an order that the claim continue as if the claimant had not used the Part 8 procedure).

Rule 8.9 Modifications to the general rules

Where the Part 8 procedure is followed:

(a) provision is made in this Part for the matters which must be stated in the claim form and the defendant is not required to file a defence and therefore:

  (i) Part 16 (statements of case) does not apply;

  (ii) Part 15 (defence and reply) does not apply;

  (iii) any time limit in these Rules which prevents the parties from taking a step before a defence is filed does not apply; and

  (iv) the requirement under rule 7.8 to serve on the defendant a form for defending the claim does not apply;

(b) the claimant may not obtain judgment by request on an admission and therefore:

  (i) rules 14.4 to 14.7 do not apply; and

  (ii) the requirement under rule 7.8 to serve on the defendant a form for admitting the claim does not apply; and

(c) the claim shall be treated as allocated to the multi-track and therefore Part 26 does not apply.

Practice Direction, Part 8

This Practice Direction supplements CPR Part 8, and Schedule 1 and Schedule 2 to the CPR

Terminology

1.1 In this practice direction 'Schedule rules' means provisions contained in the Schedules to the CPR, which were previously contained in the Rules of the Supreme Court (1965) or the County Court Rules (1981).

Contents of this Practice Direction

2.1 This practice direction explains:
(1) how to start the claims referred to in Sections A and B;
(2) which form to use as the claim form;
(3) the procedure which those claims will follow; and
(4) how to start the appeals referred to in Section C.

(Further guidance about Forms other than claim forms can be found in the practice direction supplementing Part 4).

How to use this Practice Direction

3.1 This Practice Direction is divided into three sections—Section A, Section B and Section C. Only one section will be relevant to how to make a particular claim or appeal.
3.2 If the claim is described in paragraph A.1—use section A.
3.3 If the claim is described in paragraph B.1—use section B.
3.4 If the appeal is described in paragraph C.1—use section C.

Section A

Application

A.1 Section A applies if:
(1) the claim is listed in Table 1 below;
(2) an Act provides that a claim or application in the High Court is to be brought by originating summons;
(3) before 26 April 1999, a claim or application in the High Court would have been brought by originating summons, and is not listed in Section C; and no other method for bringing the claim or application on and after 26 April 1999 is specified in a Schedule rule or practice direction.

A.2(1) The claimant must use the Part 8 procedure unless an Act, Schedule rule, or practice direction, makes any additional or contrary provision.

(2) Where such additional or contrary provision is made the claimant must comply with it and modify the Part 8 procedure accordingly.

Claim form

A.3 The claimant must use the Part 8 claim form.

TABLE 1

... RSC O 92, r 2 The Landlord and Tenant Acts 1927, 1954 and 1987 (Assignment of proceedings to Chancery Division, etc)
RSC O 97, r 5 The Landlord and Tenant Acts 1927, 1954 and 1987 (Proceedings under Part 1 of the Act of 1927) ...

Section B

Application

B.1 Section B applies if the claim:

(1) is listed in Table 2;

(2) in the county court is for, or includes, a claim for:

  (a) the recovery of possession of land; or

  (b) for damages for harassment under Section 3 of the Protection for Harassment Act 1997;

(3) would have been brought before 26 April 1999:

  (a) in the High Court, by originating motion and is not listed in Section C;

  (b) in the county court:

    (i) by originating application; or

    (ii) by petition, and

  no other procedure is prescribed in an Act, a Schedule or rule or a practice direction.

TABLE 2

Schedule Rule	Claim Form
... CCR O 43, r 2(1)	The Landlord and Tenant Acts 1927, 1954, 1985 and 1987 (Commencement of proceedings and answer) ...

Special provisions take precedence

B.2 The claimant must first comply with any special provision set out in the Schedule rules, practice direction or any Act relating to the claim.

(In Schedule 2, CCR O 6 makes special provision for service, for certain types of claim).

B.3 Special provisions contained in Schedule rules or an Act may set out:

(1) where the claim may be started;

(2) the contents of the claim form;

(3) whether a hearing is required;

(4) the nature of evidence required in support of the claim, and when it must be filed or served;

(5) the method of service of the claim form and evidence;

(6) persons on whom service must or may be affected;

(7) the form and content of Notices, and when they must or may be filed, and on whom served;

(8) the form and content of any affidavit, answer, or reply when they must or may be filed or served;

(9) persons who may apply to be joined as parties to the claim;

(10) minimum periods of notice before the hearing date.

B.4 Where a Schedule rule makes special provision for the contents of particulars of claim, those particulars must be attached to the claim form and served with it.

B.5 Subject to any special or contrary provision in an Act or Schedule rule, the claimant must use the procedure set out in the remainder of this section.

Restrictions on where to start the claim

B.6 Where the claimant is bringing a claim in a county court that claim may only be started:

(1) in the county court for the district in which:

(a) the defendants or one of the defendants lives or carries on business; or

(b) the subject matter of the claim is situated; or

(2) if there is no defendant named in the claim form, in the county court for the district in which the claimant or one of the claimants lives or carries on business.

B.7 Where the claimant is making a claim in the county court for:

(1) the recovery of land;

(2) the foreclosure or redemption of any mortgage;

(3) enforcing any charge or lien on land;

(4) the recovery of moneys secure by a mortgage or charge on land,

the claim must be started in the court for the district in which the land, or any part of it, is situated.

Claim form

B.8 This paragraph sets out which Form is to be used as the claim form:

(1) where a claim form number is listed against a particular claim in Table 2, the claimant must use that numbered form as the claim form;

(2) where the claimant intends to make a claim in the county court which is for, or includes, the recovery of possession of land, the claimant must use the claim form numbered in the practice direction supplementing Part 4 (Forms), and

(3) in every other claim, the claimant must use the Part 8 claim form.

Court will fix a date

B.9 When the court issues the claim form it will:

(1) fix a date for the hearing; and

(2) prepare a notice of the hearing date for each party.

Service of the claim form

B.10 The claim form must be served not less than 21 days before the hearing date.

B.11 Where the claimant serves the claim form, he must serve notice of the hearing date at the same time, unless the hearing date is specified in the claim form. CPR, Rule 3.1(2)(a) and (b) provide for the court to extend or shorten the time for compliance with any rule or practice direction, and to adjourn to bring forward a hearing.

Defendant is not required to respond

B.12 The defendant is not required to serve an acknowledgment of service.

At the hearing

B.13 The court may on the hearing date:

(1) proceed to hear the case and dispose of the claim; or

(2) give case management directions.

B.14 Case management directions given under paragraph B.13 will, if the defendant has filed a defence, include the allocation of a case to a track, or directions to enable the case to be allocated.

(A defended county court claim for possession of land, where it has been allocated to the multi-track, will not normally be transferred to the Civil Trial Centre: see paragraph 10(1) of the Part 26 (Case Management preliminary stages practice direction).)

B.15 CPR rule 26.5(3) and CPR rules 26.6 to 26.10 apply to the allocation of a claim under paragraph B.14.

RSC Ord 97, CPR Schedule 1

r 1 Interpretation

(1) In this Order, 'the Act of 1927' means the Landlord and Tenant Act 1927, 'the Act of 1954' means the Landlord and Tenant Act 1954 and 'the Act of 1987' means the Landlord and Tenant Act 1987.

(2) In relation to any proceedings under Part II of the Act of 1954, any reference in this Order to a landlord shall, if the interest of the landlord in question is subject to a mortgage and the mortgagee is in possession or a receiver appointed by the mortgagee or by the court is in receipt of the rents and profits, be construed as a reference to the mortgagee.

r 2 Assignment of proceedings to Chancery Division, etc

All proceedings in the High Court under Part I of the Act of 1927 or Part II of the Act of 1954 or the Act of 1987 shall be assigned to the Chancery Division and, subject to rules 9A and 12, be begun by claim form.

r 3 Issue, etc, of claim form

(1) Any claim or application under Part I of the Act of 1927 or Part II of the Act of 1954 or the Act of 1987 may be issued out of the district registry for the district in which the premises to which the claim or application relates are situated instead of Chancery Chambers.

(3) The court will set a day for the hearing of such a claim which shall be a day which will allow an interval of at least 14 days between the date of service of the claim form and the day so fixed.

r 14 Application under section 19 of the Act of 1987

A copy of the notice served under section 19(2)(a) of the Act of 1987 shall be appended to the claim form issued under section 19(1) thereof, and an additional copy of the notice shall be filed.

r 18 Service of notices in proceedings under the Act of 1987

Where a notice is to be served in or before proceedings under the Act of 1987, it shall be served in accordance with section 54 and, in the case of service on a landlord, it shall be served at the address furnished under section 48(1).

CCR Ord 43, CPR Schedule 2

r 1 Interpretation

(1) In this order 'the Act of 1927' means the Landlord and Tenant Act 1927, 'the Act of 1954' means the Landlord and Tenant Act 1954, 'the Act of 1985' means the Landlord and Tenant Act 1985 and 'the Act of 1987' means the Landlord and Tenant Act 1987.

r 2 Commencement of proceedings and answer

(1) Proceedings in a county court under the Act of 1927 or of 1954, or of 1985 or of 1987 shall be commenced by claim form and the respondent shall file an answer.

(2) The court shall fix a return day which, unless it otherwise directs, shall be a day fixed for the case management hearing of the proceedings.

r 17 Application under section 19 of the Act of 1987

A copy of the notice served under section 19(2)(a) of the Act of 1987 shall be appended to the claim form seeking an order under section 19(1) thereof, and an additional copy of the notice shall be filed.

r 21 Service of documents in proceedings under the Act of 1987

(1) Where a claim form or answer is to be served in proceedings under the Act of 1987 it shall be served by the applicant or, as the case may be, by the respondent.

(2) Where a notice is to be served in or before proceedings under the Act of 1987, it shall be served in accordance with section 54 and, in the case of service on a landlord, it shall be served at the address furnished under section 48(1).

Civil Procedure (Amendment) Rules 2001, SI 2001/256

Civil Procedure Rules 1998, Part 56

Scope and interpretation

56.1

(1) In this Section of this Part 'landlord and tenant claim' means a claim under:

- (a) the Landlord and Tenant Act 1927;
- (b) the Leasehold Property (Repairs) Act 1938;
- (c) the Landlord and Tenant Act 1954;
- (d) the Landlord and Tenant Act 1985; or
- (e) the Landlord and Tenant Act 1987.

Starting the claim

56.2

(1) The claim must be started in the county court for the district in which the land is situated unless paragraphs (2) or (4) apply or an enactment provides otherwise.

(2) The claim may be started in the High Court if the claimant files with his claim form a certificate stating the reasons for bringing the claim in that court verified by a statement of truth in accordance with rule 22.1(1).

(3) The practice direction refers to circumstances which may justify starting the claim in the High Court.

Pre-contract tenancy enquiries (Form E2, parts 66–76)*

Part I of the Landlord and Tenant Act 1987

[Note: where the Property comprises or includes a part but not the whole of a building, references in the following Enquiries to "building" means such part of a building only]

In respect of each building comprised in the Property:

66. What is the total number of flats in the building?

67. How many of those flats are held by:
67.1 protected shorthold tenants?
67.2 business tenants?
67.3 tenants whose tenancies are terminable on cessation of their employment?
67.4 assured tenants or assured agricultural occupants within the meaning of the Housing Act 1988?
67.5 tenants not falling within categories 67.1, 67.2, 67.3 and 67.4 each of whom is a tenant of at least 3 flats in the building (and for this purpose associated companies are to be treated as one tenant only)?

68. How many of the flats in the building are not demised or let?

69. Do the flats in the building which are not covered by the Replies to Enquiries 67 and 68 exceed 50 per cent of the total number of flats in the building?

70. If the reply to Enquiry 69 is: yes, does the internal floor area of all those parts of the building occupied or intended to be occupied otherwise than for residential purposes exceed 50 per cent of the internal floor area of the building taken as a whole (disregarding all common parts)?

71. Is the Seller an exempt or resident landlord within the meaning of S.58 of the 1987 Act? If yes, please give details.

72. Does the Seller consider that the proposed disposal by the Seller to the Buyer will be a relevant disposal (within the meaning of S.4 of the 1987 Act) of premises to which the 1987 Act applies?

73. If the reply to Enquiry 72 is: no, please explain why.

74. If the reply to Enquiry 72 is: yes, please supply copies of all notices served by and on the Seller in accordance with or purportedly in accordance with any provision contained in Part I of the 1987 Act.

75. Can the Seller confirm that the proposed disposal by the Seller to the Buyer will not contravene Part I of the 1987 Act?

76. Please give full details of each relevant disposal made by the Seller or any predecessor in title of his since 14th February 1988 of any estate or interest in the building or any part of it and in the case of each such disposal:
76.1 state whether or not the disposal was made in respect of premises to which at the time Part I of the 1987 Act applied and if not, why not, but if Part I did apply at the time, then
76.2 state whether or not the disposal was made in contravention of Part I, and please supply copies of all notices served in accordance with or purportedly in accordance with provisions contained in Part I.

Index

References in this index are to paragraph numbers.